Best Backpacking Vacations
in the
Northern Rockies

BOOKS BY BILL SCHNEIDER

Where the Grizzly Walks, 1977

Hiking Montana, coauthor, 1979

The Dakota Image, 1980

The Yellowstone River, 1985

Best Hikes on the Continental Divide, coauthor, 1998

The Flight of the Nez Perce, 1988

The Tree Giants, 1988

Hiking the Beartooths, 1995

Bear Aware, A Quick Reference Bear Country Survival Guide, 1996

Hiking Carlsbad Caverns & Guadalupe Mountains National Parks, 1996

Best Easy Day Hikes Canyonlands & Arches National Parks, 1997

Best Easy Day Hikes Yellowstone, 1997

Exploring Canyonlands & Arches National Parks, 1997

Hiking Yellowstone National Park, 1997

Backpacking Tips, coauthor, 1998

Best Easy Day Hikes Beartooths, 1998

Best Easy Day Hikes Grand Teton, 1999

Hiking Grand Teton National Park, 1999

Hiking Montana 20th Anniversary Edition, coauthor, 1999

Learn more about Bill Schneider's books at www.billschneider.net.

Best Backpacking Vacations in the Northern Rockies

Bill Schneider

FALCON®

GUILFORD, CONNECTICUT
HELENA, MONTANA
AN IMPRINT OF THE GLOBE PEQUOT PRESS

A FALCON GUIDE ®

Library of Congress Cataloging-in-Publication Data is available.

ISBN 0-7627-2355-6

Manufactured in the United States of America

First Edition/First Printing

WILDERNESS is . . .

The FREEDOM to experience true wildness . . . to hear only nature's music . . . to study the little secrets of the natural world . . . and to enjoy the quiet and solitude so rare in the stressful life we now live.

The CHALLENGE to learn and respect wild country . . . to be self-reliant . . . to take your time . . . to test your physical abilities . . . to courteously share the last blank spots on the map with others . . . and to fully enjoy your wilderness experience while leaving no trace of your passing.

The OPPORTUNITY to discover why wilderness is priceless . . . to see the threats to your wilderness . . . to devote part of yourself to preserving it . . . and to encourage others to do the same.

—Bill Schneider

CONTENTS

Map Legend

══🛡15══	Interstate
-(2)(93)(191)-	U.S. highway
-(83)(200)-	State highway
───────	Paved road
╌╌╌╌╌╌	Trail
━━ ━ ━	Park / Wilderness Boundary
●╌╌╌╌╌●	Tramway
🔥	Campsite
≋	Falls
╰	Pass
△	Peak
🛏	Picnic area
🚽	Pit toilet
◈	Point of interest
໐ᢋ	Spring
◆T	Trailhead
Start End	Trail start/finish

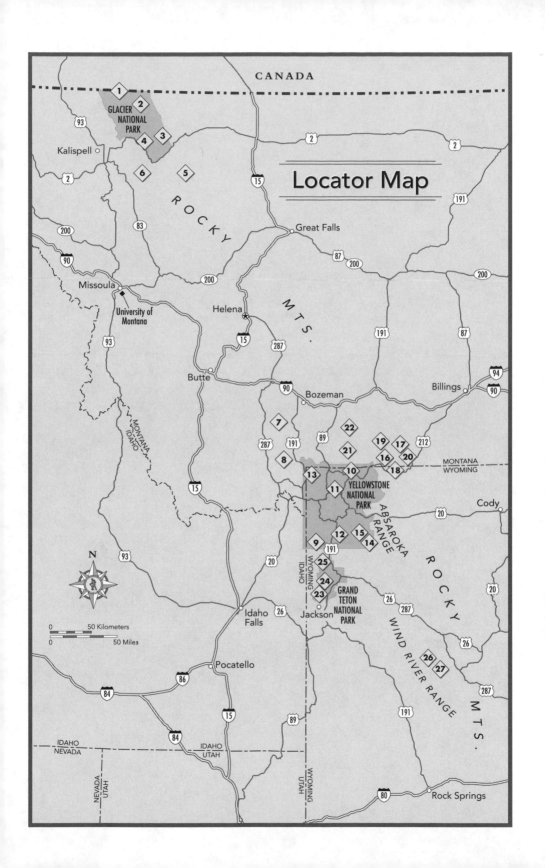

What Is a Best Backpacking Vacation? And Why?

Of all the hiking I've done over the past thirty-three years, these are my favorite backpacking trips in the northern Rockies. But they are only twenty-six trips out of hundreds of quality backpacking trips in this region. Some wonderful hiking areas like the Sawtooths, the High Uintas, Selway-Bitterroot, and Anaconda-Pintlar aren't even in this book; I hope to include some of them in a future edition.

Most routes require four nights or more in the backcountry, but I have included several trips for beginners or people with only three days to spend. I didn't include overnighters, although power hikers could cover some of these routes in two days or even in a long day hike.

But why? Why a backpacking vacation? Why not sit by a pool and read a novel or go to Las Vegas or Disneyland or Europe instead?

One reason is economics. That's right—economics. Like any outdoor activity, you can make backpacking expensive. On the other hand, you can make it one of the most economical forms of recreation. For example, you can buy fancy brand name backpacking clothes or you can get by with what's buried in your closet. You can buy expensive freeze-dried food or you can use staple foods you normally buy in bulk and already have in your cupboard.

Why backpack? Most people, like these hikers on the Grand Teton Loop, relish the opportunity to get away from it all.

The cost of a weeklong vacation with motel stays and restaurant meals would be sufficient to outfit an entire family for backpacking—and this equipment would last for many years. After that initial investment, you could see millions of acres of spectacular, roadless country without spending more on equipment. You would only need to spend a few dollars for food and for transportation to the trailheads, and after that the trips would be free. Imagine. A free vacation. Those words do not go together very often, right?

And by the way, that's another reason to do it—freedom. You can be by yourself. You can avoid being herded or overregulated, and you won't fret about check-out times, traffic jams, or waiting in line. You can control your own schedule. You can do whatever you want to do, whenever you want to do it. You can't even hear the bad news on the radio.

We occasionally hear claims that only the young and fit can enjoy backpacking, but these statements obviously come from people who haven't been out there. Quite the reverse is true. Families spend many pleasurable nights backpacking far from their vehicles. And many elderly people enjoy backpacking. The new breed of lightweight backpacking equipment and a new emphasis on going light make backpacking available to anybody of even close to average fitness level.

It's all about choice. Smell the fragrance of wildflowers or the fumes of diesel fuel, hear the wind whistling through mature pines or the screams of sirens, see the sunset reflected in a mountain lake or trying to shine through the smog, catch a native trout or get an upset stomach from eating junk food.

That's why you should take a backpacking vacation.

Why backpack? It's fun and a great way to build lasting bonds with family and friends.

BACKCOUNTRY REGULATIONS

Backcountry-use regulations aren't intended to complicate your life. They help preserve the natural landscape and protect human visitors. Be sure to know and follow all regulations covering the route of your trip. Keep in mind that these regulations vary, sometimes widely, among agencies and national parks or forests. Call the local ranger district before leaving to get the latest regulations, and check the information board at the trailhead.

BACKCOUNTRY PERMITS

If you need a permit, try to get it in advance. In some cases you don't need permits, and in other cases, you can't get them in advance, but if you can reserve your route and campsites in advance, do it. This saves time when you get to the visitor center or ranger station, and you have a better chance of getting the trip you want. I provide general information about park regulations and permits in each regional introduction.

TYPE OF TRIPS

Backpacking trips have been split into the following categories:

Loop. Starts and finishes at the same trailhead, with no (or very little) retracing of your steps. Sometimes the definition of loop is stretched to include trips that involve a short walk on a road at the end of the hike to get back to your vehicle.

Shuttle. A point-to-point trip that requires two vehicles (one left at the other end of the trail) or a prearranged pick-up at a designated time and place. One effective way to manage the logistical problems of shuttles is to arrange for another party to start at the other end of the trail. The two parties meet at a predetermined point and trade vehicle keys. When finished, they drive each other's vehicles home.

Out-and-back. Traveling to a specific destination, then retracing your steps back to the trailhead.

Base camp. A hike where you spend several nights at the same campsite, using the extra days for fishing, climbing, day hiking or, of course, just relaxing.

DISTANCES

In this guidebook most distances came from agency signs and brochures, but some trail mileage was estimated. Since it's difficult and time consuming to precisely measure trails, most distances listed in any guidebook, on trail signs, and in agency brochures are somebody's estimate. Keep in mind that distance is often less important than difficulty. A rocky, 5-mile, uphill section of trail can take longer and require more effort than 10 miles of well-contoured trail on flat terrain. The moral of this story is don't get too excited if it seems like the distance is slightly off. It usually is.

DIFFICULTY RATINGS

To help you plan your trip, trails are rated according to difficulty. However, difficulty ratings serve as a general guide only, not the final word. What is difficult to one hiker may be easy to the next. In this guidebook difficulty ratings consider both how long and how strenuous a route is. Also, keep in mind that a long, strenuous route can be made easy by taking two or three more days to cover it.

Here are general definitions of the ratings.

Easy. Suitable for any hiker, including children or elderly persons, without serious elevation gain, hazardous sections, or places where the trail is faint.

Moderate. Suitable for hikers who have some experience and at least an average fitness level. These routes might not be suitable for children or the elderly unless they have an above-average level of fitness. The route may have some short sections where the trail is difficult to follow and often includes some hills.

Difficult. Suitable for experienced hikers with above-average fitness level, often with sections of the trail that are difficult to follow or even some off-trail sections that could require knowledge of route-finding with topo map and compass; sometimes with serious elevation gain, and possibly some hazardous conditions.

FINDING MAPS

The maps printed in this book serve as a general guide only—you won't necessarily find every key point mentioned in the text on these maps. You definitely should take a more detailed map with you on your hike. If the park or wilderness area has a good commercial topographic map, this might suffice. Ditto for any map the National Park Service or USDA Forest Service has published covering the entire area. Even if it isn't a topo map, it could have some current information on new trails or trailhead relocation.

For the hikes listed in this book, I recommend taking at least two maps—United States Geological Survey quadrangles covering the route and one agency or commercial map covering the entire hiking area. Each trip in this book has specific map recommendations.

USGS maps can be ordered directly from the USGS's Denver Distribution Center or purchased at sport stores and visitor centers throughout the Northern Rockies. Since popular maps are sometimes out of stock, try to have your USGS quads in hand before you leave for the trailhead.

To obtain free map indexes and catalogs or to order topographic maps available from the USGS, contact:

USGS Map Distribution
Box 25286, Federal Center
Denver, CO 80225
Phone: (303) 236–7477
Fax: (303) 236–1972

You can also order at www.usgs.gov, but even the USGS admits that buying from a retailer is usually the fastest way to obtain a USGS topographic map.

TRAFFIC/SHARING

Hikers always hope to have the wilderness all to themselves, but that rarely happens. Instead, we have to share the trails with other hikers and backcountry horsemen, including large stock parties led by an outfitter. If you meet a stock party on the trail, move off the trail on the downhill side and quietly let the stock animals pass. It's too difficult (and sometimes dangerous) for the stock animals to yield. Hikers should always yield to horses.

RATING THE HILLS

In the process of publishing dozens of FalconGuide hiking books, we have sought to come up with a consistent rating system to help hikers determine how difficult those "big hills" really are. Such a system will help hikers decide how far they want to hike a given day or even whether they want to take a trail at all. In the past guidebook authors have described hills to the best of their ability, but subjectively. What is a big hill to one hiker might be a slight upgrade to the next.

And it isn't only going up that matters. Some hikers hate going down steep hills and the knee problems that result from descending with a big pack. These hikers might want to avoid Category 1 and Category H hills, as described below.

This new system plugs the elevation gain and the length of that section of trail into a mathematical formula to come up with a numerical hill rating similar to the system used by cyclists. The system only works for climbs of 0.5 mile or longer, not for short, steep hills.

Here is a rough description of the categories, listed from easiest to hardest.

Category 5: A slight upgrade.

Category 4: Usually within the capabilities of any hiker.

Category 3: A well-conditioned hiker might describe a Category 3 climb as "gradual," but a poorly conditioned hiker might complain about the steepness. It's definitely not steep enough to deter you from hiking the trail, but these climbs will slow you down.

Category 2: Most hikers would consider these "big hills," steep enough, in some cases, to make hikers choose an alternative trail, but these are still not the real lung-busting, calf-stretching hills.

Many trails in the northern Rockies have steep sections, such as this one on the Static Peak Divide in Grand Teton National Park, so always stay alert and watch your step.

Category 1: These are among the steepest hills you'll find. If you have heart or breathing problems, or simply dislike climbing big hills, you might look for an alternative trail.

Category H: These are hills that make you wonder about the person who laid out the trail. Any trail with a Category H hill is steeper than any trail should be. (Incidentally, "H" stands for "Horrible.")

The hills in this book are rated according to the following chart. Some climbs are rated in the hike descriptions of this book, but if a climb is not included (or to use this formula in other hiking areas), take the mileage and elevation gain from the topo map and look them up on this chart.

FALCON HILL RATING CHART

MILES

ELEVATION GAIN	0.5	1.0	1.5	2.0	2.5	3.0	3.5	4.0	4.5	5.0	5.5	6.0
200	4.2	5.0	5.4	5.5	5.6	5.6	5.7	5.7	5.7	5.7	5.7	5.7
300	3.3	4.5	4.9	5.2	5.3	5.4	5.5	5.5	5.5	5.5	5.6	5.6
400	1.8	4.0	4.5	4.8	5.1	5.2	5.3	5.3	5.4	5.4	5.4	5.4
500	1.0	3.5	4.2	4.5	4.7	5.0	5.1	5.2	5.2	5.2	5.3	5.3
600	H	3.0	3.8	4.2	4.4	4.6	4.9	4.9	5.0	5.1	5.1	5.1
700	H	2.5	3.4	3.9	4.2	4.3	4.5	4.8	4.9	4.9	4.9	5.0
800	H	1.4	3.1	3.6	3.9	4.1	4.2	4.3	4.7	4.7	4.8	4.9
900	H	H	2.7	3.3	3.6	3.9	4.0	4.1	4.2	4.6	4.7	4.7
1,000	H	H	2.3	2.9	3.4	3.6	3.8	3.9	4.0	4.1	4.5	4.6
1,100	H	H	1.9	2.7	3.1	3.4	3.6	3.7	3.8	3.9	3.9	4.5
1,200	H	H	H	2.4	2.8	3.1	3.4	3.5	3.6	3.7	3.8	3.9
1,300	H	H	H	2.1	2.6	2.9	3.2	3.3	3.5	3.5	3.6	3.7
1,400	H	H	H	1.8	2.3	2.7	2.9	3.1	3.3	3.4	3.5	3.5
1,500	H	H	H	1.6	2.1	2.4	2.7	2.9	3.1	3.2	3.3	3.3
1,600	H	H	H	H	1.9	2.2	2.3	2.7	2.9	2.9	3.1	3.2
1,700	H	H	H	H	1.7	1.9	2.3	2.5	2.7	2.8	2.9	3.0
1,800	H	H	H	H	1.5	1.8	2.0	2.3	2.5	2.6	2.7	2.8
1,900	H	H	H	H	1.3	1.7	1.9	2.1	2.3	2.4	2.6	2.6
2,000	H	H	H	H	H	1.5	1.7	1.9	2.1	2.2	2.4	2.5
2,100	H	H	H	H	H	1.3	1.6	1.8	1.9	2.0	2.2	2.3
2,200	H	H	H	H	H	1.2	1.4	1.6	1.8	1.9	1.9	2.1
2,300	H	H	H	H	H	1.0	1.3	1.5	1.7	1.8	1.9	1.9
2,400	H	H	H	H	H	H	1.2	1.4	1.5	1.6	1.8	1.8
2,500	H	H	H	H	H	H	1.0	1.2	1.4	1.5	1.6	1.7
2,600	H	H	H	H	H	H	H	1.1	1.3	1.4	1.5	1.6
2,700	H	H	H	H	H	H	H	H	1.1	1.3	1.4	1.5
2,800	H	H	H	H	H	H	H	H	1.1	1.3	1.4
2,900	H	H	H	H	H	H	H	H	H	1.0	1.2	1.3
3,000	H	H	H	H	H	H	H	H	H	H	1.0	1.1

CAMPSITES

If you're like most hikers coming to Yellowstone and Glacier National Parks, you want detailed information about the campsites, but specific information on campsites is difficult to find. You want to know if they have good views, how far you have to carry water, how sheltered they are, if there is firewood around, etc. However, unless you're lucky enough to know somebody who has been at a campsite or find a backcountry ranger to help you before you get your permit, campsites will only be numbers on a map.

Backcountry rangers are, of course, familiar with the campsites, but they're usually in the backcountry, not at the visitor center giving out permits. NPS personnel stationed at the visitor centers commonly do not have specific information on campsites or trail conditions.

For the most part, the NPS has done a superb job of locating campsites, so there aren't many bad choices. Nonetheless, some campsites are definitely better than others. If you plan to carry a big pack 10 miles into a mountain lake with several designated campsites, you really want a nice one, right? That's why I checked out most campsites along the routes in Glacier and Yellowstone National Parks while researching this guidebook.

The campsites are rated with five-star (5★) campsite being the best and one star (1★) the worst. These ratings are, of course, subjective. When you go to the campsite, you might have a higher or lower opinion of it. In most cases I was at these campsites only once, so weather conditions on that day doubtless influenced my attitude. Also, a campsite might be under water with swarms of mosquitoes in June and July but dry and bug-free in August and September. The rating system is certainly not scientific, but it should give you some useful guidelines for selecting your evening accommodations.

Before you reserve a campsite in Glacier or Yellowstone, make sure you've checked the restrictions. Many campsites don't allow campfires, and others are closed until late in the season due to weather conditions, or to protect fragile wildlife resources, or for safety considerations.

As listed in the handout from Yellowstone's backcountry office, the NPS has split that park's campsites into four categories: hiker-only, stock-party-only, boater-access-only, and mixed. The latter can be reserved by backpackers, boaters, or backcountry horsemen. This book only includes information on hiker-only or mixed campsites. Glacier has no such categorization.

Numerous campsites in Yellowstone, Glacier, and Grand Teton National Parks have tent sites located too close to the food area or bear pole. For bear safety considerations, use another tent site at least 100 feet away from the food area or bear pole.

All campsites in Yellowstone have bear poles or other secure food storage devices, but they aren't always easy to find, so look carefully around before you assume there isn't one at your campsite. In some cases a hard-to-see cable has been strung between two trees to serve as a food storage device. All campsites in Grand Teton have pit toilets, except on the Moose Basin Divide route.

Don't assume either that all campsites are easy to find or have a noticeable trailside sign. These signs sometimes get knocked down or stolen. Keep the topo map out. When you get close to the campsite, watch carefully for it, so you don't have to backtrack to find it. In addition, ask the ranger giving you the permit for specific instructions to the campsite and mark the exact location on your topo map. This is particularly true in Yellowstone where the park has some off-trail campsites varying from about a quarter-mile to a mile from the trail. These campsites are not always easy to find, and some do not have maintained spur trails. Again, ask about this when getting your permit.

One last note on campsites: Glacier sometimes rotates campsite locations to minimize resource damage and in Yellowstone, the NPS is in the process of moving campsites located too close to trails. This means some of the information listed in the campsite-rating sections of this book for both parks might be outdated when you get your permit. Make sure you ask the ranger if the site has been moved. Bears use trails at night as travel corridors, so camping near a trail increases the chance of an encounter.

FINDING THE IDEAL TRIP

To help you find the ideal trip, I've organized the hikes into groups based on backpackers' common preferences.

For Backpackers Who Like Photography

Boulder Pass	Sundance Pass
Fifty Mountain	The Teton Crest
Three Passes in Glacier	The Grand Teton Loop
Hilgard Basin	Sky Pilot
The Beaten Path	Lizard Head

For Backpackers Who Like Fishing

Jewel Basin	The Thorofare
Spanish Peaks	Two Ocean Loop
Hilgard Basin	Aero Lakes
Bechler River	The Beaten Path
Black Canyon of the Yellowstone	Green Lake
Chain of Lakes	Lake Plateau
Heart Lake	Sky Pilot

Mount Moran and Jackson Lake in Grand Teton National Park.

For Backpackers Who Like Climbing and Peak Bagging

Boulder Pass
Fifty Mountain
Three Passes in Glacier
Hilgard Basin
Aero Lakes
The Gallatin Skyline
The Beaten Path
Lake Plateau
The Teton Crest
The Grand Teton Loop
Sky Pilot
Lizard Head

For Backpackers Who Like High-Altitude Scenery

Boulder Pass
Fifty Mountain
Three Passes in Glacier
Hilgard Basin
Aero Lakes
The Beaten Path
The Gallatin Skyline
Lake Plateau
Sundance Pass
The Teton Crest
The Grand Teton Loop
Sky Pilot
Lizard Head

For Backpackers Who Like to See Wildlife

Fifty Mountain
Three Passes in Glacier
Black Canyon of the Yellowstone
The Gallatin Skyline
The Thorofare
Two Ocean Plateau
The Hellroaring
Moose Basin Divide

For Backpackers Who Like Wildflowers

Boulder Pass
Fifty Mountain
Spanish Peaks
Hilgard Basin
Chain of Lakes
The Gallatin Skyline
The Beaten Path
Green Lake
Lake Plateau
The Teton Crest
The Grand Teton Loop
Moose Basin Divide

For Backpackers Who Like Wilderness Lakes

Jewel Basin
Spanish Peaks
Hilgard Basin
Chain of Lakes
Heart Lake
Aero Lakes
The Beaten Path
Green Lake
Lake Plateau
Sky Pilot
Lizard Head

For Backpackers Who Like Hiking along Streams

Nyack Loop
Double Divide
Bechler River
Black Canyon of the Yellowstone
The Thorofare
Two Ocean Plateau
The Beaten Path
Sundance Pass
The Hellroaring
Three Passes in the Absaroka
Moose Basin Divide

For Backpackers Who Like Waterfalls
Bechler River
Black Canyon of the Yellowstone

The Beaten Path
Sky Pilot

For Backpackers Who Like to Base Camp
Jewel Basin
Hilgard Basin
Heart Lake
The Beaten Path

Aero Lakes
Lake Plateau
Sky Pilot
Lizard Head

For Beginning Backpackers
Three Passes in Glacier
Jewel Basin
Hilgard Basin

Black Canyon of the Yellowstone
Chain of Lakes
Heart Lake

For Backpackers Who Like Grizzly Bears
Boulder Pass
Fifty Mountain
Three Passes in Glacier
Nyack Loop
Double Divide
Black Canyon of the Yellowstone

Heart Lake
The Gallatin Skyline
The Thorofare
Two Ocean Plateau
The Hellroaring
Moose Basin Divide

Why backpack? To hear only nature's voice.

For Backpackers Who Don't Like Grizzly Bears

Spanish Peaks
Aero Lakes
The Beaten Path
Green Lake
Lake Plateau

Sundance Pass
The Teton Crest
The Grand Teton Loop
Sky Pilot
Lizard Head

For Backpackers Who Don't Mind Fording Big Rivers

Nyack Loop
Bechler River
Black Canyon of the Yellowstone
Heart Lake

The Thorofare
Two Ocean Plateau
Green Lake
Three Passes in the Absaroka

For Backpackers Who Want a Real Wilderness Adventure

Nyack Loop
Double Divide
The Thorofare
Two Ocean Plateau

The Hellroaring
Three Passes in the Absaroka
Moose Basin Divide

For Backpackers Who Don't Want to See Many People

Nyack Loop
Double Divide
The Gallatin Skyline
The Thorofare

Two Ocean Plateau
The Hellroaring
Three Passes in the Absaroka
Moose Basin Divide

For Backpackers Who Don't Mind Seeing Lots of People

Boulder Pass
Fifty Mountain
Three Passes in Glacier
Jewel Basin
Hilgard Basin
Black Canyon of the Yellowstone
Chain of Lakes

The Beaten Path
Green Lake
Sundance Pass
The Teton Crest
The Grand Teton Loop
Sky Pilot
Lizard Head

For Backpackers Who Don't Mind Seeing Lots of Horses

Double Divide
Hilgard Basin
Black Canyon of the Yellowstone
The Thorofare

Two Ocean Plateau
Lake Plateau
The Hellroaring

MAKE IT A SAFE TRIP

Perhaps the best single piece of safety advice I can offer you is—Be Prepared! For starters, this means carrying survival and first-aid materials, proper clothing, a compass, and topographic maps—and knowing how to use them.

Perhaps the second-best piece of safety advice is to tell somebody where you're going and when you plan to return. Pilots file flight plans before every trip, and anybody venturing into a blank spot on a map should do the same. File your "flight plan" with a friend or relative before taking off.

Close behind your flight plan and being prepared with proper equipment is physical conditioning. Being fit not only makes wilderness travel more fun, it makes it safer. To whet your appetite for more knowledge of wilderness safety and preparedness, here are a few more tips.

- Check the weather forecast. Be careful not to get caught at high altitude by a bad storm or along a stream in a flash flood. Watch cloud formations closely, so you don't get stranded on a ridgeline during a lightning storm. Avoid traveling during prolonged periods of cold weather.
- Avoid traveling alone in the wilderness.
- Keep your party together.
- In Yellowstone be extremely careful around thermal areas. In some cases a thin crust can break and cause a severe burn or death.
- Study basic survival and first-aid skills before leaving home.
- Don't eat wild plants unless you have positively identified them and know they are safe to consume.
- Before you leave for the trailhead, find out as much as you can about the route, especially any potential hazards.
- Don't exhaust yourself or other members of your party by traveling too far or too fast. Let the slowest person set the pace.
- Don't wait until you're confused to look at your maps. Follow them as you go along from the moment you start moving up the trail, so you have a continual fix on your location.
- If you get lost, don't panic. Sit down and relax for a few minutes while you carefully check your topo map and take a reading with your compass. Confidently plan your next move. It's often smart to retrace your steps until you find familiar ground, even if you think it might lengthen your trip. Lots of people get temporarily lost in the wilderness and survive—usually by calmly and rationally dealing with the situation.
- Stay clear of all wild animals.
- Take a first-aid kit (See p. 264).
- Take a survival kit (See pp. 265).

Last but not least, don't forget that the best defense against unexpected hazards is knowledge. Read up on the latest in wilderness safety information.

Lightning: You Might Never Know What Hit You

The high altitude topography of the northern Rockies is prone to sudden thunderstorms, especially in July and August. If you get caught by a lightning storm, take special precautions. Remember:

- Lightning can travel far ahead of a storm, so be sure to take cover before the storm hits.
- Don't try to make it back to your vehicle ahead of the storm. It isn't worth the risk. Instead, seek shelter even if there is only a short distance back to the trailhead. Lightning storms usually don't last long, and from a safe vantage point, you might enjoy the sights and sounds.
- Be especially careful not to get caught on a mountaintop or exposed ridge, under large solitary trees, in the open, or near standing water.
- Seek shelter in a low-lying area, ideally in a dense stand of small, uniformly sized trees.
- Stay away from anything that might attract lightning, such as metal tent poles, graphite fishing rods, or pack frames.
- Get in a crouch position and place both feet firmly on the ground.
- If you have a pack (without a metal frame) or a sleeping pad with you, put your feet on it for extra insulation against shock.
- Don't walk or huddle together. Instead, stay 50 feet or more from each other, so if somebody gets hit by lightning, others in your party can give first aid.
- If you're in a tent, stay there, in your sleeping bag with your feet on your sleeping pad.

Hypothermia: The Silent Killer

Be aware of the danger of hypothermia—a condition in which the body's internal temperature drops below normal. It can lead to mental and physical collapse and death.

Hypothermia is caused by exposure to cold and is aggravated by wetness, wind, and exhaustion. The moment you begin to lose heat faster than your body produces it, you're suffering from exposure. Your body starts involuntary exercise, such as shivering, to stay warm and makes involuntary adjustments to preserve normal temperature in vital organs, restricting blood flow in the extremities. Both responses drain your energy reserves. The only way to stop the drain is to reduce the degree of exposure.

With full-blown hypothermia, as energy reserves are exhausted, cold reaches the brain, depriving you of good judgment and reasoning power. You won't be aware that this is happening. You lose control of your hands. Your internal temperature slides downward. Without treatment, this slide leads to stupor, collapse, and death.

To defend against hypothermia, stay dry. When clothes get wet, they lose about 90 percent of their insulating value. Wool loses relatively less heat; cotton, down, and some synthetics lose more. Choose rain clothes that cover the head, neck, body, and legs and provide good protection against wind-driven rain. Most hypothermia cases develop in air temperatures between 30 and 50 degrees Fahrenheit, but hypothermia can also develop in warmer temperatures.

If your party is exposed to wind, cold, and wet, think hypothermia. Watch yourself and others for these symptoms: uncontrollable fits of shivering; vague, slow, slurred speech; memory lapses; incoherence; immobile, fumbling hands; frequent stumbling or a lurching gait; drowsiness (to sleep is to die); apparent exhaustion; and inability to get up after a rest. When a member of your party has hypothermia, he or she may deny any problem. Believe the symptoms, not the victim. Even mild symptoms demand treatment, as follows:

- Get the victim out of the wind and rain.
- If the victim is only mildly impaired, give him or her warm drinks. Get the victim into warm clothes and a warm sleeping bag. Place well-wrapped water bottles filled with heated water close to the victim.
- If the victim is badly impaired, attempt to keep him or her awake. Put the victim in a sleeping bag with another person—both naked. If you have a double bag, put two warm people in with the victim.

Fording Rivers

When done correctly and carefully, crossing a big river can be safe, but you must know your limits. So, be smart and cautious. There are cases where you simply should turn back. Even if only one member of your party (such as a child) might not be able to follow taller, stronger members, you might not want to try a risky ford. Never be embarrassed to be overly cautious.

One key to fording rivers safely is confidence. If you aren't a strong swimmer, you should be. This not only allows you to safely get across a river that is a little deeper and stronger than you thought, but it gives you the confidence to avoid panic. Just like getting lost, panic can easily make a situation worse.

Another way to build confidence is to practice. Find a river near your home and carefully practice crossing it both with a pack and without one. You can also start with a smaller stream and work up to a major river. After you've become a strong swimmer, get used to swimming in the current.

Here is some sound advice for safely fording rivers in the northern Rockies:

- When you get to the ford, carefully assess the situation. Don't automatically cross at the point where the trail comes to the stream and head on a straight line for the marker on the other side. A mountain river can reform itself every spring during high run-off, so a ford that was safe last year might be too deep this year. Study upstream and downstream and look for a place where the stream widens and the water is not more than waist-deep on the shortest member of your party. The tail end of an island is usually a good place, as is a long riffle. The inside of a meander sometimes makes a safe ford, but in other cases a long shallow section can be followed by a short, deep section next to the outside of the bend where the current picks up speed and carves out a deep channel.
- Before starting any serious ford, make sure your matches, camera, billfold, clothes, sleeping bag, and other items you must keep dry are in watertight bags.
- In the northern Rockies most streams are cold, so have dry clothes ready for when you get to the other side to minimize the risk of hypothermia, especially on a cold, rainy day.

Safely fording rivers can be a challenge.

- Minimize the amount of time you spend in the water, but don't rush across. Instead, go slowly and deliberately, taking one step at a time, being careful to get each foot securely planted before lifting the other foot. Take a 45-degree angle instead of going straight across, following a riffle line if possible.
- Don't try a ford with bare feet. Wear hiking boots without socks, sneakers, or tightly strapped sandals.
- Stay sideways with the current. Turning upstream or downstream greatly increases the force of the current.
- In some cases two or three people can cross together, locking forearms, with the strongest person on the upstream side.
- If you have a choice, ford in the early morning when the stream isn't as deep. In the mountains, cool evening temperatures slow snow melt and reduce the water flow into the rivers.
- On small streams a sturdy walking stick used on the upstream side for balance helps prevent a fall, but in a major river with a fast current, a walking stick offers little help.
- Loosen the belt and straps on your pack. If you fall or get washed downstream, a waterlogged pack can lead to drowning by anchoring you to the bottom, so you must be able to easily get out of your pack. For a short period your pack might actually help you become buoyant and float across a deep channel, but in a minute or two, it could become an anchor.
- If you're 6 feet 4 inches tall and a strong swimmer, you might feel secure crossing

a big river, but you might have children or vertically challenged hikers in your party. In this case the strongest person can cross first and string a line across the river to aid those who follow. This line (with the help of a carabiner) can also be used to float packs across instead of taking a chance of a waterlogged pack dragging you under. (If you know about the ford in advance, you can pack along a lightweight rubber raft or inner tube for this purpose.) Depending on the size and strength, you might also want to carry children.

- Be prepared for the worst. Sometimes circumstances can arise where you simply must cross instead of going back, even though the ford looks dangerous. Also, you can underestimate the depth of the channel or strength of the current, especially after a thunderstorm when a muddy river hides its true depth. In these cases, whether you like it or not, you might be swimming. It's certainly recommended to avoid these situations, but if it happens, be prepared. Don't panic. The second rule is not to try to swim directly across. Instead, pick a long angle and gradually cross or swim to the other side, taking as much as 100 yards or more to finally get across. If your pack starts to drag you down, get out of it immediately, even if you have to abandon it. If you lose control and get washed downstream, go feet first, so you don't hit your head on rocks or logs.

- And finally, be sure to report any dangerous ford as soon as you finish your trip.

Routes with Serious Fords

Nyack Loop	The Thorofare
Bechler River	Two Ocean Plateau
Black Canyon of the Yellowstone	Green Lake
Heart Lake	Three Passes in the Absaroka

ZERO IMPACT

Going into a national park or wilderness area is like visiting a famous museum. You wouldn't leave your mark on an art treasure in the museum. If everybody going through the museum left one little mark, the piece of art would be quickly destroyed—and of what value is a big building full of trashed art? The same goes for a pristine wilderness, which is as magnificent as any masterpiece. If we all left just one little mark on the landscape, the wilderness would soon be despoiled.

A wilderness can accommodate human use as long as everybody behaves. But a few thoughtless or uninformed visitors can ruin it for everybody who follows. All wilderness users have a responsibility to know and follow the rules of zero-impact camping. An important source of these guidelines, including the most updated research, can be found in the book *Leave No Trace*. Visit your favorite bookseller or outdoor retailer to purchase this book.

Nowadays most wilderness users want to walk softly, but some aren't aware that they have poor manners. Often their actions are dictated by the outdated habits of a past generation of campers who cut green boughs for evening shelters, built campfires with fire rings, and dug trenches around tents. In the 1950s these "camping rules" may have been acceptable. But they leave long-lasting scars, and today such behavior is absolutely unacceptable. The wilderness is shrinking, and the number of users is mushrooming. More and more camping areas show unsightly signs of heavy use.

Consequently, a new code of ethics is growing out of the necessity of coping with the unending waves of people who want a perfect wilderness experience. Today, we all must leave no clues that we have gone before. Canoeists can look behind the canoe and see no sign of their passing. Hikers, mountain bikers, and four-wheelers should have the same goal. Enjoy the wildness, but make it a zero-impact visit.

Falcon's Zero-Impact Principles

- Leave with everything you brought in.
- Leave no sign of your visit.
- Leave the landscape as you found it.

Most of us know better than to litter—in or out of the wilderness. Be sure you leave nothing, regardless of how small it is, along the trail or at the campsite. This means you should pack out everything, including orange peels, flip tops, cigarette butts, and gum wrappers. Also, pick up any trash that others leave behind. In addition, please follow this zero-impact advice.

- Follow the main trail. Avoid cutting switchbacks and walking on vegetation beside the trail.
- Don't pick up "souvenirs," such as rocks, antlers, or wildflowers. The next person wants to see them, too, and collecting such souvenirs violates national park regulations.
- Avoid making loud noises that may disturb others. Remember, sound travels easily to the other side of a lake. Be courteous.
- Carry a lightweight trowel to bury human waste 6 to 8 inches deep and pack out used toilet paper. Keep human waste at least 300 feet from any water source.
- Finally, and perhaps most importantly, strictly follow the pack-in/pack-out rule. If you carry something into the backcountry, consume it or carry it out.

Leave zero impact of your passing—and put your ear to the ground in the wilderness and listen carefully. Thousands of people coming behind you are thanking you for your courtesy and good sense.

BE BEAR AWARE

The first step of any hike in bear country is an attitude adjustment. Nothing guarantees total safety. Hiking in bear country adds a small additional risk to your trip. However, that risk can be greatly minimized by adhering to this age-old piece of advice: Be prepared. And being prepared doesn't only mean having the right equipment. It also means having the right information. Knowledge is your best defense.

You can—and should—thoroughly enjoy your trip to bear country. Don't let the fear of bears ruin your vacation. This fear can accompany you every step of the way. It can be constantly lurking in the back of your mind, preventing you from enjoying the wildest and most beautiful places left on Earth. And even worse, some bear experts think bears might actually be able to sense your fear.

Being prepared and being knowledgeable give you confidence. And this confidence allows you to fight back the fear that can burden you throughout your stay in bear country. You won't—nor should you—forget about bears and the basic rules of safety, but proper preparation allows you to keep the fear of bears at bay and let enjoyment rule the day.

And on top of that, do we really want to be totally safe? If we did, we probably would never go hiking in the wilderness—bears or no bears. We certainly wouldn't, at much greater risk, drive hundreds of miles to get to the trailhead. Perhaps a tinge of danger adds a desired element to our wilderness trip.

Hiking in Bear Country

Nobody likes surprises, and bears dislike them, too. The majority of bear maulings occur when a hiker surprises a bear. Therefore, it's vital to do everything possible to avoid these surprise meetings. Perhaps the best way is to know the five-part system. If you follow these five rules, the chance of encountering a bear on the trail sinks to the slimmest possible margin.

- Be alert.
- Go in with a group and stay together.
- Stay on the trail.
- Hike in the middle of the day.
- Make noise.

No substitute for alertness: As you hike, watch ahead and to the sides. Don't fall into the all-too-common and particularly nasty habit of fixating on the trail 10 feet ahead. It's especially easy to do this when dragging a heavy pack up a long hill or when carefully watching your step on a heavily eroded trail.

Using your knowledge of bear habitat and habits, be especially alert in areas most likely to be frequented by bears, such as avalanche chutes, berry patches, streambeds, and stands of whitebark pine.

Watch carefully for bear signs and be especially watchful (and noisy) if you see any. If you see a track or a scat, but it doesn't look fresh, pretend it's fresh. Such an area is obviously frequented by bears.

Watch the wind: The wind can be a friend or foe. The strength and direction of the wind can make a significant difference in your chances of an encounter with a bear. When the wind is blowing at your back, your smell travels ahead of you, alerting any bear that might be on or near the trail ahead. Conversely, when the wind blows in your face, your chances of a surprise meeting with a bear increase, so make more noise and be more alert.

A strong wind can also be noisy and limit a bear's ability to hear you coming. If a bear can't smell or hear you, the chances of an encounter greatly increase, so watch the wind.

Safety in numbers: There have been very few instances where a large group has had an encounter with a bear. On the other hand, a large percentage of hikers mauled by bears were hiking alone. Large groups naturally make more noise and put out more smell and probably appear more threatening to bears. In addition, if you're hiking alone and get injured, there is nobody to go for help. For these reasons rangers often recommend parties of four or more hikers when going into bear country.

If the large party splits up, the advantage is lost, so stay together. If you're on a family hike, keep the kids from running ahead. If you're in a large group, keep the stronger members from going ahead or weaker members from lagging behind. The best way to prevent this natural separation is to ask one of the slowest members of the group to lead. This keeps everybody together.

Stay on the trail: Although bears use trails, they don't often travel on them during midday when hikers commonly use them. Through generations of associating trails with people, bears probably expect to find hikers on trails, especially during midday.

Contrarily, bears probably don't expect to find hikers off trails. Bears rarely settle down in a day bed right along a heavily used trail. However, if you wander around in thickets off the trail, you are more likely to stumble into an occupied day bed or cross paths with a traveling bear.

Sleeping late: Bears—and most other wildlife—usually aren't active during the middle of the day, especially on a hot summer day. Wild animals are most active around dawn and dusk. Therefore, hiking early in the morning or late afternoon increases your chances of seeing wildlife, including bears. Likewise, hiking during the middle of a hot August day greatly reduces the chance of an encounter.

Be noisy: Perhaps the best way to avoid a surprise meeting with a bear is to make sure the bear knows you're coming, so make lots of noise. Some experts think metallic noise is superior to human voices, which can be muffled by natural conditions, but the important issue is making lots of noise, regardless of what kind.

In addition to the five rules described above, there are other precautions you can take to avoid an encounter.

Running: Many avid runners like to get off paved roads and running tracks and onto backcountry trails. But running on trails in bear country can be seriously hazardous to your health. Bears can't hear you coming and you approach them faster than expected, and of course, it's nearly impossible to be fully alert when you have to watch the trail closely to keep from falling.

Leave the night to the bears: Like running on trails, hiking at night can be very risky. Bears are more active after dark, and you can't see them until it's too late. If you get caught at night, be sure to make lots of noise, and remember that bears commonly travel on hiking trails at night.

You can be dead meat, too: If you see or smell a carcass of a dead animal when hiking, immediately vacate the area. Don't let your curiosity keep you near the carcass a second longer than necessary. Bears commonly hang around a carcass, guarding it and feeding on it for days until it's completely consumed. Your presence could easily be interpreted as a threat to the bear's food supply, and a vicious attack could be imminent.

Most routes in this book pass through grizzly bear habitat, so always be bear aware.

If you see a carcass ahead of you on the trail, don't go any closer. Instead, abandon your hike and return to the trailhead. If the carcass is between you and the trailhead, take a very long detour around it, upwind from the carcass, making lots of noise along the way. Be sure to report the carcass to the local ranger. This might prompt a temporary trail closure or special warnings and prevent injury to other hikers. Rangers will, in some cases, go in and drag the carcass away from the trail.

Cute, cuddly, and lethal: If you see a bear cub, don't go 1 inch closer to it. It might seem abandoned, but it most likely is not. Mother bear is probably close by, and female bears fiercely defend their young.

It doesn't do you any good in your pack: If you brought a repellent such as pepper spray, don't bury it in your pack. Keep it as accessible as possible. Most pepper spray comes in a holster or somehow conveniently attaches to your belt or pack. Such protection won't do you any good if you can't have it ready to fire in one or two seconds. Before hitting the trail, read the directions carefully and test fire the spray.

Regulations: Nobody likes rules and regulations. However, national parks have a few related to hiking and camping in bear country that you must follow. These rules aren't meant to take the freedom out of your trip. They are meant to help bring you back safely.

"But I didn't see any bears": You know how to be safe: Walk up the trail constantly clanging two metal pans together. It works every time. You won't see a bear, but you'll hate your "wilderness experience." Didn't you leave the city to get away from loud noise? Yes, you can be very safe, but how safe do you want to be and still be able to enjoy your trip? It's a balancing act. First, be knowledgeable and then decide how far you want to go. Everybody has to make his or her own personal choice.

Here's another conflict. If you do everything listed here, you most likely will not see any bears—or any deer, moose, eagles, or any other wildlife. Again, you make the choice. If you want to be as safe as possible, follow these rules religiously. If you want to see wildlife, including bears, do all of this in reverse, but then, you are increasing your chances of an encounter instead of decreasing it.

Camping in Bear Country

Staying overnight in bear country is not dangerous, but it adds a slight additional risk to your trip. The main difference is the presence of more food, cooking, and garbage. Plus, you are in bear country at night when bears are usually most active. Once again, however, following a few basic rules greatly minimizes this risk.

Storing food and garbage: If the campsite doesn't have a bear-proof storage box or bear pole, be sure to set one up or at least locate one before it gets dark. It's not only difficult to store food after darkness falls, but it's easier to overlook a juicy morsel on the ground. Also, be sure to store food in airtight, waterproof bags to prevent food odors from circulating throughout the forest. For double protection, put food and garbage in securely closed zip-locked bags and then seal tightly in a larger plastic bag.

The illustrations on page 25 depict three popular methods for hanging food bags. In any case, try to get food and garbage at least 10 feet off the ground.

Special equipment: It's not really that special, but one piece of equipment you definitely need is a good supply of zip-locked bags. This handy invention is perfect for keeping food smell to a minimum and helps keep food from spilling on your pack, clothing, or other gear.

Take a special bag for storing food. The bag must be sturdy and waterproof. You can get "dry" bags at most outdoor specialty stores, but you can get by with a trash compactor bag. Regular garbage bags can break and leave your food spread on the ground.

You also need 50 feet of nylon cord. You don't need a heavy climbing rope to store food. Go light instead. Parachute cord will usually suffice unless you plan to hang large quantities of food and gear (which might be the case on a long backpacking excursion with a large group).

You can also buy a small pulley system to make hoisting a heavy load easier. Again, you can usually get by without this extra weight in your pack unless you have a massive load to hang.

What to hang: To be as safe as possible, store everything that has any food smell. This includes cooking gear, eating utensils, bags used to keep food in your pack, all garbage, toiletries, and even clothes with food smells on them. If you spilled something on your clothes, change into other clothes for sleeping and hang clothes with food smells with the food and garbage. If you take these items into the tent, you aren't separating your sleeping area from food smells. Try to keep food odors off your pack, but if you can't, put the food bag inside and hang the pack.

What to keep in your tent: You can't be too careful in keeping food smells out of the tent. Just in case a bear has become accustomed to coming into that campsite looking for food, it's vital to keep all food smells out of the tent. This often includes your pack, which is hard to keep odor-free. Usually only take valuables (like cameras and binoculars), clothing, and sleeping gear into the tent.

If you brought a bear repellent, such as pepper spray, sleep with it. Also, keep a flashlight in the tent. If an animal comes into camp and wakes you up, you need the flashlight to identify it.

The campfire: In many areas, regulations prohibit campfires, but if you're in an area where fires are allowed, treat yourself. Besides adding the nightly entertainment, the fire might make your camp safer from bears.

The campfire provides the best possible way to get rid of food smells. Build a small but hot fire and thoroughly burn everything that smells of food—garbage, leftovers, fish entrails, everything. If you brought food in cans or other incombustible containers, burn those, too. You can even dump extra water from cooking or dish water on the edge of the fire to erase the smell.

Be very sure you have the fire hot enough to completely burn everything. If you leave partially burned food scraps in the fire, you are setting up a dangerous situation for the next camper who uses this site.

Before leaving camp the next morning, dig out the fire pit and pack out anything that has not completely burned, even if you believe it no longer carries food smells. For example, many foods like dried soup or hot chocolate come in foil packages that might seem like they burn, but they really don't. Pack out the scorched foil and cans (now with very minor food smells). Also, pack out foil and cans left by other campers.

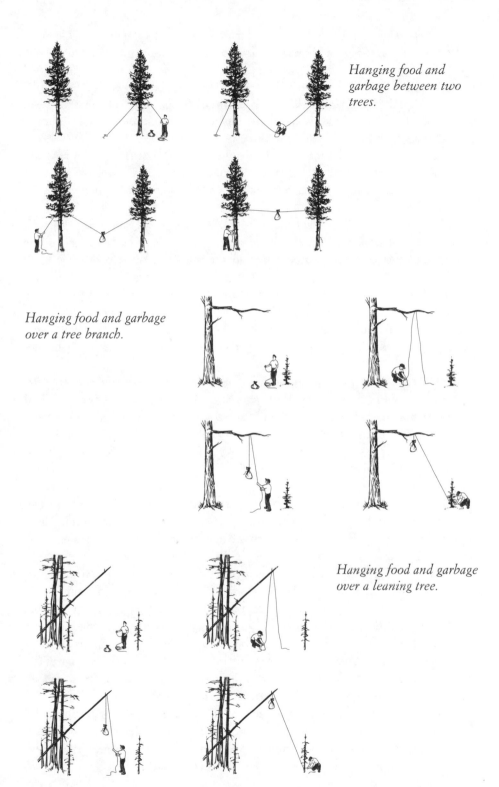

Hanging food and garbage between two trees.

Hanging food and garbage over a tree branch.

Hanging food and garbage over a leaning tree.

Types of food: Perhaps the safest option is freeze-dried food. It carries very little smell, and it comes in convenient envelopes that allow you to "cook it" by merely adding boiling water. This means you don't have cooking pans to wash or store. However, freeze-dried food is expensive. Many backpackers don't use it, but they still safely enjoy bear country.

Dry, prepacked meals (often pasta- or rice-based) offer an affordable compromise to freeze-dried foods. Also, take your favorite high-energy snack. Avoid fresh fruit and canned meats and fish.

The key point is this: What food you have along is much less critical than how you handle it, cook it, and store it. An open can of tuna fish has a strong smell, but if you eat all of it in one meal, don't spill it on the ground or on your clothes, and burn the can later, it can be quite safe.

Hanging food at night is not the only storage issue. Make sure you place food correctly in your pack. Use airtight packages as much as possible. Store food in the containers it came in or, when opened, in zip-locked bags. This keeps food smells out of your pack and off your camping gear and clothes.

How to cook: The overriding philosophy of cooking in bear country is to create as little odor as possible. Keep it simple. Use as few pans and dishes as you can.

Unless it's a weather emergency, don't cook in the tent. If you like winter backpacking, you probably cook in the tent, but you should have a different tent for summer backpacking.

If you can have a campfire and decide to cook fish, try cooking in aluminum foil envelopes instead of frying them. Then, after removing the cooked fish, quickly and completely burn the fish scraps off the foil. Using foil also means you don't have to wash the pan you used to cook the fish.

Be careful not to spill on yourself while cooking. If you do, change clothes and hang the clothes with food odor with the food and garbage. Wash your hands thoroughly before retiring to the tent.

Don't cook too much food, so you don't have to deal with leftovers. If you do end up with extra food, however, you only have two choices. Carry it out or burn it. Don't bury it or throw it in a lake or leave it anywhere in bear country. A bear will most likely find and dig up any buried food or garbage.

Taking out the garbage: In bear country, you have only two choices—burn garbage or carry it out. Prepare for garbage problems before you leave home. Bring along airtight zip-locked bags to store garbage. Be sure to hang your garbage at night along with your food. Also, carry in as little garbage as possible by discarding excess packaging while packing.

Washing dishes: This can be a problem, but there is one easy solution. If you don't dirty dishes, you don't have to wash them. So try to minimize food smells by using as few dishes and pans as possible. If you use the principles of zero-impact camping, you are probably doing as much as you can to reduce food smells from dishes.

If you brought paper towels, use one to carefully remove food scraps from pans and dishes before washing them. Then, when you wash dishes, you have much less food smell. Burn the dirty towels or store them in zip-locked bags with other garbage. Put pans and dishes in zip-locked bags before putting them back in your pack.

If you end up with lots of food scraps in the dishwater, drain out the scraps and store them in zip-locked bags with other garbage or burn them. You can bring a lightweight screen to filter out food scraps from dishwater, but be sure to store the screen with the food and garbage. If you have a campfire, pour the dishwater around the edge of the fire. If you don't have a fire, take the dishwater at least 200 feet downwind and downhill from camp and pour it on the ground or in a small hole. Don't put dishwater or food scraps in a lake or stream.

Although possibly counter to accepted rules of cleanliness for many people, you can skip washing dishes altogether on the last night of your trip. Instead, simply use the paper towels to clean the dirty dishes as much as possible. You can wash them when you get home. Pack dirty dishes in zip-locked bags before putting them back in your pack.

Finally, don't put it off. Do dishes immediately after eating, so a minimum of food smell lingers in the area.

Choosing a tent site: Try to keep your tent site at least 100 feet from your cooking area. Unfortunately, some campsites do not adequately separate the cooking area from the tent site. Store food at least 100 yards from the tent. You can store it near the cooking area to concentrate food smells further.

Not under the stars: Some people prefer to sleep out under the stars instead of using a tent. This might be okay in areas not frequented by bears, but it's not a good idea in bear country. The thin fabric of a tent certainly isn't any real physical protection from a bear, but it does present a psychological barrier to a bear that wants to come closer.

Do somebody a big favor: Report all bear sightings to the ranger after your trip. This might not help you, but it could save another camper's life. If rangers get enough reports to spot a pattern, they will manage the area to prevent potentially hazardous situations.

In sum, these are the bear essentials of backpacking in bear country:

- Knowledge is the best defense.
- There is no substitute for alertness.
- Hike with a large group and stay together.
- Don't hike alone.
- Stay on the trail.
- Hike in the middle of the day.
- Make lots of noise while hiking.
- Never approach a bear.
- Females with cubs are very dangerous.
- Stay away from carcasses.
- Defensive hiking works. Try it.
- Choose a safe campsite.
- Camp below timberline.
- Separate sleeping and cooking areas.
- Sleep in a tent.

- Cook just the right amount of food and eat it all.
- Store food and garbage out of reach of bears.
- Never feed bears.
- Keep food odors out of the tent.
- Leave the campsite cleaner than you found it.
- Leave no food rewards for bears.

BE MOUNTAIN LION AWARE, TOO

The most important safety element for recreation in mountain lion country is simply recognizing their habitat. Mountain lions primarily feed on deer, so these common ungulates are a key element in cougar habitat. Basically, where you have a high deer population, you can expect to find mountain lions. Fish and wildlife agencies usually have good information about deer distribution from population surveys and hunting results.

If you are not familiar with identifying deer tracks, seek the advice of someone knowledgeable, or refer to a book on animal tracks such as FalconGuide's *Scats and Tracks* series.

Safety Guidelines for Traveling in Mountain Lion Country

To stay as safe as possible when hiking in mountain lion country, follow this advice.
- Travel with a friend or group. There's safety in numbers, so stay together.
- Don't let small children wander away by themselves.
- Don't let pets run unleashed.
- Avoid hiking at dawn and dusk—the times mountain lions are most active.
- Watch for warning signs of mountain lion activity.
- Know how to behave if you encounter a mountain lion.

What to Do If You Encounter a Mountain Lion

In the vast majority of mountain lion encounters, these animals exhibit avoidance, indifference, or curiosity that never results in human injury. But it is natural to be alarmed if you have an encounter of any kind. Try to keep your cool and consider the following:

Recognize threatening mountain lion behavior. There are a few cues that may help you gauge the risk of attack. If a mountain lion is more than 50 yards away, and it directs its attention to you, it may be only curious. This situation represents only a slight risk for adults, but a more serious risk to unaccompanied children. At this point, you should move away, while keeping the animal in your peripheral vision. Also, look for rocks, sticks, or something to use as a weapon, just in case.

If a mountain lion is crouched and staring intensely at you less than 50 yards away, it may be assessing the chances of a successful attack. If this behavior continues, the risk of attack may be high.

Do not approach a mountain lion. Instead, give the animal the opportunity to move on. Slowly back away, but maintain eye contact if close. Mountain lions are not known to attack humans to defend young or a kill, but they have been reported to "charge" in rare instances and may want to stay in the area. It's best to choose another route or time to hike through the area.

Do not run from a mountain lion. Running may stimulate a predatory response from the mountain lion.

Make noise. If you encounter a mountain lion, be vocal and talk or yell loudly and regularly. Try not to panic. Shout in a way that makes others in the area aware of the situation.

Maintain eye contact. Eye contact presents a challenge to the mountain lion, showing you are aware of its presence. Eye contact also helps you know where the animal is. However, if the behavior of the mountain lion is not threatening (if it is, for example, grooming or periodically looking away), maintain visual contact through your peripheral vision and move away.

Appear larger than you are. Raise your arms above your head and make steady waving motions. Raise your jacket or another object above your head. Do not bend over, as this will make you appear smaller and more "prey-like."

If you are with small children, pick them up. First, bring children close to you, maintaining eye contact with the mountain lion, and pull the children up without bending over. If you are with other adults or children, band together.

Defend yourself and others. If attacked, fight back. Try to remain standing. Do not feign death. Pick up a branch or rock; pull out a knife, pepper spray, or other deterrent device. Remember that everything is a potential weapon, and individuals have fended off mountain lions with blows from rocks, tree limbs, and even cameras. In past attacks on

HOW TO GET REALLY BEAR AND MOUNTAIN LION AWARE

Most of the information in this chapter comes from *Bear Aware* and *Mountain Lion Alert,* handy, inexpensive FalconGuides®. These small, "packable" books contains the essential tips you need to reduce the risk of being injured by a bear or mountain lion to the slimmest possible margin, and they are written for both beginner and expert:

- Day Hikers
- Tent Campers
- Hunters
- Anglers
- Outfitters
- Backpackers
- Backcountry Horsemen
- Mountain Bikers
- Trail Runners
- Photographers

In addition to covering the all-important subject of how to prevent an encounter, these books include advice on what to do if you are involved in an encounter.

You can buy these books at booksellers specializing in outdoor recreation and at national park visitor centers.

children, adults have successfully stopped attacks. Physically defending a pet is not recommended.

Respect any warning signs posted by agencies.

Before leaving on your hike, discuss lions and teach others in your group how to behave in case of a mountain lion encounter. For example, anyone who starts running could bring on an attack.

Report encounters. If you have an encounter with a mountain lion, record your location and the details of the encounter, and notify the nearest land owner or land-managing agency. The land management agency (federal, state, or county) may want to visit the site and, if appropriate, post education/warning signs. Fish and wildlife agencies should also be notified because they record and track such encounters. If physical injury occurs, it is important to leave the area and not disturb the site of attack. Mountain lions that have attacked people must be killed, and an undisturbed site is critical for effectively locating the dangerous mountain lion.

BACKPACKING WITH STYLE

What is backpacking with style? It's performing random little acts of courtesy, things that usually go unspoken, but that make a trip much more pleasant for everybody. In general try to backpack in a way that makes it comfortable, convenient, and safe for everybody. Also, do things to fit naturally into your wilderness environment instead of conflict with it.

Here are a few examples, but this is by no means a complete list.

- In the wilderness safety always wins out over convenience, vanity, or speed. Don't suggest anything to the contrary.

- Strive for the highest level of organization, regardless of how disorganized or messy your office or home is. Whether you're on the trail or in camp, know where every single piece of your equipment is at every second of the day and night. Spend the appropriate amount of time planning out what you need to take along and packing your pack so it is as small and efficient as possible. Know how much you have and where everything is at all times.

- Avoid neon colors in your clothing, tents, sleeping bags, and other gear. Instead, go for natural colors. A drab, dull wardrobe works just find. Avoid T-shirts with messages others might not want to read in the depth of the wilderness.

- Don't have stuff hanging on your back or belt. It looks tacky and unorganized, and backpackers strive for extreme organization. Instead, pack everything neatly inside your pack or in appropriate side pockets.

- Don't make others wait while you constantly pack or repack or look for something in your pack in the morning or on rest stops. Keep the items you need during the day easily accessible and know where they are. Be ready to go when others are ready to go. Don't suddenly remember to do something or get something after others have already hoisted their packs.

- If you have to stop on the trail, say "pack down" so others know you have stopped and can also unload, but don't stop unnecessarily if the group wants to keep going.

- If you're a slow hiker, volunteer to go first to keep the group together (especially in bear and mountain lion country) and to make sure nobody gets too tired, including you while trying to keep up. Safety and style always outweigh vanity in the wilderness.

- People go to the wilderness to escape noise, so please respect the silence of others. Try to be as quiet as possible at all times. There is nothing better than the sound of silence.

- Drink profusely during the day to stay well-hydrated but back off in the evening so you can avoid getting up at night and waking up your tent mates.

- If you don't have a well-behaved dog, leave it at home. A barking dog can destroy the sound of silence. If you take your dog, don't let it chase wildlife or bother other hikers or their equipment.

- Pleasantly greet other hikers on the trail, but if they don't want to be social, don't take it personally. Many backpackers want only to enjoy a wild, people-free experience, so don't babble on when they want to be alone with nature. However, always warn hikers you meet of any hazardous or confusing sections of the trail.

- If you're super-fit, help weaker members of the group and be careful not to wear them out. You can run hills or do push-ups at night if you don't feel like you had a good enough workout during the day!

- If you're a weaker member of the group, don't be vain and reject offers from stronger members to help you or lighten your load.

- Always take care of your own stuff only. Don't try to be helpful and organize other people's stuff. While backpacking, everybody takes care of his or her own stuff.

- Help others get their packs on.

- Always do your share in communal activities like cleaning camp, cooking, filtering, washing dishes, setting up the tent, or cleaning group equipment. But don't do more than your share, lest you cause others to develop bad habits or make them feel uncomfortable about not doing their part.

- Don't sleep late and make others do more than their share of the communal work or wait for you.

- Don't take radios, CD players, PDAs, or other electronic gadgets. If you take a cell phone, use it strictly for emergencies, not to call Mom or check stock quotes or sports scores.

- On rocky trails kick off a rock or two when it's convenient to do so. If every hiker does this, the rocky trail will no longer be rocky.

- If possible, pitch your tent where other campers or hikers can't see it.

- Avoid wearing a bear bell unless your really need it for your self-confidence; even then put it away in areas where there is obviously no chance of encountering a bear, or when in camp. Keeping your group together and practicing other proven bear awareness techniques can keep you safe without annoying others.

- Eat your own food unless you've packed food as a group.
- When taking a rest, don't block the trail, bridges, or entries to stream crossings with your pack.
- Remember the stuff you need so you don't have to sponge on others. Use a checklist.
- Make sure your equipment works and is in good shape so it doesn't break on the trail and inconvenience the group or create a hazardous situation. In severe weather a leaky tent or a stove that won't start could kill the entire group. Ditto for a compass that doesn't work.
- And never pick the M&Ms out of the gorp.

These are just a few suggestions for becoming a stylish backpacker. You'll think of others. After becoming more stylish, you might enjoy your backpacking vacation a little more than you expected—and others in your group will, too.

BILL'S GUARANTEED WEIGHT-LOSS DIET FOR BACKPACKERS

Ever wish your jeans weren't so tight? Well, I have the solution.

In addition to loosening tight jeans, this special backpacking diet solves two more problems. It allows you to carry less weight, which means you can finally take that ten-day backpacking trip you have always wanted to tackle (but could never carry enough food for), and it allows you to spend more time hiking, fishing, mountain climbing, and wildlife viewing, instead of spending two or three hours every day cooking and washing dishes.

Through the years it has become clear to me that this diet won't work for everybody—and could be considered radical by some backpackers. Nutritionists might not recommend it, and I'm sure those who fret about "germs" will hate it. Nonetheless, it's worked for me for thirty years, and I wouldn't do it any other way.

This diet works for me because I'm a guy who hates cooking—and washing dishes. Both seem like a huge waste of time. Therefore, to avoid these two time-wasters, I spend almost every daylight hour fishing, exploring, or watching wildlife, not cooking or washing dishes. Unless there is a concern with finding a good campsite, I often hike late into the day. Even if I set up camp early, I prefer to sit by a stream and read or take a nap, rather than cook.

Here's another reason to do it my way. I've spent most of my nights in the wilderness in grizzly country. Dirty dishes, leftover food, and dishwater all tend to attract bears.

And, there is even one more reason. One of the basic principles of backpacking is self-reliance. People might not think they can get by on almost nothing, but they can—and enjoy it, too. I've been proving it for years.

The basis of this diet is snacks and hot drinks. I essentially snack all day, but in the morning and evening I combine my snacks with hot drinks. I never stop to cook lunch, but I do crank up the stove in the morning for several cups of hot tea. At night, I munch on bread and drink hot soup, cider, and herbal tea.

I choose snacks with nutrition in mind. I take raisins or dried fruit (so I can continue to be a regular guy), organic nuts, granola bars, bread and cheese, and jerky. I also take gorp and hard candy, but I'm careful not to eat too many high-sugar, empty-calorie snacks at the expense of high-nutrition food.

As for hot drinks, I can't live without my caffeinated tea in the morning and my green or herbal tea at night. I drink at least two mugs of dried soup each night. (Be sure to get the kind of soup you mix in your mug just like hot chocolate.) My family likes hot chocolate, and this fits well into the diet. I also take packets of hot cider mix for a change of pace.

I always take bread, and this is really the staple of my diet in the backcountry. I like Scottish oat or sourdough rolls that tend to stay fresh for several days. I also take French bread, but it gets hard enough to beat off a bear after a few days, so I usually eat it the first two days. I eat my bread with cheese at night and with strawberry jam in the morning (from the little jelly packets I get from restaurants). Sometimes, I take bagels for breakfast, toasted over the stove and covered with jelly or cream cheese.

Concerning dishes, I only get my camp mug and spoon dirty. I only use my pan for boiling water, not for cooking.

Sometimes, I eat fish, but I still do not dirty any pans or dishes. I cook fish in aluminum foil in a campfire. After I finish eating my fill (out of the foil), I burn away all the fishy odors by tossing the foil and all leftover fish parts into the campfire. I dig the foil out of the ashes in the morning and pack it out. If regulations or natural conditions dictate no campfires, I do not eat fish.

Before turning in I "wash" my mug and spoon by pouring in about a tablespoon of boiling water, and swab it out with a paper towel. I dip my spoon in hot water and clean it with a paper towel. Then, I burn the paper towel. If I don't have a campfire, I pack it out. I hang my mug with my food and garbage.

If I'm with a group who won't buy into this diet (and this happens frequently), I compromise by adding dried pasta- and rice-based prepackaged dinner to the evening meal. Although I frequently don't eat these easy-to-fix dinners, my hiking companions usually enjoy them. This means, heaven forbid, a pan to wash, but I still use small amounts of boiling water and paper towels to clean it. I suppose this might offend some people, but I've backpacked for thirty years without taking soap.

I'm not a professional nutritionist, so I don't know if this diet is a nutritional nightmare or not. Just to be safe, I take a multiple vitamin, calcium, and vitamin C each night. I've never noticed any problems with this diet except, of course, weight loss. Considering how many calories you burn backpacking, you will definitely lose at least one-half pound per day, and those jeans will fit better when you get home. If you spend a lot of time backpacking and use this diet, you can hide behind a lodgepole pine.

For hikers, million-acre Glacier National Park, "the crown of the continent," is probably the most popular destination in the northern Rockies. And it deserves its recommendation. The scenery is spectacular, and the park has a terrific trail system. Locals have been known to say of Glacier that, "God had to live somewhere while he made the rest of the world."

Many hiking routes in Glacier take you above the timberline and offer some cathedralistic views of the park's peaks. Other routes take you through the "V" shaped valleys through lush vegetation. Wildflower fans and photographers will think they're in heaven—geology buffs, too. Anglers can find some great fishing in Glacier. The park considers hiking a high priority recreational use, so consequently, trail crews keep most trails in excellent condition.

GETTING TO GLACIER

Straddling the Canadian border in northernmost Montana, Glacier is a long way from most places, and in most cases, it's a long drive to get there. If you're flying, the Glacier Park International Airport in Kalispell (25 miles west of the park) is the best choice, but many people use slightly larger airports in Great Falls or Missoula.

Lake Janet.

In addition to the driving and flying options, Glacier offers another intriguing alternative. Amtrak stops year-round in West Glacier and in East Glacier in the summer, so you could ride the train to Glacier.

BACKPACKING IN GLACIER

Along with this popularity and scenic grandeur has come very heavy use in many areas of the park. The National Park Service has responded with a carefully managed back-country permit system that limits the number of permits and designated campsites. The NPS doesn't require permits for day hiking, but all overnight backpackers must get a backcountry permit.

Backpacking in Glacier means hiking in grizzly country, and it requires knowledge and preparation. Be bear aware. Read up on this before going to the park. You can start by reading the bear awareness section in this book.

Bears might add a small slice of risk to your trip to Glacier, but not nearly as much as the weather. It's usually great weather in July and August in Glacier, but it can also snow any day of the year. So regardless of how nice it is when you leave the trailhead, be prepared for nasty weather.

One regulation of special note is the ban on leaving your pack unattended. Don't leave your pack unattended while you take a side trip unless you remove the food and take it with you or store it in a bear-resistant food container. If a ranger discovers you've left a pack with food in it unattended, you'll be cited. So, you need to leave somebody with the packs or hang them in one of the established food-storage devices in designated campsites. If you do leave your pack unattended, it might be prudent to attach a note to the ranger explaining that all the food has been removed.

With the exception of the Nyack Loop, backpackers must use designated campsites. These campsites are a mixed bag. In some sites you can enjoy a heavenly scenery. In others you are regulated to a lodgepole thicket. All campsites have pit toilets as well as designated tent sites, food preparation areas, and food/garbage storage devices, all of which you are required to use. Campfires are allowed in some campsites, but you must use fire pits.

FINDING MAPS

In addition to the USGS quadrangles (specific maps are listed with each trip), the USGS publishes an excellent map covering all of Glacier National Park. Make sure you have this map or the Trails Illustrated map for the park. You can get these maps at park visitor centers or local sport stores. You can also order large USGS and Trails Illustrated maps (and many other publications) from the Glacier Natural History Association whose proceeds go back to the park. You can also order maps online from the association's Web site (www.glacierassociation.org) or you can call or write for a free catalog and membership information:

Glacier Natural History Association
P.O. Box 310
West Glacier, MT 59936
Phone: (406) 888–5756
e-mail: gnha@glacierassociation.org

GETTING A PERMIT

The easiest way to get a backcountry camping permit is to walk into one of the park's ranger stations or visitor centers, apply right there, and pay the $4.00 per person per night backcountry camping fee. However, waiting until the last minute is risky because many popular campsites are reserved long in advance; if you can't get a permit for your preferred campsite, you might have to drastically change your planned route.

You can get permits at the following park facilities:

Apgar Backcountry Permit Center (Summer only—May through October)

St. Mary Visitor Center (Summer only—May through September)

Park Headquarters (Winter weekdays—October through April)

Apgar Visitor Center (Winter weekends—October through April)

Many Glacier, Polebridge, and Two Medicine ranger stations (Memorial Day to Labor Day)

Waterton Lakes National Park Visitor Reception Centre (Memorial Day to Labor Day)

The safest (but by no means the easiest) way to get your permit is by using the National Park Service's advance reservation system. Refer to Glacier's Web site (www. nps.gov/glac/activity.htm) for the details of the reservation system. You can also download an application from the Web site.

Reservations are issued on a first-come, first-served basis, so apply early. However, no applications are accepted if they are postmarked earlier than mid-April. Call 406–888–7857 for the specific date, which varies slightly year-to-year. In 2001 the reservation fee was $20.00 per trip. This is in addition to a $4.00 per person per night backcountry camping fee. Don't send the per person/per night fee with the reservation fee. You pay this when you pick up the permit. You must pick up the permit by 10:00 A.M. the morning your trip starts or the campsites will go back in the pool and be available to the long line of backpackers waiting for a permit at the visitor center, so don't be late. You also can't pick up permits sooner than the day before your trip starts.

If you can't, heaven forbid, get to Glacier to take your backpacking trip, please call the backcountry office (406–888–7857) and cancel your reservation so others might enjoy these campsites. Reservation fees are nonrefundable unless your application is unsuccessful or the park officially closes the trail you have chosen.

Getting a permit for early in the season (late June to early July) can be unpredictable. Each campground opens according to weather and snow conditions, which, of course, vary from year to year. A late-season snow can change these "earliest available dates," which are listed on the park's Web site.

Given all this uncertainty, the NPS strongly recommends that you have a "back-up plan" (an alternative hiking route) ready before you get to the park.

BACKCOUNTRY REGULATIONS

You can get a complete list of backcountry regulations when you get your permit or from the park's Web site. Here are a few of the most relevant rules for backpackers:

- Pets, firearms, moterboats, snowmobiles, and wheeled vehicles (including bicycles and canoe carts) are prohibited.
- Do not leave your backpack unattended if it has food in it.
- All natural features are protected. Fish and edible berries may be harvested for personal consumption only. Picking mushrooms is prohibited.
- Wood fires are permitted in designated fire pits only.
- Pack out all refuse, including uneaten food and scraps.
- Feeding, disturbing, or harassing wildlife is unsafe and illegal.
- Fishing does not require a license. Obtain fishing regulations when you pick up your backcountry camping permit.
- Shortcutting switchbacks is unsafe, destructive, and illegal.
- Human waste must be deposited in a toilet when available. When not, use a cathole at least 200 feet from water sources and pack out toilet paper.

FOR MORE INFORMATION

You can get much of the basic information you need from the *Waterton-Glacier Guide,* a free newspaper published by the Glacier and Waterton Natural History Associations and given out at entrance stations. You can also contact the NPS directly:

National Park Service, Park Headquarters, West Glacier, MT 59935; (406) 888–7800; fax: (406) 888–7808; e-mail: glac_park_info@nps.gov; Web site: www. nps.gov/glac.

Contact the Glacier Natural History Association at this address.

Glacier Natural History Association, P.O. Box 310, West Glacier, MT 59936; (406) 888–5756; e-mail: gnha@glacierassociation.org.

For lodging at historic hotels in the park, contact Glacier Park, Inc.:

Glacier Park, Inc., 106 Cooperative Way, Suite 104, Kalispell, MT 59901; (406) 756–2444; www.glacierparkinc.com.

1

Boulder Pass

General description: A long, scenic shuttle starting in Canada and ending in the United States

Special attractions: Incredible alpine scenery and remoteness; a classic backpacking trip

Type of trip: Shuttle

Total distance: 30.6 miles

Difficulty: Moderately strenuous

Traffic: Moderate

Maps: Kintla Lake, Kintla Peak, Porcupine Ridge, and Mount Carter USGS quads and either the USGS or Trails Illustrated map for the entire park

Starting point: Goat Haunt Trailhead at the south end of Waterton Lake

Finding the trailhead: To reach the trailhead you cross through customs into Canada at the Chief Mountain station, drive to the Waterton town site in Waterton Lakes National Park, and, for a modest fee, take the tour boat to Goat Haunt. The boat leaves from the marina on Emerald Bay (also called Divers Bay). The cruise runs several times during the day and takes two hours and fifteen minutes. Call or e-mail the Waterton Shoreline Cruise Company (403–859–2362; wscruise@cadvision.com) for an updated schedule and fees. You can also check the information at www.watertoninfo.ab.ca/m/cruise.html. Alternatively, you can hike from the Waterton town site along the west shore of Waterton Lake, but the cruise is worth the money.

Leave a vehicle or arrange for a pick-up at Kintla Lake Campground at the foot of Kintla Lake. To reach this trailhead drive north of Columbia Falls on County Road 486 (known locally as the "North Fork Road") for 30 miles until you see the sign for Polebridge. Turn right here, and cross the North Fork of the Flathead River at the Polebridge Ranger Station. After you pass through the NPS facilities, you intersect with the gravel road along the east side of the North Fork within the park. Turn left (north) here and drive 13 miles to the end of the road at the Kintla Lake Campground.

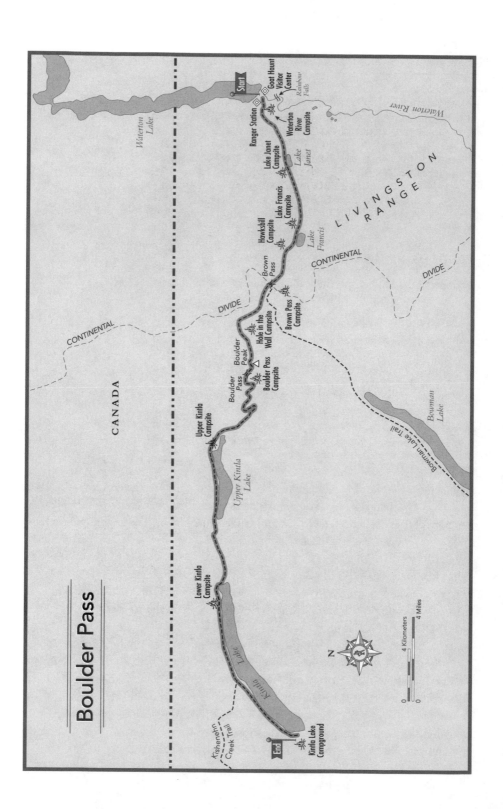

Boulder Pass

Waterton Lake

CANADA

Start

Goat Haunt Visitor Center

Rainbow Falls

Ranger Station

Waterton River Campsite

Waterton River

Lake Janet Campsite

Lake Janet

LIVINGSTON RANGE

Lake Francis Campsite

Hawksbill Campsite

Lake Francis

Brown Pass

CONTINENTAL

DIVIDE

Brown Pass Campsite

DIVIDE

Hole in the Wall Campsite

CONTINENTAL

Boulder Peak

Boulder Pass

Boulder Pass Campsite

Upper Kintla Campsite

Upper Kintla Lake

Bowman Lake Trail

Bowman Lake

Lower Kintla Campsite

Kintla Lake

Kishenehn Creek Trail

End

Kintla Lake Campground

N

4 Kilometers

4 Miles

0

0

0.4 m.	Junction with Rainbow Falls Trail; turn right
0.6	Waterton River Campsite (2★)
0.9	Junction with Boulder Pass Trail, turn left
3.1	Lake Janet and Campsite (2★)
5.6	Lake Francis and Campsite (4★)
6.2	Hawksbill Campsite (3★)
7.7	Junction with Brown Pass Trail and campsite (3★); turn right
10.5	Trail to Hole-in-the-Wall Campsite (5★); turn right
13.0	Boulder Pass
13.6	Boulder Pass Campsite (5★)
18.8	Upper Kintla Lake and Campsite (4★)
21.6	Lower end of Upper Kintla Lake
24.3	Lower Kintla Lake and Campsite (4★)
27.0	Junction with trail to Kishenehn Creek; turn left
31.0	Kintla Lake Campground

Parking and trailhead facilities: At Goat Haunt, a visitor center and rest rooms. Ample parking at the marina. At Kintla Lake a vehicle campground and toilets, but limited parking, so be careful not to take more than one space.

Recommended itinerary: Take the earliest boat you can get in order to get a good start on your hike and so you have time to reach Lake Francis, which has a nicer campsite than those at Waterton River, Lake Janet, or Hawksbill.

First night:	Lake Francis
Second night:	Boulder Pass or Hole-in-the-Wall
Third night:	Upper Kintla Lake
Fourth night:	Lower Kintla Lake

The spacing of the campsites on the west side of Boulder Pass makes deciding between a four- or five-day trip a difficult choice. You could cut back to a four-day trip by hiking from Boulder Pass Camp to Lower Kintla Lake. This is 11 miles, but it's almost all downhill. If you can't get Boulder Pass Campsite and you stay at Hole-in-the-Wall, it's best to take five days.

The hike: Boulder Pass is a truly classic trip and has achieved some widespread popularity because of it. The NPS limits use with the number of designated campsites and permits, so if you're lucky enough to get one, you won't feel crowded.

The hike itself is difficult to beat, but the preparation can test your patience. Use the park's backcountry permit reservation system to try for a permit in advance. Showing up

The Boulder Pass Trail is challenging near the top.

at a ranger station looking for a permit to start the hike the next day might be fruitless, and you probably will be using your alternative route. When you do get a permit, you have to arrange a long, problematic shuttle. The best way to manage this is to take this trip with another party, so you can start at opposite ends of the route and meet at Boulder Pass or Hole-in-the-Wall camps to exchange car keys. Then, of course, you both have to get permits, so more patience is required.

Another special planning task is watching the weather forecast. You really don't want to be up on Boulder Pass in a summer snowstorm. Because of the elevation, snow claims the area until at least late July. It can come back any day, so always prepare for the worst weather.

And keep in mind that this is prime grizzly country, so study up on bear awareness advice before hitting the trail.

But take some solace in the fact that this route is worth any amount of frustration in planning and preparation!

The first leg of the route climbs gradually through the lush Olson Creek valley, thick with thimbleberry and false hellebore. If you leave early, before the sun gets a chance to dry the dew, plan on getting as wet as if it had rained. There are plenty of water sources, which is, in general, true for the entire route.

At Lake Janet you get a great view of The Sentinel over the lake, but you get a poor view of Lake Francis from the trail. Just past Lake Francis, at the foot of an unnamed lake, the trail starts switchbacking out of the forest into the alpine wonderland you'll enjoy until you plunge down to the Kintla Valley on the other side of Boulder Pass. Here you walk out of the thimbleberry forests onto the wildflower carpet. Off to your left (south), Thunderbird Falls cascades down from the mountain and glacier of the same name (originating from several Indian legends about a great bird spirit with lightning flashing from its eyes that creates thunder by flapping its wings) into the unnamed lake. You might think this is scenery at its best, but it gets even better as you proceed uphill. It's a gentle, Category 4 climb to Brown Pass.

When you reach the junction with the Brown Pass Trail, bear right. If you have a permit for the Brown Pass campsite, you must have bug netting and repellent to keep the infamously vicious Brown Pass mosquitoes at bay. They are little brown mutants that go right for your eyeballs.

After Browns Pass you are in the high country as you gradually climb to Boulder Pass, again only a Category 4 climb. About 2 miles from the pass, the wildflowers give way to sheer rock, with a few hard phlox hanging on to the soil-less landscape. Mighty Kintla Peak and its slightly shorter but more austere companion, Kinnerly Peak, dominate the southern horizon most of the way to the top. You can look back and see the park's highest peak, Cleveland, and nearby Stoney Indian Peaks with their thirteen distinct spires.

The trail is in great shape considering the rugged environment. You have to follow cairns in a few places, but the route is easy to find. Earlier in the season (mid- to late-July), you may encounter a few dangerous snow banks.

After enjoying some special time on top of the pass, start down the giant decline to Upper Kintla Lake. This trail is rougher, rockier, and steeper than the east side trail, but it isn't as brushy.

Along Upper Kintla Lake you get a constant view of the Matahorn-like Kinnerly Peak. With the exception of a small hill between the lakes and a few hills along Lower Kintla Lake, it's essentially a gradual downhill the rest of the trip.

Watch for bald eagles around the upper end of Lower Kintla Lake, but be careful not to disturb them.

Options: You can do this trip in reverse, of course, but the climb up from Upper Kintla Lake is more strenuous than coming up from the east side, a Category 1 hill. Plus, coming down to the Kintla Valley offers some fantastic scenery that you miss if you're struggling uphill staring at your next foot plant.

Side trips: If you have time at the beginning of the trip, take the short spur trail over to see Rainbow Falls. Otherwise, there aren't really any logical side trips except some casual exploring amid the scenic grandeur of Boulder Pass.

Camping: You must use designated campsites on this route. All have pit toilets and food/garbage storage devices. I have unscientifically rated the sites as follows:

Waterton River: (2★) Slightly difficult to find. Go west of the ranger station, past the corral, and past the camp you can see on the other side of the stream. Walk about another quarter-mile past the camp all the way to the junction with the Boulder Pass Trail, then take a right onto a spur trail and cross the stream on a suspension bridge and hike back east to the camp. No view. Five tent sites. Good water sources. Private enough. Heaven for mosquito in July.

Lake Janet: (2★) Marginal view. Two tent sites. Good water source. Private enough.

Lake Francis: (4★) At the west end of the lake with a great view of unnamed falls tumbling down from Dixon Glacier, Thunderbird Mountain and The Sentinel. Two campsites. Pit toilet. Private. Good water source. About a half mile steep downhill to the campsite.

Hawksbill: (3★) Nice view from tent sites. No view from food preparation area. Two campsites. Private enough. A short walk to water.

Browns Pass: (3★). Good view from food preparation area. No view from tent sites. Lots of mosquitoes. Short walk to water. Minimally private.

Hole-in-the-Wall: (5★) Doesn't get much better than this. A fantastic view from all sections of the campground, which sits in a big notch in the south flank of Mount Custer. Five campsites. Good water source. Fairly private. Only drawback is the steep, mile-long spur trail down to the campground from the main trail, which, of course, you need to climb the next morning.

Boulder Pass: (5★) Like Hole-in-the-Wall, it doesn't get any better. Fabulous view all around, especially from the open-air pit toilet. Only two campsites. Good water source. Not well protected, so plan on having good weather. About 0.2 mile off the trail. The NPS should get a medal for placing this camp in the ideal spot.

Upper Kintla Lake: (4★) Great view of mighty Kinnerly Peak from food preparation area and tent sites. Four campsites all fairly close to the lake instead of tucked back in a thicket with no view. Minimal privacy. Easy water source.

Lower Kintla Lake: (4★) Close to lake with good view. Six campsites. Easy water source. Campfires allowed in fire pits. Minimally private. Shows signs of overuse.

Fishing: Normally, this route doesn't attract anglers, but Lake Francis has some good fishing for rainbows. They can get up to four pounds but are difficult to catch. You can also fish Lower Kintla Lake where you stand a good chance of getting a nice cutthroat from the west shore. Upper Kintla is closed to fishing.

2

Fifty Mountain

General description: A long trek through the alpine heart of Glacier National Park

Special attractions: Perhaps the best mountain scenery in the park. Plus, you start at high elevation, so there are no big climbs. It's basically a downhill backpacking trip.

Type of trip: Shuttle

Total distance: 30.5 miles

Difficulty: Moderate

Traffic: Heavy considering the length and remoteness of the trip, especially near Logan Pass, Granite Park Chalet, and Kootenai Lake

Maps: Ahern Pass, Logan Pass, Many Glacier, Porcupine Ridge, Mount Geduhn USGS quads and either the USGS or Trails Illustrated map for the entire park

Starting point: Logan Pass

Finding the trailhead: The trailhead is across the highway from the Logan Pass Visitor Center.

When you reach Goat Haunt at the end of your hike, take the boat tour back to Waterton. You'll need to leave a vehicle or arrange for a pick-up at the marina in Waterton. This means you'll pass through customs at the Chief Mountain station. There is a modest fee to take the tour boat from Goat Haunt. The boat leaves from the marina on Emerald Bay (also called Divers Bay). The cruise runs several times during the day and takes two hours and fifteen minutes. Call or e-mail the Waterton Shoreline Cruise Company (403–859–2362; wscruise@cadvision.com) for an updated schedule and fees. You can also check the information at www.watertoninfo.ab.ca/m/cruise.html. Alternatively, you can hike from the Waterton town site along the west shore of Waterton Lake, but the cruise is worth the money.

Parking and trailhead facilities: Logan Pass Visitor Center has drinking water and rest rooms. Ample parking. At Goat Haunt, small visitor center, ranger station, drinking water, and rest rooms. No vehicle access to trailhead.

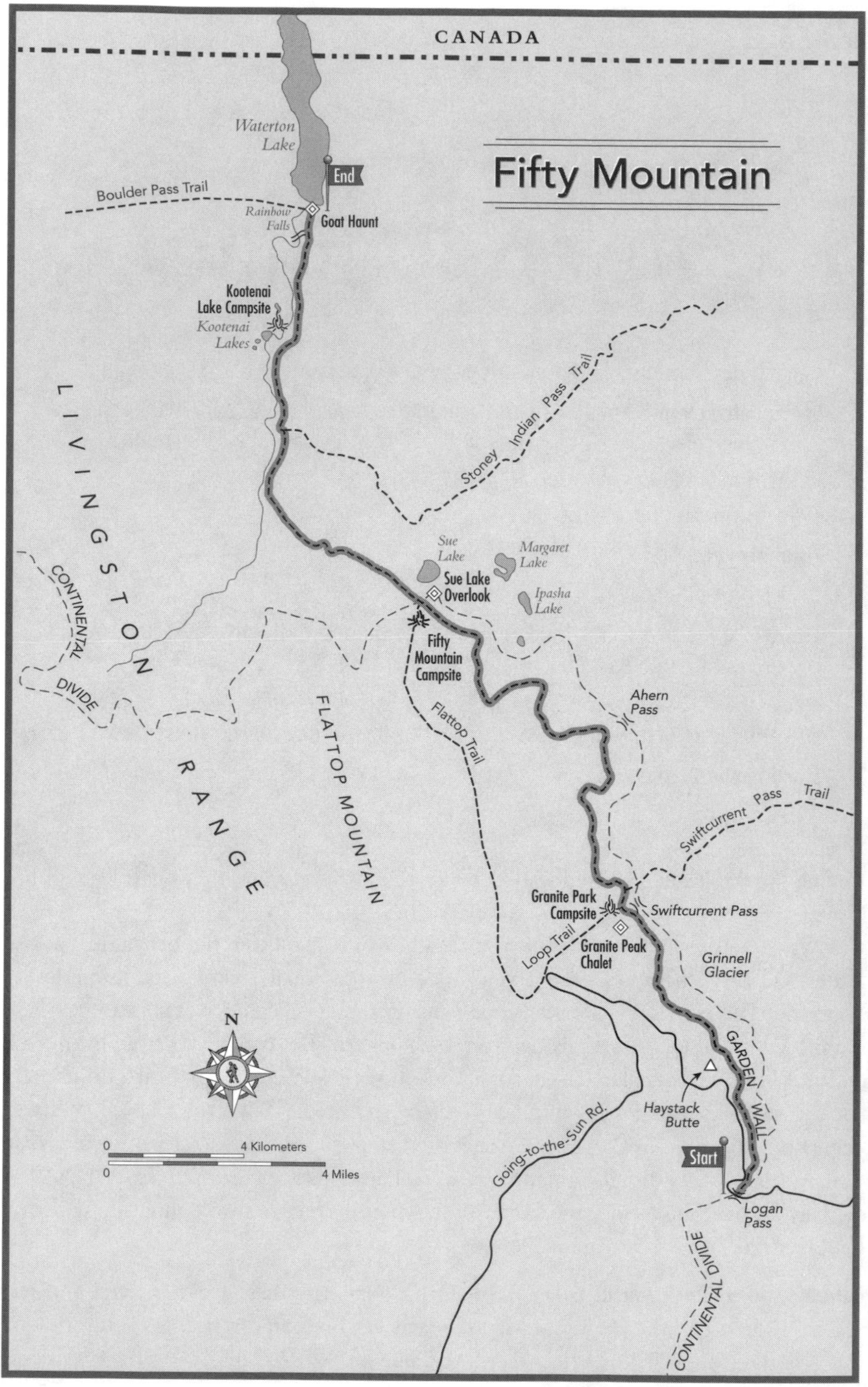

CANADA

Waterton Lake

Boulder Pass Trail

End

Fifty Mountain

Rainbow Falls

Goat Haunt

Kootenai Lake Campsite

Kootenai Lakes

Stoney Indian Pass Trail

L I V I N G S T O N

Sue Lake

Margaret Lake

CONTINENTAL

Sue Lake Overlook

Ipasha Lake

Fifty Mountain Campsite

DIVIDE

Ahern Pass

R A N G E

Flattop Trail

FLATTOP MOUNTAIN

Swiftcurrent Pass Trail

Granite Park Campsite

Swiftcurrent Pass

Loop Trail

Granite Peak Chalet

Grinnell Glacier

N

GARDEN WALL

Haystack Butte

0   4 Kilometers

0   4 Miles

Start

Going-to-the-Sun Rd.

Logan Pass

CONTINENTAL DIVIDE

6.8 m.	Junction with Glacier Overlook Trail; turn left
7.6	Granite Park Chalet
7.8	Junction with Swiftcurrent Pass Trail; turn left
8.0	Junction with trail to Granite Park Campsite (5★); turn right
11.8	Junction with Ahern Pass Trail; turn left
18.3	Junction with trail to Sue Lake Overlook; turn left
19.3	Fifty Mountain Camp (5★) and junction with Flattop trail; turn right
22.1	Junction with Stoney Indian Pass Trail; turn left
27.3	Kootenai Lakes and Campsite (3★)
30.5	Goat Haunt Ranger Station, Visitor Center, and Waterton Lake

Recommended itinerary: This trip can be easily done in four days, but while in the middle of paradise, why not take an extra day for relaxing and day hiking?

First night:	Granite Park Chalet or Campsite
Second night:	Fifty Mountain Campsite
Third night:	Fifty Mountain Campsite
Fourth night:	Kootenai Lakes

The hike: When you get your backcountry permit, ask the ranger if the Ahern Drift has been blasted. This is an extremely steep and dangerous snowfield that clings to a precipitous slope about a mile before Ahern Pass. Trail crews usually blast out a safe path in early July before this route opens, but you'll want to be sure of this.

The first 3 miles of the trail go along the Garden Wall directly above Going-to-the-Sun Highway. Some of this is on ledge, which can be a little nerve-wracking but beautifully unique. Then, the trail gradually climbs up to Granite Park Chalet across the flanks of Haystack Butte and in the shadow of mighty Mount Gould to the north. (There has never been a haystack on Haystack Butte, but it looks like one.)

To the south Heavens Peak, Longfellow Peak, and others dominate a fantastic horizon. You can also see McDonald Creek tumbling down to the huge lake with the same name. The first leg of this trip to Granite Park follows the Continental Divide. Don't forget to look behind you on this section for some stunning views.

You can see the wonderfully positioned chalet about 1.5 miles before you get there. Locals appropriately call this stretch of trail "Bear Valley" because you can often see grizzly bears here from the trail and the chalet.

After leaving Granite Park, you hike on a nearly flat route to Ahern Creek (crossing Ahern Drift just before the creek) and then move gradually downhill to Cattle Queen Creek, which is the lowest point on the Continental Divide in Glacier Park. From here, it's a fairly steep uphill (Category 3 hill) to a plateau (sometimes called Fifty Mountain

Leaving Fifty Mountain Campsite on a carpet of wildflowers.

Pass) overlooking Fifty Mountain Camp. After enjoying the scenery (perhaps trying to count all fifty mountains you are supposed to be able to see from here), hike down a short decline to the campsite.

You might not be able to see all fifty peaks, but you certainly can see many of them with no chance of finding the scenery disappointing. This is all prime grizzly habitat, and you can frequently see bears at safe distances. Heavens Peak again dominates the southern horizon; only this time you're looking at the other side of the mountain. Alpine wildflower enthusiasts will think they're in heaven.

After leaving Fifty Mountain Campsite, you hike through a spectacular, wildflower-carpeted flat for about a mile before launching down toward Kootenai Lakes. This 4-mile stretch of trail can be difficult hiking because the vegetation (thimbleberry, cow parsnip, and false hellebore) gets so thick you can't see your next step on this often-rocky trail. As you descend, however, you'll be thrilled that you didn't do this route in reverse because you'd be struggling up a Category 1 hill.

The trail flattens out just before the junction with the Stoney Indian Pass trail and remains an easy grade the rest of the way. This might be the time to get out your mosquito head net because the pesky insects can be thick enough to blot out the sun. Also watch for moose frequenting the Kootenai Lakes area.

Start checking the time so you can catch the boat, which runs about every three hours. If you miss the last boat, check with the ranger on duty at Goat Haunt to see if you can stay at the Waterton River Campsite, just west of the ranger station.

Options: You don't want to do this hike in reverse because you face a huge climb (Category 1) up to Fifty Mountain from Goat Haunt. As an option you can take the Loop Trail up to Granite Park to shorten the trip by about 3 miles, but again, you would face a tough ascent to Granite Park, which can be avoided by taking the more scenic Highline Trail from Logan Pass. You can avoid the hassle of going into Canada and taking the boat trip down Waterton Lake by adding two nights to the trip and starting at the Chief Mountain Trailhead, hiking up the Belly River and over Stoney Indian Pass and down to Kootenai Lakes.

Side trips: You won't want to miss the terrific view from the Grinnell Glacier Overlook. It's a short (0.6 mile one way) but steep hike, and worth the effort, perhaps something to do after supper at the Granite Park Chalet. From the overlook you can hike on an unofficial trail along the ridge to another saddle and look down into Lake Sherburne, Lake Josephine, and Lake McDonald.

Sue Lake (0.3 mile one way) is another must-do side trip, but it comes near the end of a long day from Granite Park to Fifty Mountain. This might be a good day hike during your rest day at Fifty Mountain. The spur trail doesn't actually go to the lake, but to an overlook, which many Glacier aficionados consider the best view in the park.

Ahern Pass is a short, off-trail scramble for those with extra energy. From here, you can look down into Elizabeth Lake, Helen Lake, and the Upper Belly River Valley. There is an unofficial trail (not shown on maps) leading up to the pass.

Even if you aren't camping at Kootenai Lakes, you can take the short spur trail over to see the lakes—because you can't seem them from the main trail.

In taking these side trips, be sure to hang your pack out of reach of grizzlies and marmots. If you can't hang packs, don't leave them unattended.

Camping: If you want to stay at Granite Park Chalet, reserve a room with Glacier Wilderness Guides, a private company managing the facility for the NPS. Contact them at Glacier Wilderness Guides, Box 535, West Glacier, MT 59936; (800) 521–7238; glguides@cyberport.net, or check out the Web site at www.glacierguides.com.

There are only three designated campsites on the route.

Granite Park: (5★) Great view, but be especially careful with food and garbage in this prime grizzly habitat.

Fifty Mountain: (5★) Great views. Six tent sites. Easy water source. Marginally private.

Kootenai Lakes: (3★) Good view of Lower Kootenai Lake. Four tent sites, one next to the toilet with no view. Lots of mosquitoes. Good water source. Fairly private.

Fishing: This is not a trip for anglers. With the possibility of catching a few brookies in Kootenai Lake, there is no fishing along this route.

3

Three Passes in Glacier

General description: A fairly short backpacking trip through outstanding mountain scenery, mostly above timberline

Special attractions: One of the most scenic and popular hikes in Glacier National Park, featuring two jewel-like mountain lakes, a traverse along the Continental Divide, and three mountain passes. Where else can you hike over three spectacular passes in 4 miles of scenic hiking?

Type of trip: Loop

Total distance: 18.8 miles

Difficulty: Short but moderately strenuous

Traffic: Heavy; also a popular day hike

Maps: Cut Bank Pass, Mount Rockwell, and Dancing Lady USGS quads and either the USGS map or Trails Illustrated map for the entire park

Starting point: Pray Lake Trailhead

Finding the trailhead: From East Glacier drive north on Montana Highway 49 about 4 miles to a well-marked turnoff for Two Medicine Road. Turn right for Two Medicine Campground. Drive through the campground to the bridge over Two Medicine River at the outlet of Pray Lake, a small lake below the outlet of Two Medicine Lake. (Pray Lake is named after Charles N. Pray, one of the congressmen who pushed hard for the establishment of Glacier National Park.) The Pray Lake Trailhead is at the outlet of the two lakes.

Parking and trailhead facilities: Plenty of parking at the Two Medicine Camp Store, ranger station, rest rooms, campground, and Glacier Park Boat Company boat rides.

Recommended itinerary: Spend the first night at Oldman Lake and the second night at No Name Lake or, if necessary, in reverse order.

The hike: The name Two Medicine comes from the Blackfeet history that refers to two medicine lodges built in the area for performing the Sun Dance. The exact site of the lodges has not been discovered.

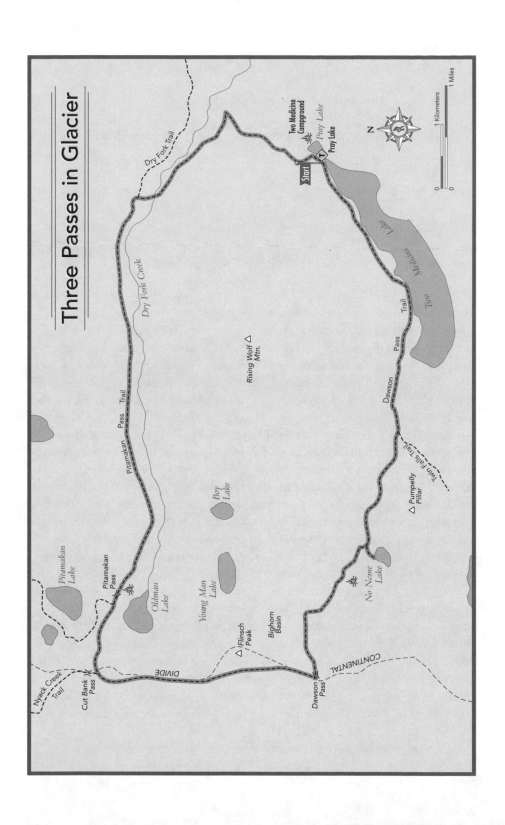

Three Passes in Glacier

Dry Fork Trail

Dry Fork Creek

Pitamakan Pass Trail

Pitamakan Lake

Pitamakan Pass

Oldman Lake

Young Man Lake

Boy Lake

Rising Wolf Mtn. △

Nyack Creek Trail

Cut Bank Pass

DIVIDE

△ Flinsch Peak

Bighorn Basin

CONTINENTAL

Dawson Pass

No Name Lake

Dawson Pass Trail

△ Pumpelly Pillar

Twin Falls Trail

Two Medicine Lake

Two Medicine Campground

Pray Lake

Pray Lake

Start

N

0   1 Kilometers

0   1 Miles

2.4 m.	Junction with Dry Fork Trail; turn left
6.4	Oldman Lake
8.2	Pitamakan Pass and junction with Cut Bank Creek Trail; turn left
8.5	Junction with Nyack Creek Trail; turn left
8.8	Cut Bank Pass
12.4	Dawson Pass
14.0	Junction with No Name Lake Trail; turn left
15.5	Junction with Twin Falls/Upper Two Medicine Lake/South Shore Trails; turn left
18.8	Pray Lake Trailhead/Two Medicine Campground

From the trailhead parking lot, cross the bridge below Pray Lake and turn right toward Oldman Lake, 6.8 miles down the trail. In the first 2.4 miles, you hike around the base of a towering mastiff called Rising Wolf Mountain (shortened vision of a Blackfeet term for "the way the wolf rises") and across the bridge over Dry Fork Creek to a marked trail junction where you turn left (west). From here, you face a steady climb up an open valley. The very wet Dry Fork Creek cascades the length of the valley, and several smaller streams drop out of hidden cirques to add to the volume. Paintbrush and lupine add splashes of color to the scene.

At the head of the valley, you enter a blister-rust–plagued whitebark pine forest. The trail splits shortly before Oldman Lake. The right fork heads directly for Pitamakan Pass while the left fork leads to the campsites on the lake. Flinsch Peak dominates the western skyline. At Oldman Lake you might see a family of beavers at the far end of the lake in the twilight hours. Twenty-inch Yellowstone cutthroat cruise the shoreline. On the northern slopes above the lake, a white cloud of beargrass stands as thick as anywhere in the park in late July. The area around Oldman Lake is prime habitat for grizzlies. Play it safe.

From Oldman Lake to No Name Lake, the trail is nearly devoid of water by early August, so fill all your bottles before leaving camp. To reach Pitamakan Pass from Oldman Lake, take the short cutoff trail almost straight north from the outhouse instead of going back to the trail junction. The Category 2 climb to Pitamakan Pass is short and steep—more than 1,000 feet up in 1.8 miles. The pass is actually a saddle in a ridge. Before following the trail up the ridge, pause for a look down at Pitamakan Lake, about 800 feet below. Pitamakan is, incidentally, Blackfeet for "Running Eagle."

Very soon after leaving the saddle, you encounter two well-marked junctions. In each case turn left (west). Just after the second junction, you reach Cut Bank Pass and cross the Continental Divide. Due west stands mighty Mount Stimson, rising 6,000 feet above the Nyack Creek Valley.

From here the trail goes in a southerly direction, paralleling the Continental Divide along the shoulders of Mount Morgan and Flinsch Peak to Dawson Pass (named for an

Oldman Lake from Pitamakan Pass Trail.

early surveyor of the park), where you cross the divide again. While nearly level through this section, the trail traverses steep slopes of roller-bearing scree, which is dangerous when wet. Some sections of the trail follow ledges with steep drops, so watch your step. Because dangerous snow bands lie across these slopes until late June or early July, the NPS opens this trail later than most. Check with the Two Medicine Ranger Station before planning an early trip.

Dawson Pass is a favorite hangout for mountain goats, which are quite tame in this region. Don't feed them and make the situation worse than it already is. You might also see bighorn sheep.

Dawson Pass is a popular cutoff spot for people who wish to make the steep walk up the south face of Flinsch Peak. While you're up high on these passes, watch the weather. You don't want to get caught in a thunderstorm (like we did).

From Dawson Pass the trail drops rapidly through Bighorn Basin to No Name Lake. The lake deserves a more descriptive "no-name," for it lies at the base of sheer Pumpelly Pillar, named after an early geologist in the park. It is an evocative pool, especially in the first moments of sunlight on a quiet morning.

Leaving No Name Lake, you move down the valley about 1.5 miles to a trail heading up to Upper Two Medicine Lake, Twin Falls, and the South Shore trail. Turn left (east) and follow the trail along the north side of Two Medicine Lake back to the Pray Lake Trailhead.

Options: You can just as easily hike this loop in reverse, and the availability of campsites might make this option necessary.

From the lower end of Two Medicine Lake, you can take a commercial tour boat to the trailhead—or back to the trailhead at the end of your hike. This cuts about 3 miles off your trip. Check on the arrangements at the boat dock near the trailhead before you leave on the hike or contact Glacier Park Boat Company: (406) 257–2426; gpboats@mountainweb.com.

You can elect to bypass camping at No Name Lake and hike all the way from Oldman Lake on the second day, making this a weekend trip. This option makes for a long day with lots of climbing, but at least it's downhill from Dawson Pass to the trailhead.

Side trips: On the way back you can take the trail up to Upper Two Medicine Lake as a side trip. From the Dawson Pass Trail it's about 1.3 miles to Upper Two Medicine Lake. Double this for the trip back, and you add 2.6 miles to your hike. You might want at least to take a break and take the short hike (about a mile round trip) to see Twin Falls. You probably do not want to take side trips down the Cut Bank Creek or Nyack Creek trails unless you like climbing huge hills to get back to this trail.

Camping: Oldman Lake and No Name Lake have designated campsites, but they are very popular and frequently reserved, so you might try the park's reservation system to make sure you can get a permit.

Fishing: Oldman Lake has some nice-size Yellowstone cutthroats. You might also attract a few fish to your fly in the stream below the lake. No Name Lake has small brookies and rainbows and can be fair fishing when conditions are right. You can also stop to fish Two Medicine Lake on the way back—you might catch a few rainbows or brookies. The brook trout can grow big in Two Medicine Lake, but you need a float tube or canoe to increase your chances of catching a big one.

4

Nyack Loop

General description: A long backpacking expedition for experienced hikers into the most remote section of Glacier National Park

Special attractions: A rare opportunity to get away from everything (and everybody) and into the heart of true wilderness

Type of trip: Loop with shuttle option

Total distance: 37.3 miles

Difficulty: Moderate

Traffic: Light

Maps: Nyack, Mount Jackson, Mount Stimson, and Mount Saint Nicholas USGS quads and either the USGS map or the Trails Illustrated map for the entire park

Starting point: Nyack Trailhead, about 10 miles southeast of West Glacier

Finding the trailhead: To reach Nyack Trailhead drive east of West Glacier on U.S. Highway 2 for about 10 miles and take the only public, well-maintained road on the left between the Moccasin and Cascadilla River accesses. Follow this gravel road for a short distance and turn right when you reach a dead end just before the railroad tracks. Then, drive about another quarter of a mile and park. Walk down the road a hundred yards or so, cross the railroad tracks, follow a trail through a cottonwood stand, and then wade the river, keeping your eyes peeled for trail markers on trees on the opposite riverbank.

To leave a vehicle (or have somebody pick you up) at the Coal Creek crossing, drive another 6 miles east on U.S. 2 until you see a gravel road to your left (north), just before the Stanton Creek Lodge. Follow this road as it takes off from the highway and crosses the tracks before merging into an old logging road. Leave your vehicle at the end of the logging road. If you're doing this trip in reverse, ford the Middle Fork about 75 yards south of where the old logging road hits the river. You should see an orange marker and trail sign on the opposite shore.

Both of these trailheads are hard to find and you should obtain a trailhead map at the same time you get your permit. Fording the Middle Fork is only possible in August or perhaps late July in a dry year. However, you can continue this hike by floating to

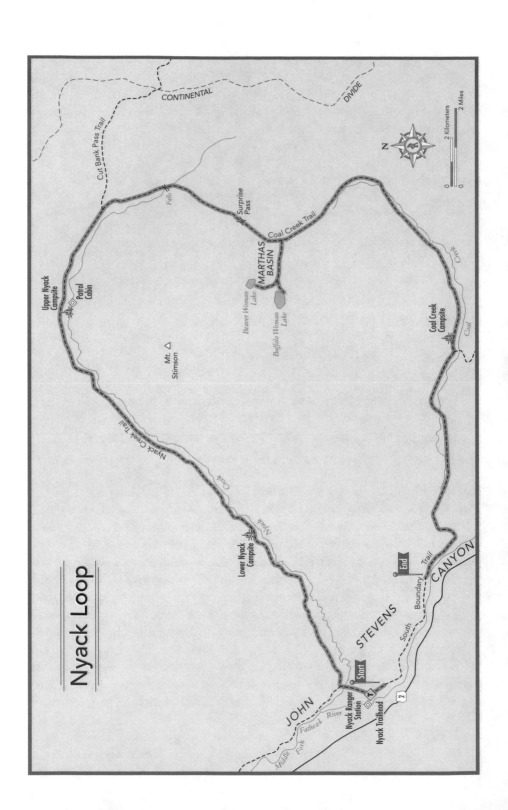

Nyack Loop

CONTINENTAL

DIVIDE

Cut Bank Pass Trail

Falls

Surprise Pass

Coal Creek Trail

MARTHAS BASIN

Upper Nyack Campsite

Patrol Cabin

Beaver Woman Lake

Buffalo Woman Lake

Mt. Stimson

Coal Creek Campsite

Coal Creek

Coal

Nyack Creek Trail

Nyack Creek

Lower Nyack Campsite

End

South Boundary Trail

STEVENS CANYON

JOHN

Start

Nyack Ranger Station

Nyack Trailhead

Middle Fork Flathead River

2

N

0   2 Kilometers

0   2 Miles

0.1 m.	South Boundary Trail; turn left
0.7	Ford Nyack Creek
0.8	Nyack Creek Trail; turn right
5.4	Lower Nyack Campsite
7.4	Lower Nyack Patrol Cabin
14.4	Upper Nyack Campsite
15.4	Upper Nyack Patrol Cabin
17.0	Cut Bank Pass Trail; turn right
21.7	Surprise Pass
22.5	Spur trail to Buffalo Woman and Beaver Woman Lakes
31.2	Coal Creek Campsite and junction with Fielding–Coal Creek Trail; turn right
33.3	Coal Creek Patrol Cabin
36.9	Junction with South Boundary Trail, turn right
37.3	Coal Creek ford of the Middle Fork

Nyack Creek from the Cascadilla River access and arranging for somebody in a raft to pick you up at the Coal Creek crossing, which is accessed by floating down from the Paola River access.

The easiest way to avoid confusion is to stop at the Walton Ranger Station for detailed and updated directions and a special hand-drawn map of both the Nyack Creek and Coal Creek trailheads. You can also get the map when getting your permit at Apgar or Saint Mary Visitor Centers.

Parking and trailhead facilities: Limited parking at both trailheads; no facilities.

Recommended itinerary: You can spend more than four nights on this route and not be disappointed, or you could hurry through with a three-night trip, but the following itinerary should be about right.

First night: Lower Nyack designated campsite or undesignated campsite somewhere along Lower Nyack Creek

Second night: Upper Nyack designated campsite or undesignated campsite somewhere along Upper Nyack Creek

Third night: Designated campground at Beaver Woman Lake or undesignated campsite at or near Buffalo Woman Lake or Beaver Woman Lake

Fourth night: Coal Creek designated campsite or undesignated campsite halfway down Coal Creek

The hike: Many trails in Glacier Park are heavily used. Others receive surprisingly little use, although they host as many backcountry rewards. The Nyack Loop is an excellent example of the latter. Keep in mind, though, that if you plan to ford the river to access the Nyack Creek and Coal Creek trailheads, you have to wait until August to take this trip.

The trail follows Nyack Creek (named after Nyack Flats on the west side of the river) as it flows over a gorgeous falls and colorful bedrock. Mount Stimson, an incredible hulk of a mountain named for a friend of George Bird Grinnell, dominates the landscape for much of the hike. And you can get a few nice views of mighty Mount St. Nicholas from the Coal Creek Trail. In addition plan on seeing more wildlife, including the grizzly, than you can find in most sections of the park. And unlike most of the park, you can camp almost anywhere instead of in often-trampled designated campsites.

So, what keeps the trail from heavy use? Well, it's a long 37 miles plus side trips—and offers no fishing. In addition it starts and ends by fording the Middle Fork of the Flathead River, which can be a stressful experience under some circumstances. But if you aren't a fanatic angler, can tolerate getting your feet wet, and do not mind long walks, this could turn out to be the backpacking vacation of your life. Plan to take at least four days, though you could easily spend a week on this hike without regretting it. The Nyack Loop is wild nature at its finest.

After crossing the Middle Fork (the former site of the Nyack Ranger Station), hike northwest on the South Boundary Trail for about three-quarters of a mile until you ford Nyack Creek. A suspension bridge used to straddle Nyack Creek, but it's long gone. Anyway, you will get your feet wet again. And get used to it—no footbridges in this, the wildest, section of the park.

Nyack Creek is a large stream. This deep ford can be dicey in July but is usually manageable in August. Right after crossing Nyack Creek, you see the Nyack Trail junction. Turn right (east). Expect several boggy sections after Nyack Creek until the trail climbs to higher ground.

The trail gradually climbs (Category 4) in thick forest along Nyack Creek all the way to Surprise Pass. Along the way, you pass through some incredibly large western larch and cottonwood groves. The trail dips down to the stream occasionally but stays high much of the way. The scenery along the trail is superb, but the scenic highlight may be Nyack Falls with massive Mount Stimson forming the backdrop.

Although there are a few dry stretches, you can usually find enough drinking water. In late summer on the way up Surprise Pass, you can gorge yourself on huckleberries. Keep very close watch for grizzlies, however, as this entire hike traverses some of the best grizzly habitat left in the world.

Soon after you drop over Surprise Pass into Coal Creek, a trail to Buffalo Woman and Beaver Woman Lakes juts off to the right. Don't miss these "beautiful women" nestled in gorgeous Martha's Basin.

After the lakes, it is a long, forested haul down Coal Creek to the Middle Fork. The last section of this trail burned in 1984 and has been difficult to keep clear of downfall.

Leave your fishing rod at home. The NPS prohibits fishing in Nyack Creek, Coal Creek, Buffalo Woman Lake, and Beaver Woman Lake. You will need the extra room in your pack for food anyway.

As a special precaution, carefully read the section of this book on hiking in bear country to reduce your chances of encountering a grizzly on unpleasant terms. Remember that this is the big bear's home, and you are the visitor. Behave accordingly.

Options: If 37 miles isn't enough, once you get to the Coal Creek Trailhead, you could take the Boundary Trail back to Nyack Creek where you started to make this a true loop. This adds 4.5 miles to the trip. This section of the South Boundary Trail is, however, lightly traveled and may be brushy and difficult to follow. This trail takes off to the right (west) about 0.4 mile before reaching the river. The South Boundary Trail heads down to ford Coal Creek shortly after the junction and then closely follows the Middle Fork most of the way to Nyack Creek.

Side trips: Be sure to take the trip to Beaver Woman and Buffalo Woman Lakes, sometimes referred to as Martha's Basin. You can take Cut Bank Pass Trail for a good view of much of southern Glacier Park. However, the trail up to Cut Bank Pass is one of the toughest climbs in the park. Perhaps the most popular side trip is a climb up Mount Stimson. Plan to take a full day to climb from timberline to the summit of Stimson and back down again. Although one of the most rigorous climbs in the park, it's nontechnical and within reach of most well-conditioned, experienced hikers.

Camping: You can set up a zero-impact camp anywhere along this route, which is not the case in most of Glacier National Park. If you prefer designated sites, however, you can apply for four campgrounds (all nice campsites) along the route. If you use an undesignated site, make sure you don't leave any mark so the next camper can think he or she is the first person ever to use this campsite. You can only stay a maximum of two nights at any campsite, which must be at least 100 feet from any lake or stream and a half mile from any patrol cabin. Also, campsites should be at least 150 feet from the trail and out of sight of the trail or other campers. And you must be prepared to hang food 12 feet off the ground and 6 feet from any tree. And as in the rest of Glacier, campfires are prohibited.

Fishing: Nyack Creek and Coal Creek are closed to fishing to protect bull trout spawning habitat.

BOB MARSHALL COUNTRY

Montana's Bob Marshall Wilderness complex is the flagship of the nation's wilderness system. This is a huge expanse of roadless country—an amazing 140 miles from Marias Pass in the north to Rogers Pass to the south with no roads. It encompasses about 2.5 million acres, including the continuous Great Bear, Bob Marshall, and Scapegoat Wilderness Areas, which make up the core of the complex, 1.5 million acres of protected wild land. The remaining million acres surround the designated wilderness, mainly on the east (Rocky Mountain Front) and west (Swan Face) flanks. These undesignated but still remote roadless areas contain some of the wildest land in Montana.

Bob Marshall Country (or the "Bob," as is called locally) is administered by four national forests (Flathead, Lewis and Clark, Lolo, and Helena). Congress designated the Bob Marshall Wilderness Area as part of the original Wilderness Act of 1964. Many credit early forester, wilderness preservation pioneer, and Wilderness Society cofounder Bob Marshall with single-handedly protecting at least 5.4 million acres of wild land. The least he deserves is to have this pristine area named for him.

The Bob is one of the most completely preserved mountain ecosystems in the world, the kind of wilderness most people can only imagine—rugged peaks, alpine lakes, cascading waterfalls, grassy meadows embellished with shimmering streams, a towering coniferous forest, and big river valleys.

The Bob includes the north and south forks of the Sun River and the middle and south forks of the Flathead River and one of the wildest sections of the Continental Divide.

Hiking over the divide between Badger Creek and the North Fork of Birch Creek.

Elevations are lower than many areas in the northern Rockies, ranging from 4,000 feet to more than 9,000 feet. A huge escarpment called the Chinese Wall, a part of the Divide, highlights the Bob's vast beauty, with an average height of more than 1,000 feet and a length of 22 miles. The Chinese Wall extends into Scapegoat Wilderness to the south.

The Bob Marshall Wilderness complex is one of the few hold outs south of Canada for the grizzly bear and provides critical habitat to the endangered gray wolf as well.

July is the most popular month for backpacking in the Bob. In mid-September, big-game hunting becomes the most popular recreational activity. Fifty-five outfitters operate in the complex.

The Bob is classic horse country because of its vastness, relatively gently terrain, and wide low-elevation river valleys with abundant forage for grazing. It is probably one of the few wildernesses where horse users still outnumber backpackers, even though the complex has more than 1,000 miles of well-developed trails.

GETTING TO THE BOB

If you're flying into Montana for the hikes it this book, fly to Great Falls for the Double Divide trip and Kalispell for the Jewel Basin hike. You can also access the area by car from Missoula or Helena.

BACKCOUNTRY REGULATIONS

In both areas covered by these hikes, follow zero-impact guidelines by camping 200 feet from streams, lakes, and trails. Also, watch the information board at the trailheads for updated regulations, especially in August and September for fire restrictions.

In Jewel Basin, you must keep your dog on a leash. Campfires are prohibited at Birch, Crater, Twin, and Picnic lakes. Group size is limited to twelve people.

FINDING MAPS

In addition to USGS quads, you should obtain the large map published by the FS entitled "Bob Marshall, Great Bear and Scapegoat Wilderness complex," which can be purchased at any Forest Service (FS) office or local sport stores. For the Jewel Basin, you need the Jewel Basin Hiking Area map/brochure published by the Glacier Natural History Association. You can get this special map/brochure for a small fee at FS offices or from visitor centers operated by the GNHA.

FOR MORE INFORMATION

For the two hikes included in this book, you can get information from the following sources:

Rocky Mountain Ranger District, 1102 Main Avenue NW, P.O. Box 340, Choteau, MT 59422; (406) 466–5341; fax: (406) 466–2237.

Flathead National Forest, Supervisors Office, 1935 3rd Avenue East, Kalispell, MT 59901; (406) 758–5200; fax: (406) 758–5363.

5

Double Divide

General description: A long loop in the Rocky Mountain Front and in the northeast corner of the Bob Marshall Wilderness

Special attractions: Two easy trips over the Continental Divide

Type of trip: Loop

Total distance: 39.5 miles

Difficulty: Moderate

Traffic: Moderate

Maps: Morningstar Mountain, Swift Reservoir, Fish Lake, Gateway Pass, and Gooseberry Park USGS quads; Bob Marshall Wilderness complex map

Starting point: Birch Creek Trailhead

Finding the trailhead: Take U.S. Highway 89 to a rest area on the north edge of Dupuyer (36 miles south of U.S. Highway 2 and 32 miles north of Choteau) and turn left (west) onto Forest Road 146 to Swift Dam. This road runs west for 18 miles to Swift Dam Trailhead—the main trailhead—on your left (south) at the foot of the dam. You can start the hike here or travel 2 miles farther around the north side of the reservoir on a rough road to a secondary trailhead. This road crosses the Blackfeet Reservation and may be closed or restricted, so check for signs near the dam. You can make it to the main trailhead in any vehicle, but you need high clearance to access the secondary trailhead on the north side of the reservoir. The following description follows the route from the main trailhead at the foot of the dam.

Parking and trailhead facilities: Pit toilet, campsite, and plenty of parking at the main trailhead. Limited parking available on the secondary trailhead with only undeveloped camping areas.

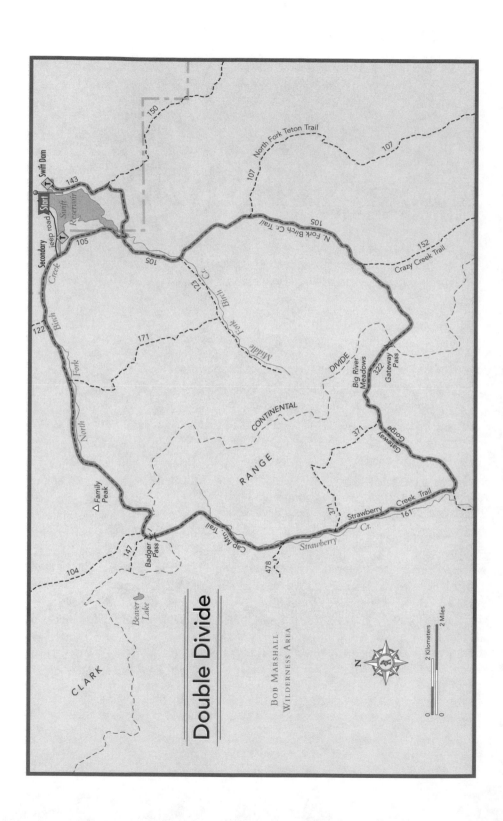

Double Divide

BOB MARSHALL
WILDERNESS AREA

Start

Swift Dam

Secondary

jeep road

Swift Reservoir

143

105

122

Birch Creek

North Fork

△ Family Peak

147

104

Beaver Lake

CLARK

Badger Pass

Cap Mtn. Trail

478

371

Strawberry Cr.

Strawberry Creek Trail

161

371

Gateway Gorge

322

Gateway Pass

Big River Meadows

DIVIDE

CONTINENTAL

RANGE

171

Middle Fork

Birch Cr.

105

N. Fork Birch Cr. Trail

105

107

North Fork Teton Trail

107

152

Crazy Creek Trail

150

N

2 Kilometers

2 Miles

2.1 m.	Junction with Trail 150; turn right
3.5	Junction with North Fork Birch Creek Trail 105; turn left
5.0	Junction with Middle Fork Birch Creek Trail 123; turn left
7.5	Junction with North Fork Teton Trail 107; turn right
12.9	Junction with Crazy Creek Trail 152; turn right
14.5	Gateway Pass, Trail 105 becomes Trail 322
15.5	Big River Meadows
16.6	Junction with East Fork Strawberry Creek Trail 371; turn left
17.5	Gateway Gorge
19.5	Junction with Strawberry Creek Trail 161; turn right
20.0	Junction with East Fork Strawberry Creek Trail 371; turn left
21.5	Junction with Cap Mountain Trail 478; turn right
24.5	Badger Pass
24.7	Junction with Beaver Lake Trail 147; turn right
24.9	Junction with Badger Creek Trail 104; turn right
30.5	Junction with Blind Tubby Trail 171; turn left
32.0	Junction with Hungry Mack Trail 122; turn right
34.0	Jeep road (trail 121 on map) on north side of Swift Reservoir and secondary trailhead
36.0	Junction with South Fork Birch Creek Trail 143; turn left
37.4	Junction with Trail 150; turn left
39.5	Swift Dam trailhead

Recommended itinerary: You can hike longer days on this trip because of the gentle terrain; a well-conditioned hiker could easily do this in three nights. Four nights, however, would be less strenuous.

First night:	Halfway up the South Fork of Birch Creek
Second night:	Big River Meadows
Third night:	Meadows just west of Badger Pass or Beaver Lake
Fourth night:	Halfway down the North Fork of Birch Creek

The hike: This trip typifies backpacking in the Bob. It travels through long, gentle, and mostly forested valleys and gradually climbs to low-elevation passes. If you develop a stronger interest in the Bob, you can expect more of the same on most routes. On this route you pass over the Continental Divide twice, but in both cases, the climb seems so slight that you hardly break into a sweat.

You can slash 7 miles off the total distance by starting the hike on the north shore of Swift Reservoir, but this is a rough jeep road requiring a high-clearance vehicle, and it crosses through Blackfeet Reservation land. Check carefully at the dam to make sure the road isn't closed.

The Bob is horse country, so expect to meet a stock party or two along the route. And expect the trails to be quite distinct because of the high horse traffic—too distinct in many places, where the trail becomes deeply rutted.

The route has adequate water sources, but some can dry up in August. Plan on carrying a full water bottle at all times.

From the main trailhead you face a short, 200-foot hill to get your heart pumping before dropping down into the South Fork of Birch Creek for the long haul to Gateway Pass. Once you ford the stream (sorry, no bridges on this route), you follow a gradual upgrade all the way to the pass. You'll find five official trail junctions and frequent social trails established by outfitters, but stay on the main trail to Gateway Pass, the most distinct choice in all cases.

The trail meanders through sparse forest of lodgepole and Douglas fir with frequent meadows, opening up more and more as you approach the pass. Be alert for campsites. You'll need to find one somewhere along the way, and there aren't an abundance of good choices.

Typically, hikers expect a short, steep pull to get over a pass, but not so with Gateway. As you approach the pass, you'll be looking ahead trying to guess where the trail goes. And then, much to your surprise, you'll see a sign on a tree indicating you're standing on the pass. Low-elevation (6,478 feet) Gateway Pass is hidden in a small grove of mixed conifers.

Immediately after the pass, you start through Big River Meadows, a logical choice for your second night out. The meadow is gorgeous and so typically Bob, but it should be named Little Brook Meadows because there's no river.

Big River Meadows.

After a pleasant night in Big River Meadows, you drop gradually toward the Gateway Gorge, taking a left (north) turn when the trail up the East Fork of Strawberry Creek veers off to the right. When you approach the gorge, the trail climbs up onto the talus slope above the stream to give you a better view. The gorge is impressive, but possibly overrated for its scenic beauty.

After the gorge the trail heads into a mature forest and stays there after you take a right (east) turn at the next junction and start the gradual upgrade along Strawberry Creek toward Badger Pass. As you approach the pass, the forest opens up into a series of meadows. You can pick one of these for your next campsite, or, if you're ambitious, go all the way to the pass and take a 1.5-mile spur trail over to Beaver Lake for your third night out. This side trip to Beaver Lake adds 3 miles to the total distance of this route.

Badger Pass resembles Gateway Pass, a gentle, forested, no-sweat pass that you hardly notice climbing—and it's very close to the same elevation, too. At the pass and shortly thereafter, stay alert to make sure you get on North Fork of Birch Creek Trail by going right (south or east) at both junctions. You'll know you're on the right trail when you start the only serious climb of this trip out of the Badger Creek over a mildly serious, Category 3 hill (about 600 feet in 1.5 miles), into the North Fork of Birch Creek. This will get your heart rate up for the first time on the trip.

When you reach the top, take a break and look around. To the north, you get a panoramic view into the expansive Badger–Two Medicine area, currently proposed for wilderness status but also proposed for extensive oil and gas development. To the south you get a sweeping view of the North Fork of Birch Creek, the boundary line of the Bob Marshall Wilderness. This means all the wild country on the north side of the stream is part of a large undesignated wild land called the Rocky Mountain Front, also proposed for wilderness and energy development.

On the way down the North Fork Trail, stay on campsite alert. Unless you have decided to hike out that day, you'll need to find one about halfway down for your fourth night out. As you watch the stream bottom for a campsite, you'll see the dramatic signs of the major flood that flushed out this area in 1964.

After you drop steeply for about 2 miles from the North Fork/Badger divide (making you happy you didn't do the trip in reverse!), the trail settles into a stream grade easy walk until you reach the road leading to the secondary trailhead on the north side of the reservoir. You probably won't see vehicles on this road as you walk along it for a quarter-mile because most users park in an open area above tiny Haywood Creek and don't drive on this last half-mile of road before it turns into a single-track trail. This section can be confusing, so be alert. You follow the road to a top of a ridge. When you see the road veering off to the left and heading down to Haywood Creek, you go straight on a distinct trail.

Shortly after you leave the jeep road, you drop down and get your feet wet fording the North Fork. Then you climb a short hill over the divide between the North Fork and South Fork, drop down, and hook up with the trail back to the main trailhead and your vehicle.

Hiking down to the North Fork of Birch Creek.

Options: You can do this route in reverse, but the climb over the North Fork/Badger divide would be make it more difficult. The climbs over the passes would still be no sweat.

Side trips: You can always find a side trip, but this route doesn't include many logical choices. A short trip over to Beaver Lake is one possibility, and if you like mountaintops, try Family Peak from the top of the North Fork/Badger divide.

Camping: Camp anywhere, but be sure to set up a zero-impact camp. This is grizzly country, so be bear aware and handle food and garbage properly.

Fishing: You can find a few cutthroats in both the South Fork and North Fork, but this trip is not known for its fishing.

6

Jewel Basin

General description: An easy trip into a popular hiking area in the Swan range in the northwestern corner of the Bob Marshall Wilderness

Special attractions: Subalpine scenery and good fishing lakes on a trail easy enough for beginners, families, or elderly hikers

Type of trip: Base camp

Total distance: 5–9 miles to the base camp, plus day trips

Difficulty: Easy

Traffic: Heavy on weekends

Maps: Jewel Basin, Big Hawk Mountain, and Crater Lake USGS quads and USFS Jewel Basin Hiking Area map/brochure

Starting point: Camp Misery Trailhead

Finding the trailhead: From Bigfork drive north for 3 miles on Montana Highway 35 and turn right (east) onto Montana Highway 83 for 2.3 miles. Turn left (north) at the Echo Lake Cafe on Foothills Road, also called the Echo Lake Road. Follow this road past Echo Lake for 3 miles and turn right (east) onto Forest Road 5392 and follow this dirt switchback road 7 miles to the Jewel Basin Hiking Area parking lot. The route is well marked, but the final stretch is bumpy, featuring whoop-dee-dos (abrupt mounds of dirt), and not recommended for RVs or trailers. The road extends beyond the Camp Misery Trailhead and parking lot, but it is closed to motorized use at the trailhead.

Parking and trailhead facilities: The trailhead has a large parking lot, but it fills up on summer weekends. Pit toilet. No camping or drinking water. A ranger cabin with a volunteer interpretive ranger usually on duty.

Recommended itinerary: This hike is ideal for an easy base camp, so the itinerary is simple. The only decisions are where to set up the base camp, how long to stay, and which day hikes to take from your base camp.

The hike: The Jewel Basin isn't a designated wilderness, but the Forest Service manages it like one—no logging, motor vehicles, or development. Because of the easy access from

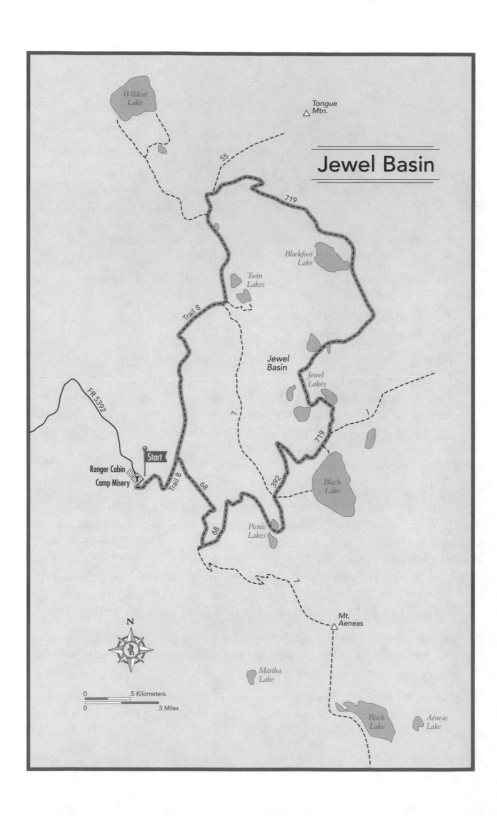

Jewel Basin

0.9 m.	Junction with trail 68; turn right
1.6	Junction with Mount Aeneas Road; turn left
2.3	Junction with trail 372; turn right
2.7	Picnic Lakes and junction with trail 392; turn left
3.4	Junction with trail 7; turn right
3.7	Black Lake
4.0	Junction with trail 719; turn left
4.3	Jewel Lakes

the Flathead Valley, this area can get crowded, but mainly on weekends. If you hike here during the week, the human population won't seem too large.

The Jewel Basin is a maze of trails, so you definitely need a map, and the special hiking map/brochure published by Glacier National History Association is by far the best.

The first order of business on this hike is to pick your base camp. Two excellent options are Black Lake, 8 miles out-and-back, and any one of the four Jewel Lakes, a 9-mile round trip. An even easier choice would be Twin Lakes, a stunningly beautiful pair of "jewels" in a small basin only a 5-mile round trip from the trailhead.

Twin Lakes, typical scenery in Jewel Basin.

Fishing Wildcat Lake.

Two trails leave the trailhead. You can get to Black Lake and Jewel Lakes on either one with no extra distance. If you prefer to hike on a trail instead of a road, take Trail 8 by the ranger cabin. After 0.6 mile, turn right (south) onto Trail 68 unless you have decided to base camp at Twin Lakes, in which case go left.

When Trail 68 junctures with Mount Aeneas Road, turn left (east) and climb up to the rim of Jewel Basin where the road ends. Two trails depart this point. You can get to Black Lake and Jewel Lakes on either one, but take the right (south) fork for a more scenic route through Picnic Lakes, where you turn left (north) onto Trail 392. Follow this trail to a junction with Trail 7 at Black Lake. Turn right onto Trail 7 and drop down to Black Lake (if you like this for your base camp) or follow it just back from Black Lake to a junction with Trail 719. Turn left (north) here and find a suitable base camp on one of the four Jewel Lakes.

After you find your way through the labyrinth of trail junctions and get your base camp set up, start checking the map for suitable day trips. You could spend a week hiking in this area, all on excellent trails with the exception of the long loop around Clayton Lake, a rough and brushy trail you might want to avoid. The FS brochure calls Clayton Lake an easy hike, but rest assured it is not. If you need a long trip, you can head over to Crater Lake or Wildcat Lake, but there are also choice short trips to Blackfoot Lake, Twin Lakes, and Birch Lake.

Jewel Basin is bear country, including the possibility of seeing a grizzly, so be bear aware and be especially careful with food and garbage.

Options: This does not have to be a base camp trip. You could move your camp from lake to lake, but since the distances are so small, a base camp provides a less strenuous option. There are several options for routes and side trips through Jewel Basin.

Side trips: Numerous side trips are possible throughout the basin. Check the map and find one that matches your interest and ability.

Camping: Campsites are not officially designated, but they are well established. To leave less impact use one of the established camps instead of camping in a virgin site—and practice zero-impact camping principles.

Fishing: Most lakes in the basin are filled with cutthroat and a few rainbow trout, but they have seen lots of artificial flies and might not be cooperative. To lower the impact you might want to release your fish so they can be caught again.

The Spanish Peaks section of the Lee Metcalf Wilderness.

LEE METCALF WILDERNESS

In the 1970s Montana wilderness advocates worked hard to win approval for a wilderness of nearly 600,000-acres. The proposed area, named after the wilderness-friendly Montana senator, Lee Metcalf, ran continuously from the western boundary of Yellowstone Park north to Spanish Creek. However, former U.S. Senator John Melcher forced conservationists to accept a bill splitting this incredible wilderness into four sections. In accepting the bill conservationists allowed an unbroken Madison Range to be split along the South Fork of the Gallatin on the east side and Jack Creek on the west side.

The result was a total of 254,288 acres of designated wilderness consisting of four separate units in the Madison Range of Montana, a huddle of high peaks rising above 10,000 feet from exquisite subalpine meadows, managed by the Bureau of Land Management and the Gallatin and Beaverhead-Deerlodge National Forests.

The BLM manages all 6,000 acres of the Bear Trap Canyon Unit, a stretch of wild canyon country along the Madison River. This was the BLM's first designated wilderness.

The Monument Mountain Unit lies on the northwest boundary of Yellowstone National Park, an isolated piece of territory rarely visited but rich in wildlife, including a large population of grizzly bears. All 30,000-plus acres lie within Gallatin National Forest.

The 78,000-acre Spanish Peaks Unit encompasses steeply rugged, glaciated peaks rising more than 11,000 feet above scenic cirques and gemlike lakes. This heavily used area, popular with bighorn sheep hunters, boasts a well-developed trail system.

The 141,000-acre Taylor-Hilgard Unit is the largest section of the Lee Metcalf Wilderness. It runs along the crest of the Madison Range, with several peaks exceeding 11,000 feet above the Hilgard Basin, and its meadows and lakes surrounded by snow-capped summits in Beaverhead National Forest.

Be especially careful with food and garbage in the Taylor-Hilgard and Monument Peak areas because grizzlies inhabit these areas. They are rarely sighted, however, in the Spanish Peaks.

GETTING TO THE LEE METCALF WILDERNESS

The Lee Metcalf Wilderness is located in relatively remote southwestern Montana. The closest large airport is in Bozeman, Montana. You could also drive up from Salt Lake City, but it will take most of a day to get to a trailhead.

BACKCOUNTRY REGULATIONS

Camping and campfires are not allowed within 200 feet of any body of water. No permit is required. Watch trailhead information boards for current regulations.

FOR MORE INFORMATION

Unfortunately, management of the Lee Metcalf Wilderness is complicated. The Beaverhead-Deerlodge National Forest manages the west side of the Taylor-Hilgard and Spanish Peaks units while the Gallatin National Forest manages the east side. Contact the Forest Service at the following locations for more information:

Beaverhead-Deerlodge National Forest, Dillon Ranger District, 420 Barrett Street, Dillon, MT 59725-3572; (406) 683–3900, fax: (406) 683–3855.

Beaverhead-Deerlodge National Forest, Madison Ranger District, 5 Forest Service Road, Ennis, MT 59729; (406) 682–4253.

Gallatin National Forest, 10 East Babcock Avenue, P.O. Box 130, Bozeman, MT 59771; (406) 587–6702, fax: (406) 587–6758.

Hebgen Lake Ranger District, Highway 287, P.O. Box 520, West Yellowstone, MT 59758; (406) 823–6961, fax: (406) 823–6990.

Taking a break at Expedition Lake with Echo Peak beyond.

7

Spanish Peaks

General description: A long circuit through the midsection of a smaller wilderness area

Special attractions: Many high alpine views, lakes, and fishing opportunities

Type of trip: Loop

Total distance: 23 miles

Difficulty: Moderately strenuous

Traffic: Moderate

Maps: Hidden Lakes, Gallatin Peak, Garnet Mountain, Beacon Point, Willow Swamp, Cherry Lake USGS quads; Lee Metcalf Wilderness Forest Service map

Starting point: South Fork of Spanish Creek Trailhead

Finding the trailhead: From Bozeman drive 7.5 miles south on U.S. Highway 191. Just before entering the Gallatin Canyon, take a right (west) up Spanish Creek at a marked turnoff. After 5.2 miles turn left (south) up the South Fork of Spanish Creek. Drive about 4 miles until you reach the trailhead.

Parking and trailhead facilities: Pit toilet, campground, picnic area, and parking lot.

Recommended itinerary: This trip is nicely suited for two nights out, but can be extended by making a base camp and exploring the high country for one or two additional days.

First night:	Upper Falls Creek Lake or Jerome Lakes
Second night:	Big Brother Lake

The hike: Spanish Peaks is a popular hiking area—and you'll probably see some stock parties, too. This route, however, skirts the most heavily used portions while still providing the same incredible scenery that has made the Spanish Peaks Wilderness nationally famous.

The Spanish Peaks could be called a pocket wilderness. It is isolated on the north edge of the massive Big Sky development. In the 1970s Montana wilderness advocates agreed to give up Jack Creek in exchange for the designation of the Lee Metcalf

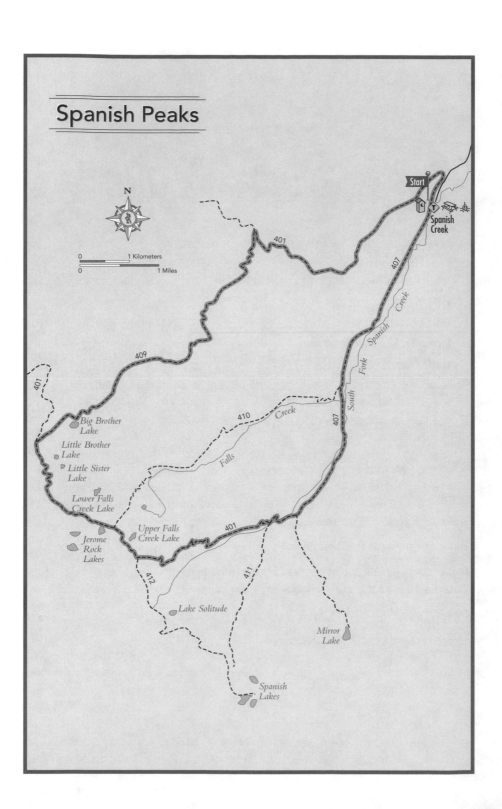

Spanish Peaks

N

| 0 | 1 Kilometers |
| 0 | 1 Miles |

401

407

Start

Spanish Creek

South Fork Spanish Creek

409

401

Big Brother Lake

Little Brother Lake

Little Sister Lake

Lower Falls Creek Lake

Jerome Rock Lakes

Upper Falls Creek Lake

410

Falls Creek

407

401

412

411

Lake Solitude

Mirror Lake

Spanish Lakes

3.0 m.	Junction with Falls Creek Trail 410; turn left
5.5	Junction with trail to Mirror Lake; turn righton Trail 401
6.0	Junction with Trail 411 to Spanish Lakes; turn right
8.5	Junction with Trail 412 to Lake Solitude; turn right
9.0	Upper Falls Creek Lake
9.3	Junction with Falls Creek Trail 410; turn left
9.5	Jerome Rock Lakes
12.0	Junction with Trail 409 to Big Brother Lake; turn right
12.9	Big Brother Lake
20.0	Junction with Trail 401 back to trailhead; turn right
23.0	Spanish Peaks Campground and Trailhead

Wilderness in two parts. The South Fork of the Gallatin (now filled with residential and commercial development associated with Big Sky) and Jack Creek form a corridor of civilization between the two sections of wilderness.

You should wait until at least early July to try this trip, preferably mid-July. Before going you might want to call the Forest Service for snow conditions. You want the snow line below 9,000 feet before taking this trip. Below 8,700 would make it easier to find a

Wait until late July to hike this route to avoid crossing dangerous snow banks.

Hiking the Spanish Peaks high country.

dry campsite and safely cross a small pass just west of Jerome Rock Lakes.

This is a 23-mile loop hike going up the South Fork of Spanish Creek and coming back to the same trailhead through the headwaters of Camp and Cuff Creeks, using Trails 407, 401, and 409 in a clockwise direction.

From the trailhead begin hiking on South Fork of Spanish Creek Trail 407, which is well maintained (thanks to local backcountry horsemen). All major creek crossings have bridges.

After 3.0 miles, turn left at the junction with the Falls Creek Trail.

At 5.5 miles, the trail to Mirror Lake heads off to the left. Stay right on the South Fork of Spanish Creek Trail 401 to Upper Falls Creek Lake. Shortly after the Mirror Lake junction, you pass another junction with Trail 411 to Spanish Lakes. Again stay right, heading southwest and uphill on Trail 401.

After 8.5 miles Trail 401 junctions with Trail 412, which heads southeast to Lake Solitude. Lake Solitude is a good side trip, with many campsites, great views, and lots of fish. Stay right on Trail 401 for Jerome Rock Lakes.

Just before Jerome Rock Lakes, Trail 401 junctions with Falls Creek Trail 410. If you want to cut your trip short, this is a possible short cut. From here it's about 8 miles back to the trailhead. However, if you haven't had enough of the spectacular high lakes of the Spanish Peaks, stay left, continuing west for Jerome Rock Lakes.

This first day (about 9 miles) can be strenuous, especially the big hill out of the South Fork of Spanish Creek. The second day is short and easy, though, and the third day is mostly downhill.

All three of Jerome Rock Lakes support smart populations of Yellowstone cutthroat trout. The lower and middle lakes have adequate campsites, but camping is marginal at the upper lake. You can find the middle lakes by following the stream. Resist the temptation to build a campfire in this high altitude area where wood is sparse and scenic. Jerome Rock Lakes is a good spot to set up a base camp to spend a day or two exploring the Spanish Peaks.

Wildflowers abound in this area, especially glacier lilies and yellow columbine. In fact I saw more glacier lilies and yellow columbine in this area than in more well-known wildflower havens like Glacier Park and the Beartooths.

After enjoying Jerome Rock Lakes, continue northwest on Trail 401 and cross a 9,200-foot pass before Brother and Sister Lakes Basin. In June and early July, there can be some potentially dangerous snow banks on both sides of the pass. Hike on snowfields in the afternoon, when soft snow allows for better footholds.

After descending from the pass, look for two cairns that mark the junction with Trail 409 and the continuation of Trail 401 to Cherry Lake. Turn right, heading northeast on Trail 409, descending to Big Brother Lake. Keep your map out because this junction is easy to miss.

The trail from Big Brother Lake is a pleasant walk in the woods for 8 miles. You pass through several open meadows with views.

Upon reaching the junction with another Trail 401 (unconnected to the 401 you previously hiked on), turn right, heading east through a logged area and open meadows, and finally looping around Ted Turner's Flying D Ranch and back to the trailhead. Stay on the trail and avoid trespassing.

Options: You can do this hike in reverse with about the same level of difficulty. You can also cut this hike short by 6 miles by coming down Falls Creek on Trail 410.

Side trips: Lake Solitude (about 2 miles round trip and easy) is close to a must-do side trip. For the especially ambitious, try making it over to Spanish Lakes and back for a long, strenuous day hike.

Camping: There are no designated campsites, so you can camp anywhere, but be sure to set up a zero-impact camp to avoid signs of overuse in this fragile area.

Fishing: Jerome Lakes have cutthroats, but they can be finicky.

8

Hilgard Basin

General description: A popular trip into the southern Madison Range

Special attractions: An unusual high-altitude, lake-filled basin

Type of trip: Out-and-back base camp

Total distance: 16 miles plus side trips from base camp

Difficulty: Moderate

Traffic: Heavy

Maps: Hilgard Peak and Pika Point USGS quads and Lee Metcalf Wilderness FS map

Starting point: Potamogeton Park Trailhead

Finding the trailhead: Drive south of Ennis on U.S. Highway 287 for 47.5 miles or 24.5 miles northwest of West Yellowstone (14.5 miles to the junction of U.S. Highways 89 and 297) and turn north on Beaver Creek Road (Forest Road 985). Follow Beaver Creek Road for about 4.5 miles until it ends at Potamogeton Park Trailhead. Three trails leave this trailhead; take Sentinel Creek Trail 202 on the north side of the parking area.

Parking and trailhead facilities: Plenty of parking, toilet, undeveloped camping along Beaver Creek and the developed Cabin Creek Campground on U.S. Highway 287 just east of the Beaver Creek turnoff.

Recommended itinerary: This could be an overnighter or even a long day hike, but it would be your big loss to head back without spending at least one day exploring, climbing, and fishing in the main basin or the south basin by making this a two- or three-night base camp.

The hike: Of all the Madison Range's natural wonders, the Hilgard Basin is one of the most beautiful and popular.

From the trailhead, Sentinel Creek Trail 202 crosses Sentinel Creek on a bridge and then climbs gradually all the way to the rim of Hilgard Basin. It really doesn't seem like you're gaining 2,700 feet. The sign at the trailhead says it's 8 miles to the basin, but it's a long 8 miles, all on a well-worn trail frequently used by stock parties. In recent years

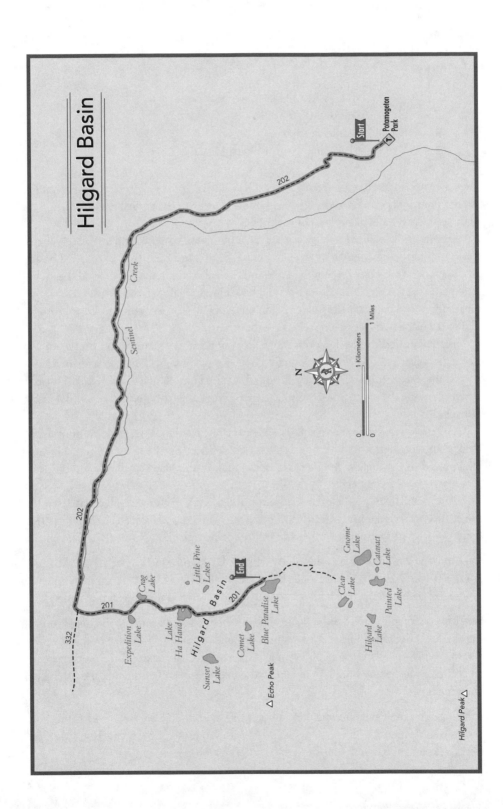

Hilgard Basin

Start

Potamogeton
Park

202

Sentinel Creek

N

1 Kilometers
1 Miles

0
0

332

202

201

Expedition
Lake

Crag
Lake

Little Pine
Lakes

End

Sunset
Lake

Lake
Ha Hand

Hilgard Basin

201

Comet
Lake

Blue Paradise
Lake

△ Echo Peak

Gnome
Lake

Cataract
Lake

Clear
Lake

Painted
Lake

Hilgard
Lake

Hilgard Peak △

KEY POINTS:

8.0 m.	Junction with Trail 201; turn left
8.5	Lake Ha Hand
9.5	Blue Paradise Lake
10.5	Clear Lake and South Hilgard Basin

several switchbacks have been added, possibly increasing the length by a mile or more. After a few miles periodic feeder streams tumble down to join Sentinel Creek, so you can plan on finding water along most of the trail.

About a mile before Expedition Pass, on a high saddle, the splendor of the Hilgard Basin unfolds before you. Newly constructed Trail 201 turns left (south) into the basin. At the saddle you can see Expedition Lake and several others in the foreground and Echo Peak, creating a perfect backdrop. Spend a few minutes taking in the views. Get out the map and start to make the difficult decision on which nearly perfect campsite you would like to try. You have at least a hundred great options.

Plan on using your backpacking stove, leaving the area's scarce wood supply intact. Recently Hilgard Basin has become increasingly popular and, with greater use, increased regulation usually follows. Camping is not allowed within 200 feet of the trail. Hilgard Basin is among the most fragile of hiking areas, so take every precaution to leave zero impact.

For peak baggers the basin acts as a base for several climbs, with 11,214-foot Echo Peak being the most popular and an easy scramble. Also nearby is 11,316-foot Hilgard Peak, which is the highest and most technical peak in the Madison Range and only for more experienced climbers.

After your hike (not before it) stop into the Grizzly Bar and Grill about 10 miles north of Quake Lake for a Grizzly Burger, which may be bigger and better than the famed Grizzly Burger of the Grizzly Bar in Roscoe near the East Rosebud Trailhead.

Options: You can make this a shuttle by coming back to Sentinel Creek Trail 201 and going left (east) down into the Finger Lakes Basin and out Moose Creek. However, this is a long shuttle and the trail here is not nearly as desirable as the one on the west side.

Side trips: Hiking into the South Hilgard Basin, where you'll find more jewel-like lakes in the shadow of mighty Hilgard Peak, is the one must-do side trip. A new trail leads past Blue Paradise Lake into the south basin and ends near Clear Lake. Also, you can spend an entire day just going from lake to lake in the main basin and testing out the fishing or climbing a peak or two.

Camping: You can camp anywhere in Hilgard Basin, and there are dozens of wonderful campsites. Make sure you set up a zero-impact camp to preserve the scenic beauty for the next backpacker to follow your steps. No campfires, please.

Open terrain provides a myriad of side trips throughout Hilgard Basin.

Fishing: Most of the lakes used to support trout populations, but the harsh winters have frozen out some lakes. The treat here is the thrill of discovery. You never know which lake has the good fishing until you try it.

As a destination for hikers, Yellowstone is unlike any other place on Earth.

In Yellowstone you can be alone. The park suffers the bad reputation of being overcrowded, but that is rarely the case on backcountry trails. While thousands drive around the Old Faithful area trying to find the bathroom, you can hike all day in the backcountry without seeing another person.

In Yellowstone you can hike to some of the best fishing in the world. And you can catch trout that have never seen a marshmallow.

In Yellowstone you can hike through perhaps the richest remaining wildlife sanctuary in the lower forty-eight states.

In Yellowstone you can hike every step within the shadow of the great bear. In fact, it's impossible to hike in Yellowstone without thinking of the majestic grizzly. If you're anxious to see one, you'll be up early and late glassing the slopes. If you're ingrained with fear of the bear, you'll be noisily hiking in the heat of the day, watching the trail ahead and at night tossing sleeplessly in your tent convincing yourself that each sound is of a bear approaching.

In Yellowstone you can come around a bend in the trail and be eyeball-to-eyeball with a 2,000-pound bison. At this point, of course, you should beat a hasty retreat off the trail. Bison never yield to hikers.

In Yellowstone you can hike through thermal areas—and not just on boardwalks in heavily used, roadside geyser basins. You can spend hours carefully exploring backcountry thermal areas, some that aren't even marked on maps. Mother Nature is in high gear in Yellowstone. New thermal areas spring up every year, and others cool off and go away. So you never know what will be around the next bend in the trail.

In Yellowstone you can see more waterfalls than in any other national park. The unique geology of the park has caused sudden uplifts and created these natural wonders.

In Yellowstone you can hear the drawn-out howl of the wolf, recently returned to its rightful place in the natural system of America's first national park. The master predator's song is like frosting on the cake for your night in the Yellowstone wilderness.

In Yellowstone you can hike along the most beautiful streams. Some are large, like the Yellowstone or Snake, or small, like the Nez Perce or Fan, but all are untamed and natural—textbook examples of what a watercourse is supposed to look like without riprap or dams or bridges or channel straightening.

In Yellowstone you have to really try hard not to have a memorable hike.

BEARS, BUGS, BISON, AND BURNT TREES

Here are a few things you might want to know about backpacking in Yellowstone.

Bears. Unlike in many parks and wilderness areas, in Yellowstone you can't just go anywhere anytime. Yellowstone is managed for natural regulation in general and more specifically for the preservation of large predators, like grizzly bears and wolves. In some areas of the park, bear management affects hiking. Some areas are closed permanently, or for part of the season, or have limited hours. In addition any hazardous situation that develops often brings temporary closures that protect both bears and people.

Bison. The abundant wildlife of Yellowstone adds a spectacular element to the hiking experience, but when you see bison on or near the trail, do not be nonchalant. Bison look tame, slow, and docile, but the opposite is true in all cases. Always give bison a wide berth.

Bugs. The mosquito populations of Yellowstone are infamous. In June and July and even occasionally in August, the clouds of mosquitoes seem like they could block out the sun, so come prepared with plenty of repellent and netting. You can also wait until August or September when most mosquitoes die off.

Prime season. The best time to hike Yellowstone is August and September—for several reasons. First, hungry mosquitoes await hikers in June and July. Second, Yellowstone gets hundreds of inches of snow annually, and you can't hike high-altitude trails until mid-July. Some low-altitude areas (most notably the Bechler) stay wet and marshy into July. (In early July Bechler Meadows can be a large lake, 1 or 2 feet deep!) Third, high water in Yellowstone streams can make fords dangerous until mid-July or later. And fourth, bear management regulations restrict entry and camping into some areas until July 1 or July 15.

Downfall. The fires of 1988 heavily burned much of Yellowstone, and now hikers are experiencing "the morning after." From a positive viewpoint, hikers can see the wonderful regeneration of a forest in many places. From a negative viewpoint, however, hikers can expect to climb over many downed snags left by the fire. Millions of burned trees will fall down in the next few years in Yellowstone, and probably a million or two will fall over trails. It's basically impossible for the Park Service trail crews to keep up with this, so expect to be climbing over—or under—a few logs on many trails in Yellowstone.

You can see a long, long way from the top of Big Horn Peak on the Gallatin Skyline trip.

Fords. Many trails in Yellowstone involve fording large rivers. If this isn't on your agenda, be sure to research your hike in advance to make sure it doesn't involve a ford. Refer to the safety section in this book for information on fording rivers more safely and for a list of trails that have fords over large streams.

Weather. It can snow any day of the year in Yellowstone, so always be prepared for it. Normal weather patterns (if there is such a thing) in the summer create clear mornings with thundershowers (or "rollers" as they're called locally) in the mid-afternoon, followed by clear, coolish evenings. This means early morning hikers usually enjoy better weather, and they more often get their tents set up before it rains.

Getting to the trailhead. If you have to drive long distances in Yellowstone, plan on about twice the normal driving time. This is especially true if you go through the Hayden Valley between Canyon and Fishing Bridge. You also save time by getting up early and driving to the trailhead before most tourists leave camp and clog the roads.

Research pays. It's amazing how pleasant and stress-free your hiking trip to Yellowstone can be when it's well planned. The following information should help you plan your Yellowstone backpacking vacation.

GETTING TO YELLOWSTONE

Yellowstone National Park crosses the boundaries of three states—Idaho, Montana, and Wyoming—and unlike most national parks, Yellowstone has five entrance stations. You can drive to the park from these five gateway communities—Red Lodge, Gardiner, and West Yellowstone (all in Montana), Cody, or Jackson (in Wyoming). In addition you can enter the park at the Bechler River Ranger Station in the far southwestern corner of the park, accessed from Ashton, Idaho. Expect to pay a fee to enter the park (this money now actually goes to the park instead of the U.S. Treasury).

The roads to the park are usually well-maintained, but only two-lanes, and often crowded with traffic, including slow-moving vehicles. If you drive during midday, don't be in a hurry.

You can fly into small airports at Jackson, Wyoming, or West Yellowstone, Montana, but most park visitors fly into larger airports at Salt Lake City, Utah, Billings or Bozeman, Montana, or Idaho Falls, Idaho.

The roads in the park are heavily used and always need repair, but they are all easily passable with any two-wheel-drive vehicle. The park speed limit is 45 mph (and strictly enforced), but in many cases, traffic moves much slower.

GETTING A BACKCOUNTRY PERMIT

In Yellowstone you must have a permit for all overnight use of the backcountry. If you use the advance reservation system, expect to pay a small fee for this permit. However, you can still walk into a visitor center without a reservation and get a free backcountry permit.

In 1996 the park installed a new computerized reservation system. This replaced a cumbersome system where hikers had to wait in line for permits and often couldn't get their preferred site. With the new system you can usually get the campsites you want—as long as you start planning long in advance.

You should get a Backcountry Trip Planner from the park; it explains the process of getting a permit. Get one by writing or calling:

Backcountry Office, P.O. Box 168, Yellowstone National Park, WY 82190; (307) 344–2160 or (307) 344–2163, e-mail: yell_park_info@nps.gov; Web site: www.nps.gov/yell (click on "publications," then "backcountry trip planner").

The reservation system is relatively new, so some specifics might change, but for now, the NPS has established the following policies:

- Reservations are made on a first-come, first-served basis, beginning April 1 each year.
- You can call for help or advice, but phone reservations won't be accepted. Reservations must be submitted by mail or in person.
- Reservation requests must be on the Trip Planning Worksheet that comes with the Backcountry Trip Planner.
- A fee (currently $15) is charged for each trip. If you return to a road and go back into the backcountry at a second trailhead, that's another trip—and another fee.
- You can pay with cash, personal check, travelers check, or money order. At this point, credit cards are not accepted. The fee is nonrefundable.
- A confirmation notice will be mailed to you. This is not a permit, but you can exchange it for your official permit when you get to the park.
- Get your permit in person at a ranger station not more than forty-eight hours in advance of the first day of your trip, but no later than 10:00 A.M. the first day of your trip. If you miss this deadline, your permit will be released to other back-country users.
- If the NPS has to close a trail or campsite for resource protection or safety reasons, the Backcountry Office will try to help you plan a comparable trip.
- You can pick up permits at the following locations in the park:
    Bechler Ranger Station
    Canyon Ranger Station/Visitor Center
    Mammoth Ranger Station/Visitor Center
    Old Faithful Ranger Station
    Tower Ranger Station
    West Entrance Ranger Station
    Grant Village Ranger Station
    Lake Ranger Station
    South Entrance Station

If possible, plan on getting your permit from one of the main locations listed above. In some cases you can also get permits at the following locations, but the rangers stationed there have other responsibilities and may not be available when you get there.

> East Entrance Ranger Station
>
> Northeast Entrance Ranger Station
>
> Bridge Bay Ranger Station

FINDING MAPS

In addition to USGS quads (specific maps listed with each trip), you have two good choices for Yellowstone maps. Both Trails Illustrated and Earthwalk Press publish excellent topo maps for the park. You can get these at park visitor centers or local sport stores, or you can order them in advance from the Yellowstone Association (the profits go back to the park) at www.yellowstoneassociation.org.

FOR MORE INFORMATION

For a great summary of basic facts on visiting Yellowstone, call the main park number and ask for a free copy of *Yellowstone Today,* a newspaper published by the Yellowstone Association. You can also get a copy at the entrance station when you enter the park. The paper contains a list of commercial services available in the park, updates on park road construction, lists of events and guided tours, campgrounds, medical and emergency services and facilities, area museums, special exhibits, and lots more useful information. *Yellowstone Today* will answer most of your questions about park services.

Because of budget cuts, the NPS is sometimes unable to keep up with all visitor inquiries, so please be patient when trying to get your questions answered. There are many books and other publications on Yellowstone that provide a wealth of excellent information, and these are often a better way to get information than calling the NPS directly. Many of these publications are available from The Yellowstone Association.

Contact Yellowstone National Park by mail, phone, or Internet:

National Park Service, Park Headquarters, P.O. Box 168, Yellowstone National Park, WY 82190; (307) 344–7381; www.nps.gov/yell, yell_visitor_services@nps.gov.

Contact The Yellowstone Association for helpful information on the park:

The Yellowstone Association, P.O. Box 117, Yellowstone National Park, WY 82190; (307) 344–2296; www.yellowstoneassociation.org; ya@yellowstoneassociation.org.

Amfac Parks and Resorts handles commercial lodging in the park. If you need accommodations in the park, Yellowstone, contact this concessionaire:

Amfac Parks & Resorts, P.O. Box 165, Yellowstone National Park, WY 82190; (307) 344–7311, fax: (307) 344–7456; www.travelyellowstone.com, info@travelyellowstone.com.

BACKCOUNTRY-USE REGULATIONS

Backcountry-use regulations aren't intended to complicate your life, but rather to help preserve the natural landscape and protect park visitors. The following backcountry-use regulations are distributed to hikers when they get their permits.

In Yellowstone, you must:

- Have a permit for all overnight use of the backcountry.
- Camp in designated campsites.
- Build campfires in established fire rings and only at campsites where campfires are allowed.
- Suspend food at least 10 feet above the ground and 4 feet horizontally from a post or tree.
- Carry out all trash. If you can pack it in, you can pack it out.
- Have a valid park fishing permit if you're fishing the waters of Yellowstone. Children eleven years or younger do not need permits.

In Yellowstone, you must not:

- Feed, touch, tease, frighten, or intentionally disturb wildlife.
- Take pets into the backcountry.
- Possess or operate a motorized vehicle, bicycle, wheeled vehicle, or cart in any undeveloped area or on any backcountry trail.
- Dispose of human waste within 100 feet of any water source, or campsite, or within sight of a trail.
- Toss, throw, or roll rocks or other items inside caves, into valleys, canyons, or caverns, down hillsides, or into thermal features.
- Possess, destroy, injure, deface, remove, dig, or disturb from its natural state any plant, rock, animal, mineral, cultural, or archaeological resource.
- Violate a closure, designation, use, or activity restriction or condition, schedule, or visiting hours, or public use limit.
- Use or possess weapons, traps, or nets.

9

Bechler River

General description: A long but easy backpack along the scenic Bechler River

Special attractions: Two trips over the Continental Divide on a trail that follows a beautiful river most of the way

Type of trip: A long shuttle

Total distance: 30.3 miles (48.8 kilometers)

Difficulty: Difficult because of the length and river fords, but easy otherwise

Traffic: Moderate

Maps: Trails Illustrated map of Old Faithful; Old Faithful, Shoshone Geyser Basin, Trischman Knob, Cave Falls, and Bechler Falls USGS quads

Starting point: Lone Star Trailhead (OK1)

Finding the trailhead: Drive east of Old Faithful 3.5 miles and park at the Lone Star Trailhead. Leave a vehicle or arrange to be picked up at the Bechler River Ranger Station in the far southwestern corner of the park.

You can reach the Bechler Ranger Station by two routes. The rough, scenic route goes from Flagg Ranch just south of the park on the Ashton-Flagg Road, past Grassy Lake Reservoir. Watch for a signed junction where you turn right (north) to the Cave Falls Road and right again (east) when you reach the Cave Falls Road. After about 2 miles on an unpaved section of Cave Falls Road, you reach a junction where the pavement starts and you can turn left (north) to the ranger station. Allow two and a half hours to drive to Bechler from Flagg Ranch.

You can also get to the Bechler Ranger Station from the west from either Ashton, Idaho, or West Yellowstone, Montana, by getting on Idaho Highway 47 and turning onto Green Timber Road, which turns into Cave Falls Road. Allow about an hour to drive the 22 miles from Ashton, Idaho.

Parking and trailhead facilities: Ample parking; no facilities. Plenty of parking and nearby toilet facilities at the exit point near the Bechler Ranger Station.

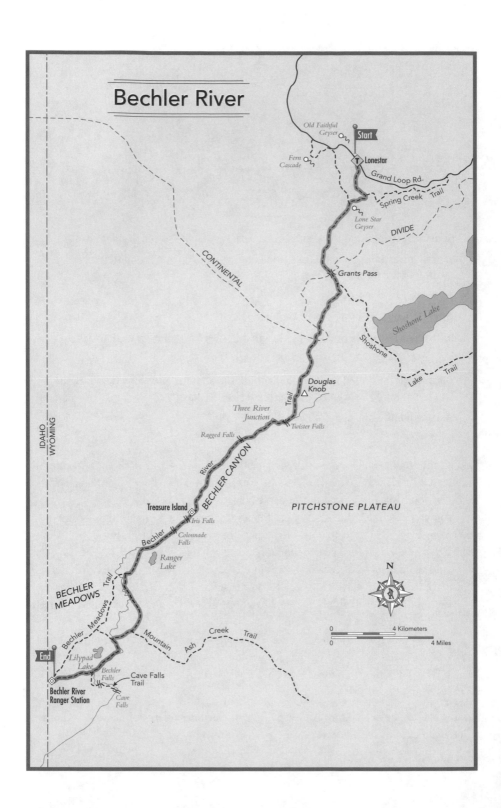

Bechler River

Old Faithful Geyser

Start

Fern Cascade

Lonestar

Grand Loop Rd.

Spring Creek Trail

Lone Star Geyser

DIVIDE

CONTINENTAL

Grants Pass

Shoshone Lake

Shoshone Lake Trail

Douglas Knob

Trail

Three River Junction

Twister Falls

Ragged Falls

BECHLER CANYON

River

PITCHSTONE PLATEAU

Treasure Island

Iris Falls

Colonnade Falls

Bechler

Ranger Lake

IDAHO

WYOMING

BECHLER MEADOWS

Bechler Meadows Trail

Mountain Ash Creek Trail

End

Lilypad Lake

Bechler Falls

Cave Falls Trail

Bechler River Ranger Station

Cave Falls

N

0   4 Kilometers

0   4 Miles

1.6 m. (2.5 k)	Junction with Spring Creek Trail; turn left
2.4 (3.8)	Lone Star Geyser and end of paved trail
2.7 (4.3)	Junction with trail to Fern Cascades Trailhead and Old Faithful; turn left
3.0 (4.8)	0A1 (3★)
3.5 (5.6)	0A2 (3★)
4.0 (6.4)	0A3 (3★)
7.0 (11.2)	Grants Pass (Continental Divide)
7.5 (12.0)	Shoshone Lake Trail; turn right, and 8G1
9.6 (15.4)	Second crossing of the Continental Divide
9.8 (15.7)	9D4 (3★)
11.6 (18.6)	9D3 (3★)
12.1 (19.4)	Douglas Knob
13.9 (22.3)	Twister Falls and 9D2 (3★)
15.2 (24.4)	Three River Junction, Ragged Falls, and 9D1(3★)
15.7 (25.2)	9B9 (3★)
16.7 (26.8)	9B8 (3★)
17.8 (28.6)	9B7 (3★)
18.4 (29.5)	9B6 (3★)
19.0 (30.5)	Treasure Island
19.2 (30.9)	Iris Falls
19.4 (31.2)	9B5 (3★)
19.6 (31.5)	Colonnade Falls
21.7 (34.9)	Ranger Lake and 9B4 (3★)
22.6 (36.3)	First cutoff trail to Bechler Meadows Trail; turn left and 9B2 (3★)
25.6 (41.2)	Junction with Mountain Ash Creek Trail
26.5 (42.6)	Rocky ford of Bechler River, junction with the second cutoff trail; turn left to Bechler Meadows and 9C1(3★)
29.3 (47.1)	Junction with Cave Falls Trail; turn right
30.3 (48.7)	Bechler Ranger Station

Recommended itinerary: A five-day trip staying at 0A1 or 0A3 the first night (which allows time for a leisurely drive to the trailhead the first day, as well as fishing the Upper Firehole or a side trip to Shoshone Geyser Basin), before heading over the Continental Divide and three nights along the Bechler River.

First night: 0A1 or 0A3
Second night: 9D4 or 9D3

| Third night: | 9B7 or 9B6 |
| Fourth night: | 9B2 or 9C1 |

The hike: Along with the Thorofare and Gallatin Skyline, the Bechler River Trail ranks among the best backpacking trips in Yellowstone. It's wild and remote, not too difficult (a good trail with no monster hills), and features good fishing and matchless scenery.

In addition this is one of the few sections of Yellowstone that escaped the fires of 1988, perhaps the only 30-mile hike you can take without walking through a burned landscape (with the exception of one small section of the canyon that burned in 1997).

You can usually find water along this trail, so unlike many long hikes, you don't have to carry an extra water bottle. The only exception to this is the Bechler Meadows route (an option on this hike), which can be a desert late in the year.

If you plan to fish, be sure to get a park fishing permit and remember all of the Bechler River Valley is catch-and-release only.

A major issue on this hike is the timing of your trip. You really don't want to be in the Bechler until late July. Before August, the mosquitoes can seem life-threatening and the water is high, which means difficult if not dangerous fords and walking on marshy trails. If you go before August, plan on having wet feet most of the time.

If you're going to carry a pack for five days, you might as well start out easy, right? The first leg of this backpacking adventure to Lone Star Geyser is as easy as it gets—2.4 miles on a flat, paved trail.

Lone Star is a well-known and heavily visited geyser—so popular that the NPS has paved the trail and opened it to mountain bikers. Even though you might see a few cyclists and more than a few hikers on this section of trail, it's still a pleasant walk along the Upper Firehole River.

At the 1.6-mile mark, stay right (south) at the junction with the Spring Creek Trail, continuing on the paved path. The pavement ends about 100 feet before the geyser and is blocked by downed trees to discourage bicycle traffic beyond this point.

Lone Star Geyser was named for its isolated location (5 miles south of Old Faithful with no other geysers in the neighborhood). The name has no link with Texas, the Lone Star state. Lone Star Geyser has a great castle and erupts 30 to 50 feet every two to three hours or so for about ten to fifteen minutes and makes gurgling sounds between eruptions.

Some maps show a little loop north of the geyser, but that loop really doesn't exist on the ground. Follow the unpaved but excellent trail past the geyser for less than a quarter mile before turning left (south) onto the main trail to the Bechler River. You could have skipped the paved section and added 1 mile to your trip by starting at the Fern Cascades Trailhead near Old Faithful and getting to the same point.

From here, the trail crosses Upper Firehole River (on a footbridge) and then continues along the river for about 2 miles before veering off to the left and climbing about 300 feet up to the Continental Divide at Grants Pass. The pass is heavily forested, effectively blocking the view.

After the pass the trail drops only slightly (about 150 feet) down to the junction with the Shoshone Lake Trail. The trail through this section is in great shape, well defined and marked.

Lone Star Geyser, shortly after the trailhead on this route.

At this junction stay right (south) and head for the Bechler River. Before you drop down to the river, however, you get to go over the Continental Divide again. Once more, the climb is gentle, hardly in line with popular images of the Great Divide.

After crossing the Divide it's all downhill for 20 miles. Hike gradually downhill into the Littles Fork, passing Douglas Knob on your left (south) at about the 12-mile mark and then over a small ridge into the Falls Fork and to Twister Falls, which is farther downstream on the Falls Fork than shown on the maps. Twister Falls makes an unusual twist as the water drops. You can't see Twister Falls from the trail, but you can take a short spur trail to a viewpoint.

Douglas Knob is forested and visible, but not as notable as its namesake, one of the most colorful and famous rangers in the early days of Yellowstone. Witness this: In the winter of 1921, Douglas tried to walk across Yellowstone Lake from West Thumb to Lake. Two miles into his trip, he fell through the ice, but crawled out, stripped off his clothes in -30° F weather, wrung out the water, and redressed himself in frozen-stiff garments. Then, he faced a tough decision—go 2 miles back to West Thumb or 15 miles to Lake. He hiked the 15 miles, and when somebody asked him why he didn't take the 2-mile option, he replied "They'd have kidded me to death."

Another 2 miles brings you to Three Rivers Junction, a flat floodplain where three forks (Ferris, Gregg, and Phillips) merge to form the Bechler River (named after the chief topographer of the Hayden survey). Ragged Falls is off to your left (south) on Ferris Fork. There is also a patrol cabin not marked on the topo maps.

You're now in the Bechler River Canyon, which is lined with cliffs, thermal areas, hot springs, cascades, waterfalls, and generally outstanding scenery. You follow the canyon for another 7 miles. Don't be surprised to see anglers casting for the wily rainbow inhabiting the scenic waterway.

The trail continues to be in great shape, well defined and well marked, but a little rocky in a few places. There are more berries (huckleberries, thimbleberries, strawberries, and others species, too) in this area than most parts of Yellowstone, which means there are bears, too, so be alert.

While in the canyon, you ford the Bechler River twice. The first ford (at about the 16.5-mile mark by 9B8) is easy and knee-deep, but the second (at about the 18-mile mark just before 9B7), is hip-deep (even in August) with a fairly fast current. Kids might have a tough time with the second ford. The NPS tries to mark the ford with posts each year, but if not marked, cross slightly downstream from where the trail hits the river.

When you get to Colonnade Falls, take a break and hike the short side trip (less than 0.25 mile) to see the magnificent double falls. You can't see Ranger Lake from the trail, but if you watch the map, you can take a half-mile off-trail jaunt to see the forest-lined

Colonnade Falls on the Bechler River.

fifty-six-acre lake. You might also try to outsmart the rainbow trout living there. Hang your packs out of reach of bears before you go.

After Ranger Lake you leave the canyon behind and head out into the incredible flat piece of wild real estate called Bechler Meadows. You basically stay on the same contour line for the last 8 miles of the hike.

At the junction with the first cutoff trail to the west over to Bechler Meadows Trail, you can go either way, but this trail description follows the Bechler River Trail, so go left (south).

From the junction the trail stays on the east side of the massive Bechler Meadows where the Bechler River splits up into several channels. In about 3 miles, you come to the junction with Mountain Ash Trail. Go right (south). In another mile or so, you reach the Rocky Ford of the Bechler River. If you cross right where the trail meets the river, you'll need dry underwear on the other side. If you cross about a 100 feet downstream, it's only knee-deep, except early in the year or after a rain when the river can come up a foot or more. The rocks are slippery, so a sturdy walking stick might prevent an embarrassing flop into the icy water.

After the ford its an easy 3.8 miles to the ranger station. After four nights out you might be thinking about a shower and a big steak, but you still should hang your pack for a few minutes and take the short out-and-back side trip over to see Bechler Falls, a huge cascade on the Bechler River with a nice steady roar to add an extra touch to the end of your adventure in Bechler River country.

Options: This trip could, of course, be done in reverse if the shuttle logistics are more convenient, but it would be a gradual upgrade most of the way.

You can finish you hike by going by Bechler Falls if you left your vehicle at the Cave Falls Trailhead instead of the ranger station. This would only shorten the hike by about a quarter mile or so. You could also shorten your trip by taking the Bechler Meadows Trail instead of staying on the Bechler River Trail, but you'd miss Rocky Ford and Bechler Falls.

Unlike many other areas of Yellowstone, in the Bechler River area there are many options for creatively building a backpacking adventure. For example, this hike can also be started or finished at the Fern Cascades, DeLacy Creek, Dogshead, Cave Falls, Fish Lake, Cascade Creek, or Grassy Lake trailheads.

Side trips: If you have the time, hang your pack and take a rewarding 2.5-mile round trip to Shoshone Geyser Basin on the west end of Shoshone Lake. Near the end of the trip, tack an extra hour on your last day with the short side trip to see Bechler Falls.

Camping: These designated campsites are on the Trails Illustrated Old Faithful map. Stock-party-only or boater-access sites are not included.

The Bechler River has an abundance of designated campsites, probably a higher density than any other area in the park, which reflects the popularity of the area. Many sites are limited to one-night stays, and some sites are minimum-impact sites, which means no campfires.

0A1 (3★) is a not-so-private, mixed site right along the trail just past Lone Star Geyser. Reasonably good water source and plenty of tent sites. Exposed campsite. Nice view of the Upper Firehole River from camp.

0A2 (3★) is a not-so-private, hiker-only site just off the trail. Nice view. Lots of tent sites. Good water source.

0A3 (2★) is a not-so-private, hiker-only site just off the trail near Firehole Springs. No view. Tent sites on hard ground—hard to get stakes in. Good water source.

8G1 (3★) is a private, hiker-only site accessed from the Shoshone Lake Trail, not the Bechler River Trail. About a 100 yards off the trail. Marginal view. Fair water source. Lots of tent sites.

9D4 (3★) is a minimum impact, hiker-only site along the trail just after crossing the Continental Divide. Marginal view. Lots of tent sites. Good water source. No campfires.

9D3 (3★) is a not-so-private, mixed site near Douglas Knob. Large campsite. Lots of tent sites, but rocky terrain. Fair view. Good water source. No campfires.

9D2 (3★) is a not-so-private, hiker-only site. No sign when we came through. Good water source. Fair view. Limited tent sites.

9D1 (3★) is a hiker-only site right along the trail. Cooking area and bear pole on one side of the trail and tent sites and toilet on the other side. Good water source. Near hot springs. No campfires. This site is scheduled to be moved.

9B9 (5★) is a large, mixed, two-party site in the Three Rivers Meadow. Incredible view of Ragged Falls from camp—and you can hear the steady roar from camp, too. Limited tent sites. Good water source. No campfires.

9B8 (4★) is a not-so-private, hiker-only site right along the trail. Nice view of a small waterfall. Good water source and tent sites.

9B7 (3★) is a mostly private, hiker-only site about 100 feet off the trail. Limited view. Good water source and tent sites.

9B6 (4★) is a not-so-private, hiker-only site right along the trail. Nice view of the river. Good water source. Lots of tent sites.

9B5 (2★) is a not-so-private, hiker-only site. Marginal view. Lots of tent sites but some too close to bear pole. Good water source.

9B4 (4★) is a semi-private, hiker-only site about 50 feet off the trail. Good view and water source. Adequate tent sites.

9B2 (4★) a mixed, two-party site right along the trail. One backpacker and one stock party allowed each night. Good view and water source. Good tent sites. Toilet. No campfires.

9C1 (3★) a private, hiker-only site. Good water source. Marginal view. Lots of tent sites.

Fishing: From Three Rivers Junction to Colonnade Falls, the river has a fairly steep gradient and rocky bottom and harbors strictly cutthroat trout in the 8 to 12 inch size class—and they're not too hard to catch. Below Colonnade Falls, you'll also find rainbows and cutthroat-rainbow hybrids and larger fish. When the river slips into Bechler Meadows, the stream smoothes out and slows down. The fish get bigger (with some reaching the 21- to 26-inch range) but more difficult to catch, so stealthy presentations are required. Boundary Creek can also have excellent fishing. August and September offer the best fishing. In July, the river is usually high and the mosquitoes vicious.

10

Black Canyon of the Yellowstone

General description: An unusual trip along the majestic Yellowstone River nearly the entire route

Special attractions: Snow gives up this area early in the year providing a rare opportunity for early season backpacking

Type of trip: Shuttle

Total distance: 18.5 miles (29.6 kilometers)

Difficulty: Moderate

Traffic: Moderate

Maps: Trails Illustrated map of Mammoth Hot Springs; Tower/Canyon and Tower Junction, Blacktail Deer Creek, Ash Mountain, and Gardiner USGS quads

Starting point: Hellroaring Trailhead (2K8)

Finding the trailhead: Drive 14.5 miles east from Mammoth or 3.5 miles west from Tower and pull into the Hellroaring Trailhead. The actual trailhead is about a half mile down a service road. To find the west trailhead in Gardiner, turn on the first road going east on the north side of the Yellowstone River and park by a sign for the Yellowstone River Trail between a private campground and a church.

Parking and trailhead facilities: Ample parking; no facilities. Limited parking and no facilities at the exit point in Gardiner.

Recommended itinerary: There are many ways to enjoy the Black Canyon, but I recommend the following three-day trip:

First night:	1R2 or 1R1
Second night:	1Y2 or 1Y1

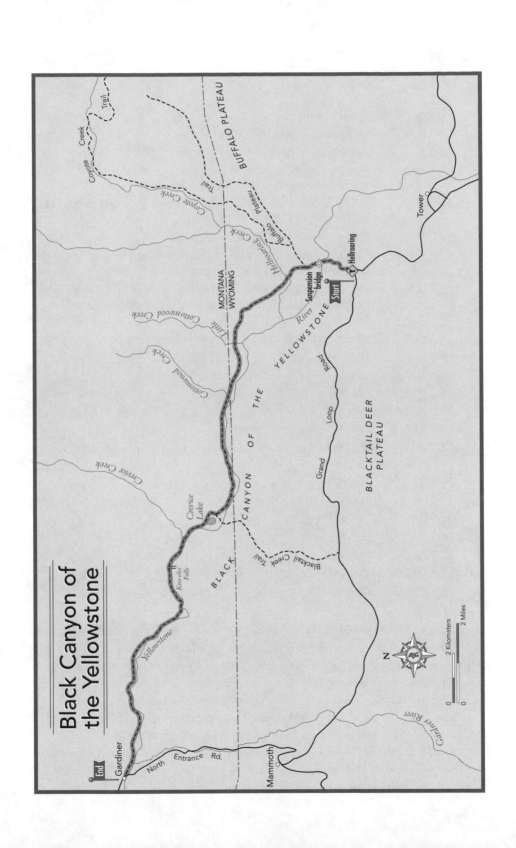

Black Canyon of the Yellowstone

0.8 m. (1.3 k)	Junction with trail to Tower; turn left
1.0 (1.6)	Suspension bridge over Yellowstone
1.6 (2.6)	Junction with trail to Coyote Creek and Buffalo Plateau; turn left
1.8 (2.9)	Spur trail going north along the east side of Hellroaring Creek to 2H6 (4★) and 2H8 (4★) and to stock bridge; turn left
1.9 (3.0)	Spur trail going south along the east side of Hellroaring Creek to 2H4 (4★) and 2H2 (5★); turn right
2.0 (3.2)	Ford of Hellroaring Creek
2.1 (3.4)	Spur trail going south along the west side of Hellroaring Creek to 2H3 (4★) and 2H1 (5★); turn right
2.2 (3.5)	Spur trail going north along the west side of Hellroaring Creek to 2H5 (4★), to the stock bridge, and into Gallatin National Forest; turn left
4.5 (7.2)	Little Cottonwood Creek, 1R3 (4★)
5.9 (9.5)	1R2 (5★)
6.0 (9.6)	Cottonwood Creek, 1R1 (5★)
8.3 (13.1)	1Y9 (5★)
9.0 (14.5)	1Y7 (4★)
9.8 (15.7)	1Y5 (4★)
10.0 (16.1)	Blacktail Creek Trail junction; trail to 1Y6 (4★) and 1Y8 (5★); turn right
10.1 (16.2)	Crevice Lake
10.5 (16.9)	1Y4 (5★)
11.6 (18.6)	Crevice Creek
11.9 (19.1)	Knowles Falls
12.3 (19.8)	1Y2 (4★)
13.2 (21.2)	1Y1 (5★)
18.5 (29.6)	Gardiner

The hike: The Black Canyon of the Yellowstone is one of the classic backpacking trips of the northern Rockies. It seems to offer everything a hiker might want. It's downhill all the way on an excellent trail with a wide choice of 4★ and 5★ campsites. Wildlife is abundant; the fishing is fantastic, and the scenery rivals almost any other hike in the park. The trail closely follows the mighty Yellowstone River most of the way.

Arranging a shuttle is the first order of business. It's better to start at the east end of the trail because you lose more than 1,000 feet in elevation along the way.

After leaving the Hellroaring Trailhead, you hike through meadows and a few stands of trees down a steep hill to the suspension bridge over the Yellowstone River, going left (north) at the junction with the trail to Tower just before reaching the bridge. Here's where you pat yourself on the back for your good plan to start at this end of the shuttle hike. If you did it in reverse, you would face this steep hill right at the end of your hike when you might not be in the mood for it.

The suspension bridge is one of the highlights of the trip, but don't conjure up images of Indiana Jones movies. This is a very sturdy metal bridge. From here to near Gardiner, you're in the Black Canyon of the Yellowstone.

Shortly after crossing the bridge, you break out into the open terrain around Hellroaring Creek. When you reach the junction with the trail up Coyote Creek, go left (west).

When you get to Hellroaring Creek, be alert or you'll get on the wrong trail. Well-defined trails go up both sides of the creek to campsites, and when we hiked this trip, many of the trail signs were missing. There used to be a footbridge across Hellroaring Creek (a large tributary to the Yellowstone), but high spring runoff claimed it a few years ago. Watch for trail markers on the west side of the creek so you know where to ford. This ford can be dangerous in June and early July, so if it looks too adventuresome for you, hike about 1 mile north along the creek and cross on a stock bridge and then back down the west side of the creek to the main trail.

After fording Hellroaring Creek you gradually climb over a ridge and drop into Little Cottonwood Creek and then over another hill into Cottonwood Creek. The section of the trail between Hellroaring and Cottonwood Creek stays high above the river on mostly open hillsides. Then, just after Cottonwood Creek, it drops down to the river's edge.

Crossing Hellroaring Creek.

Also, just before Cottonwood Creek, you pass from Wyoming to Montana. If you're an angler, though, this doesn't matter, as long as you have a park fishing license and know the regulations.

From Cottonwood Creek to the Blacktail Trail Junction, the trail stays close to the river, offering up some spectacular scenery and plenty of pleasant resting places. You might notice frequent carcasses and scattered bones along this trail. That's because this is winter range for the park's large ungulates. Each year, winter kills some weaker members of the herd, and wolves, bears, and cougars take down a few more.

At the Blacktail Trail junction, continue straight (west) along the north side of the river, passing Crevice Lake just after the junction. Then, 1.6 miles later, cross Crevice Creek on a sturdy footbridge. Some older maps show a trail going up Crevice Creek to the park boundary, but this route has been abandoned. Shortly after Crevice Creek, take a short side trip on a spur trail down to see majestic Knowles Falls, a 15-foot drop on the Yellowstone.

From the falls to where the trail ends at Gardiner, the trail continues close to the river, except one short section just after 1Y2, where the trail climbs over a rocky ridge. The river goes through a narrows here, getting white and frothy, so you might feel a bit safer being farther away. Just before Gardiner, you can see the confluence of the Gardner and Yellowstone Rivers. (Yes, Gardiner the town and Gardner the river have different spellings for no clearly definable reason. Interestingly, Jim Bridger originally called the river "Gardener Creek.")

The trail is in superb condition the entire way with the exception of one short section between Bear Creek and Gardiner. Here, the trail is etched out of a steep, clay hillside. If you draw a rainy day, this stretch can be slippery, so be careful.

Options: In addition to the three-day trip described here, this route makes an excellent four-day trip. You could stay the first night at one of the six excellent campsites along Hellroaring Creek, the second at 1R2 or 1R1, and the third at 1Y2 or 1Y1 before hiking out on the fourth day. This gives you plenty of time for fishing and relaxing. If you only have two days, stay overnight at 1Y9, 1Y7, or 1Y5. You can trim about 4 miles off the trip by leaving Black Canyon at the Blacktail Trail Junction.

Side trips: If you stay at Hellroaring Creek, you might enjoy a short day hike up the creek to the park boundary.

Camping: These designated campsites are on the Mammoth Hot Springs Trails Illustrated map. Stock-party-only or boater-access sites are not included.

All nine campsites along Hellroaring Creek are excellent hiker-only sites. On the Trails Illustrated map it's difficult to see this, but the odd-numbered campsites are on the west side of the stream and the even-numbered on the east side. All of the sites are close to Hellroaring Creek, with the stream serving as a readily accessible water source. None of the campsites allow campfires, but these campsites (as well as others farther down the river) prove that you can have a five-star camping experience without a campfire.

Enjoying one of the five-star campsites along this route.

2H1 (5★) is at the confluence of Hellroaring Creek and the Yellowstone and has all the elements of a great campsite.

2H2 (5★) is also right at the confluence and even has a beach for lounging on a hot day. Tent sites are somewhat limited, so you might be tempted to pitch your tent on the beach, which would be a bad idea if it rained up in the headwaters of Hellroaring Creek.

2H3 (4★) is about a quarter mile from the main trail and has a great view from the food area under a spreading spruce tree. Even though there is a trail going around the campsite, hikers going to 2H1 might pass through your camp.

2H4 (4★) is on your left as you approach Hellroaring Creek. In fact the trail naturally goes downstream toward 2H4 and 2H2, so you might accidentally see this site when you're looking for the ford. It's a private site except for people going to 2H2 who come right through your camp.

2H5 (4★) is similar to 2H6, but it doesn't have quite as nice of a food area or view, and you have to labor down a very steep slope to get there.

2H6 (4★) is on your right about a half mile up Hellroaring Creek. It's private, and the food area and the view are slightly better than 2H5, which is just upstream on the other side of the creek.

Hiking along the Yellowstone River.

2H7 (4★) is not quite as private as other campsites along Hellroaring Creek (about 100 yards off trail), but it is similar to the other sites in most respects. It lacks a well-defined food area.

2H8 (4★) is a private, hiker-only site about a half mile north of the Hellroaring footbridge on a good spur trail right at the confluence of Hellroaring and Coyote Creeks. Good water source. No campfires allowed.

2H9 (3★) was closed when we hiked Hellroaring Creek because a lightning fire had burned right through the campsite. However, the NPS plans to keep it open. It's a hiker-only site about 50 feet off the trail on the west bank of Hellroaring Creek. Good water source and fair view, but a little too close to the trail.

1R1 (5★) is a charming, mixed site right on the bank of the Yellowstone River and nicely private (about 200 yards off the trail) with plenty of tent sites. The bear pole is on a steep slope, making hanging food difficult. Good water source. No campfires.

1R2 (5★) is a hiker-only site very similar to 1R1. No campfires.

1R3 (4★) is a mixed site along Little Cottonwood Creek on a bench far above the Yellowstone with plenty of tent sites but close enough to the trail to make it only semiprivate. Great view of the open country above the river from the food area where you should be able to see elk from camp—and maybe some wolves chasing them. If you're an angler, you might not like this campsite because it's a steep climb down to the river. A good choice for a large party. No campfires.

1Y1 (5★) is the westernmost, near-perfect campsite on this trip. The trail is a little too close to the site for complete privacy. Great view. Easy water source (the river). Good tent sites. Even a little beach formed by the still-water pool just below a big rapids. No campfires.

1Y2 (4★) has everything but privacy. The trail actually goes between the tent sites and bear pole. This hiker-only site has a sensational view of the rapids starting just below camp. The high water in 1996 deposited fresh sand on the tent sites, which makes it so soft you won't notice if you forgot your sleeping pad. Good water source. No campfires.

1Y4 (5★) is a private, hiker-only site along a slow section of the river just above Knowles Falls. Great view and excellent tent sites. Good water source. No campfires.

1Y5 (4★) is a private, hiker-only site right along the river. Limited tent sites. It might be a marginal choice for a party with more than two tents. Good water source and view, but no campfires. 1Y5, 1Y7, and 1Y9 are similar sites.

1Y6 (3★) is the first hiker-only campsite on the spur trail 0.3 mile from the Blacktail Creek Trail on the south side of the river over the suspension bridge. Private site in sparse juniper and Douglas fir with a good view of the river. Good water source. Adequate tent sites. No campfires.

1Y7 (5★) is similar to 1Y5, a private, mixed site along the river with a special tent site under a big Douglas fir. Good view and water source.

1Y8 (4★) is the second hiker-only campsite on the spur trail 0.8 mile from the main trail on the south side of the river. It's more open and has a better view than 1Y6. Very private and appears to receive lighter use than 1Y6. Good water source and tent sites. No campfires.

1Y9 (5★) is another great campsite right along the river with privacy, lots of good tent sites, easy water source, and a great view. No campfires.

Fishing: The Black Canyon of the Yellowstone offers terrific fishing. From Hellroaring Creek to Knowles Falls, it's strictly a cutthroat fishery. Most fish range in the 10- to 14-inch range and are usually suckers for almost any fly or lure. Below Knowles Falls, you start to find a few rainbows and hybrids and a few browns, with trout getting up to 17 inches or more, but they are harder to catch. You also find large numbers of whitefish below Knowles Falls. Even though this drier section of the park is suitable for hiking in May and June, the Yellowstone often runs high and murky during the early season, and this limits fishing success.

11

Chain of Lakes

General description: A short, easy backpacking trip to four of Yellowstone's mountain lakes

Special attractions: The only hike in Yellowstone that goes to more than two lakes

Type of trip: Shuttle

Total distance: 10.3 miles (16.6 kilometers)

Difficulty: Easy

Traffic: Heavy

Maps: Trails Illustrated map of Mammoth Hot Springs; Norris Junction, Crystal Falls, and Cook Peak USGS quads

Starting point: Cascade Creek Trailhead (4K4)

Finding the trailhead: Drive about a half mile west of Canyon Junction and park in the parking area on the north side of the road. Leave a vehicle or arrange to be picked up at the Ice Lake Trailhead (on the north side of the road) 8.5 miles west of Canyon Junction.

Parking and trailhead facilities: Ample parking; no facilities, although Canyon Village is nearby. Limited parking and no facilities at exit point, but there is a pit toilet at Ice Lake.

Recommended itinerary: This route is best suited for a weekend backpacking trip, staying overnight at any of the four excellent campsites at Grebe Lake. If you want to spend more time fishing (and not too much time carrying your pack each day), extend this to three days by staying at Cascade and Wolf Lakes—although, in general, the campsites aren't as nice at these two lakes as they are at Grebe Lake.

The hike: This is the only hike in Yellowstone where you can see four mountain lakes in 10 miles. In fact there is no other hike in the park where you can see more than two. It's also an ideal trip for beginning backpackers, especially those who like to have extra time for fishing.

Be sure to bring lots of insect repellent and netting. This area, particularly Grebe Lake, produces hordes of mosquitoes. When we did this hike in early July, we were

Chain of Lakes

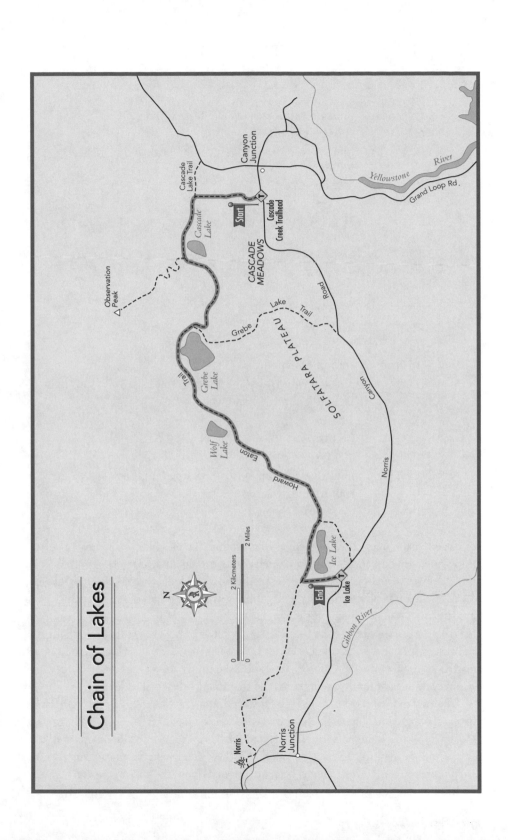

2.1 m. (3.4 k)	Junction with Cascade Lake Trail; turn left
2.3 (3.7)	Spur trail to 4E4 (2★)
2.4 (3.8)	Junction with trail to Observation Peak and to 4E3 (3★); turn left
2.5 (4.0)	Cascade Lake
2.7 (4.3)	4E2 (2★)
4.9 (7.9)	4G3 (4★); junction with Grebe Lake Trail and 4G2 (5★); turn right
5.0 (8.0)	Grebe Lake
5.2 (8.4)	4G4 (5★)
5.4 (8.7)	4G5 (5★)
6.4 (10.3)	4G6 (5★)
6.5 (10.4)	Wolf Lake
6.6 (10.6)	4G7 (3★)
7.5 (12.0)	Ford of Gibbon River
8.6 (13.8)	Junction with Little Gibbon Falls/Wolf Lake Trail; turn right
9.3 (14.9)	Second ford of Gibbon River
9.5 (15.3)	4D2 (5★)
9.6 (15.4)	Ice Lake
9.7 (15.7)	4D1 (4★)
9.8 (15.8)	Junction with trail to Norris campground; turn left
10.1 (16.2)	Spur trail to 4D3 (5★)
10.3 (16.6)	Ice Lake Trailhead

convinced that Grebe Lake served as the factory for all the mosquitoes in all of Yellowstone. If you want to avoid bugs, delay your trip until mid-August.

The first 2.1 miles go through intermittently burned lodgepole and scenic Cascade Meadows. The trail is in terrific shape the entire way, with bridges over all marshy spots. This stretch of trail gets heavy stock use.

About a half mile before the lake, the Cascade Lake Trail joins from the east. Take a left (west) and head for Cascade Lake. Just before the lake, the trail to Observation Peak and 4E3 turns off to the right (north). Cascade Lake (thirty-six acres and deep) is in a big open park (just right for fly casting), and the trail follows the north side of it.

The trail to Grebe Lake, called the Howard Eaton Trail on maps, is flat with some marshy spots and not quite as nice as the trail to Cascade Lake. Grebe Lake is a huge lake (136 acres), also in an open park nicely suited for fly casting. Some older maps may still show a trail heading off to the left (south) to the Grebe Lake Trailhead, just before reaching Grebe Lake. This trail has been abandoned. Now, the trail to the Grebe Lake Trailhead follows the east edge of Grebe Lake, turning off just before reaching 4D3.

Nearing Cascade Lake.

Grebe Lake is full of fish (rainbow and grayling) that have a super-abundant food source—the clouds of bugs produced in the marshy areas around the lake. Consequently, this lake attracts fish-eating birds—mergansers, pelicans, ospreys, and, of course, grebes.

Walking around Grebe Lake can be a real challenge because the west end features a nearly impassable marsh. However, you can easily walk the shoreline on the other three sides of the lake.

The trail between Grebe Lake and Wolf Lake (also in excellent shape) passes through burned forest before opening up into a gorgeous meadow at the inlet of the lake. You have to ford the inlet stream and a long but shallow backwater (actually the Gibbon River as it leaves the lake) to get to 4G7 and to continue on the trail. Wolf Lake is also large (fifty-one acres), fairly deep, with a fairly open shoreline (although not as open as those of Cascade and Grebe Lakes) and good fishing.

After leaving Wolf Lake you head into the unburned timber and climb a fairly serious hill and then drop back into the Gibbon River valley. You have to ford the river, but it's only a small stream at this point after mid-July. After the ford the trail follows the stream for about a half mile before going into a heavily burned forest. Just before Ice Lake (after you've taken a right (west) at the Little Gibbon Falls/Wolf Lake Trail Junction), you ford the Gibbon River once more, but it's still an easy, safe crossing after mid-July.

Ice Lake contrasts with the other three lakes on this trip. It's completely surrounded by trees—mostly victims of the 1988 fires. The lake contains no trout, but if it did, it would be a fly caster's nightmare.

At the west end of Ice Lake, take a left (south) at the junction with the trail going straight (east) to Norris campground. From here it's an easy half mile hike back to the trailhead and the Norris-Canyon Road.

Fording the Gibbon River.

Options: This shuttle hike can be done from either direction with no added difficulty. You can also start at the Cascade Lake Trailhead (4K5). If you want a shorter hike, you can hike out to the Grebe Lake or Wolf Lake trailheads.

If you want a longer hike, you can hike out to Norris, but that trail goes through burnt forest with no views for the first half of the 4.5-mile trip from Ice Lake to Norris. After 4F1 the trail goes through the huge Norris Meadow, and just before reaching the junction with the Solfatara Creek Trail, you ford the Gibbon River one more time. Here, however, the river has grown to the point where the ford can be difficult and dangerous early in the year.

Side trips: Observation Peak makes a nice side trip for hikers staying at Cascade Lake.

Camping: These designated campsites are on the Mammoth Hot Springs Trails Illustrated map. Stock-party-only or boater-access sites are not included.

4E2 (1★) is a private, hiker-only site on the north side of the trail just west of Cascade Lake. It's tucked away in the trees, with no view, on a steep hillside with only one good tent site, which is probably why it's limited to small groups of no more than four people. Parties with two tents will have a hard time finding another tent site. There is a 300-yard walk to water.

4E3 (3★) is a hiker-only site about 200 yards up the trail to Observation Peak. This private site has a good view of Cascade Lake, but you have to haul water up from the stream along the trail.

4E4 (2★) is a mixed site southeast of the lake. It's a private site (about 200 yards off the trail) with the food and sleeping areas separated by a marshy meadow, which means early in the year you might get your feet wet every time you travel between the two. Marginal view and water source.

4P1 (3★) is an unusual campsite. It's a hiker-only site essentially on the summit of Observation Peak. You don't have a view from camp, but it's only about 50 yards to the summit where you get an incredible view of the Yellowstone River valley. Lots of tent sites, but no water source unless you get there early enough in the year to find snowbanks. Otherwise, be sure to carry enough water with you for your overnight stay.

All four Grebe Lake campsites (4G2, 4G3, 4G4, 4G5) are excellent. They are located along the shore of the lake (the readily accessible water source) with good views.

4G2 (5★) is the only hiker-only site at Grebe Lake. It's a private site on the south side of the lake. Great view from the food area and you can almost fish from camp.

4G3 (4★) is a not-so-private, mixed site right along the trail on the north side of Grebe Lake. If you're an angler, you can almost fish from camp. Firewood is sparse.

4G4 (5★) is nestled in the trees on the north side of the lake. This private, mixed site doesn't appear to get much use from stock parties.

4G5 (5★) is very similar to 4G4.

4G6 (5★) is about 50 yards north of the trail on the edge of the meadow that holds Wolf Lake. It's a semi-private, mixed site with a good view of the lake, an easy water source, and good tent sites.

4G7 (3★) is an exposed, hiker-only site on the south side of the trail on the west side of the outlet. Lacks privacy. Good view of the lake and easy water source.

4D1 (4★) is a hiker-only site on the south side of the trail at the west end of Ice Lake. It has a good view and easy water source, but limited tent sites and little privacy (right along the trail).

4D2 (5★) is a private, hiker-only site on a bench above the east end of Ice Lake with good tent sites and easy access to water. Good view of the lake.

4D3 (5★) is the only backcountry campsite in Yellowstone accessible by wheelchair. This private, hiker-only site has a good view of the lake, good tent sites, and believe it or not, a luxurious outdoor privy.

4F1 (5★) is incorrectly marked as 4N1 on some older maps. This private, hiker-only site is on a small bench overlooking Norris Meadows—ideal for wildlife watching. Good water source and tent sites. This trail gets little use, so you probably won't see many people coming through the meadow.

Fishing: Cascade Lake has cutthroats and a few grayling and is fair fishing. Grebe Lake can be great fishing for rainbows and grayling, but be prepared for clouds of mosquitoes. Ditto for Wolf Lake, although fishing is usually not as good as it is at Grebe Lake. Ice Lake is barren.

12

Heart Lake

General description: A popular backpacking trip around a massive mountain lake

Special attractions: Variety—lakes, fishing (lake and stream), wildlife viewing, mountain climbs, thermal areas—all in one trip

Type of trip: Loop

Total distance: 33.9 miles (54.5 kilometers)

Difficulty: Moderate

Traffic: Moderate

Maps: Trails Illustrated map of Yellowstone Lake; Mount Sheridan and Heart Lake USGS quads

Starting point: Heart Lake Trailhead (8N1)

Finding the trailhead: Drive 5.2 miles south of Grant Village Junction and park in the trailhead parking area on the east side of the road.

Parking and trailhead facilities: Ample parking; no facilities.

Recommended itinerary: I recommend a five-day trip with two nights on the west shore of Heart Lake (using the extra day to climb Mount Sheridan), taking three more nights to complete the loop.

First night:	8H6, 8H5, 8H4, 8H3, or 8H2
Second night:	same campsite
Third night:	8B2, 8B5, or 8C5
Fourth night:	8J4, 8J6, or 8J1

The hike: This is a superb, moderately difficult backpacking trip especially suited for anglers—and one of the few major backpacking trips in Yellowstone that doesn't require a bothersome vehicle shuttle.

Heart Lake sort of looks like the big heart of Yellowstone, but it isn't named for its shape. Instead, it's named after Hart Humey, an old trapper who frequented the area before the park was created. Through the years, "Hart" Lake became Heart Lake.

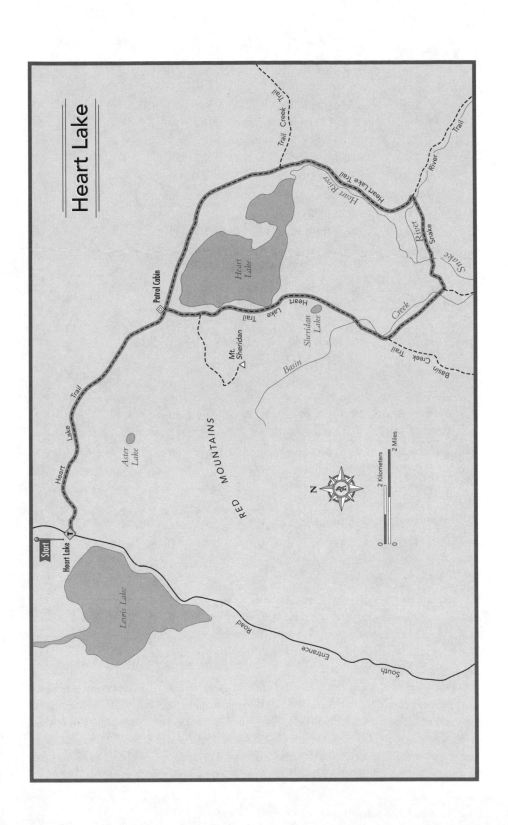

Heart Lake

5.0 m. (8.0 k)	Viewpoint down Witch Creek to Heart Lake
7.8 (12.5)	Heart Lake patrol cabin
8.0 (12.8)	Trail Creek Trail Junction; turn right
8.2 (13.2)	Rustic Geyser
8.3 (13.3)	Trail to 8H6 (4★)
8.7 (14.0)	Trail to 8H5 (4★) and spur trail to Mount Sheridan
9.0 (14.5)	Trail to 8H4 (4★)
9.5 (15.3)	Spur trails to 8H3 (4★) and 8H2 (4★)
10.5 (16.9)	8H1 (2★)
11.5 (18.5)	Sheridan Lake
13.0 (20.9)	8B1 (4★)
13.5 (21.7)	Basin Creek Trail Junction; turn left
15.6 (25.1)	8B5 (3★)
16.0 (25.7)	Junction with Snake River Trail; turn left
16.9 (27.2)	Ford the Snake River
18.2 (27.3)	Ford the Snake River
18.3 (29.4)	8C5 (4★)
18.4 (29.6)	Junction with Heart River Trail; turn left
19.0 (30.5)	Ford the Heart River
21.5 (34.6)	Ford the Heart River and Outlet Creek
21.7 (34.9)	Junction with Trail Creek Trail and 8J4 (3★); turn left
22.0 (35.4)	8J6 (4★)
24.2 (38.9)	8J1 (5★)
25.7 (41.3)	Junction with Heart Lake Trail; turn right
25.9 (41.6)	Heart Lake patrol cabin
33.9 (54.5)	Heart Lake Trailhead

Regardless of the name, however, this seems like the heart of the southeastern section of Yellowstone. It's a uniquely large and beautiful mountain lake in the shadow of stately Mount Sheridan. Anglers love the healthy population of large cutthroat and lake trout. Bald eagles and loons love it, too, looking for the same fish, and grizzlies roam the slopes of Mount Sheridan.

Heart Lake is a truly monstrous mountain lake. It spans 2,160 acres and gets down to 180 feet deep. It has also become a popular destination for hikers, so don't plan on having the lake or the trail to yourself. The trail is in great shape all the way with bridges over all streams. It goes through unburned forest interrupted here and there by small meadows for the first 5 miles. Then, the trail passes through a small burn from the 1988 fires to a great viewpoint of the lake, Factory Hill, and Witch Creek, probably named for the numerous hot springs and steam vents that line most of its course. At this viewpoint, it seems like you're closer to the lake because it's so large, but you actually have more than 2 miles to go.

From this point on the trail goes through open terrain with great scenery as you drop down to the lake. If you stop to investigate thermal areas, be careful not to disturb delicate ecosystems or burn yourself. On a cold day the thermal areas kick up so much steam that it clouds views of the lake. Factory Hill (named for the steam vents that resemble smoke stacks) partly blocks the view of Mount Sheridan.

Just before you reach the lake and the junction with the Trail Creek Trail, you'll see the Heart Lake patrol cabin off to the left. A ranger stays there most of the summer.

The trail follows the shoreline through the Witch Creek bottomlands and by the overflow of Rustic Geyser and several hot pools off to your right. Again, these thermal areas are fascinating to explore, but be cautious. At the first junction the left fork goes to 8H6. You turn right to the other campsites and to the Mount Sheridan spur trail, about 200 yards farther down the trail.

If you're taking the counterclockwise route for the loop around the lake, turn right (south) at the junction just past the patrol cabin and stay at one of the six campsites on the west side of the lake. If you plan on hiking up to the summit of Mount Sheridan (and you'll be sorry if you don't), reserve the campsite for two nights.

The hike along the west side of the lake climbs slightly away from the lakeshore after 8H6 and then drops back to the shoreline before 8H1. You climb a little hill when leaving the lake before dropping into Sheridan Lake, a small, marsh-lined lake off to your right (west). In the spring the trail gets boggy in spots near the lake.

The trail continues through mostly open terrain and meadows along Basin Creek. At the junction with the Basin Creek Trail, go left (southeast) and continue following Basin Creek through mostly burned timber until you see the Snake River and the junction with the Heart River Trail. The trail through this section is well-defined, with frequent stream crossings.

Here, turn left (northeast) and hike along the Snake River through a big meadow for about 1 mile until you reach the ford. The trail is a little rocky, but in fair shape. Early in the season, the ford might be hazardous, but after mid-July, it's usually knee-deep.

After fording the Snake, the trail angles away from the river into a heavily burned area until you reach the junction with the trail going south to the headwaters of the Snake. Turn left (north) and head toward Heart Lake on the Heart River Trail. You ford the Snake River again just before the junction, but it's an even smaller stream because the Heart River hasn't joined yet.

This section of trail is in good shape as it closely follows the Heart River and passes through lightly burned forest most of the way to Heart Lake. About halfway to the lake you ford this river, and then again, as well as Outlet Creek just before reaching Heart Lake. All of these fords are easier than the Snake River ford.

When you reach the Trail Creek Trail, go left (west) and finish your circle of Heart Lake back to the junction at the patrol cabin. The trail is in great shape through this section. It stays in the timber much of the way, but a few openings in the trees provide for some great views of the lake with its incredible backdrop, Mount Sheridan.

Heart Lake and Mount Sheridan.

From here, retrace your steps to the Heart Lake Trailhead.

Options: You can take the loop in either direction with no increased difficulty.

Side trips: The obvious (and spectacular) side trip is the out-and-back trail up Mount Sheridan. It's 6 miles round trip and a tough, Category H, 2,700-foot climb. The spur trail takes off from Heart Lake Trail 0.7 mile south of the Trail Creek Junction.

The hike up to the lookout on 10,308-foot Mount Sheridan may be the most scenic mountain top hike in the park. It definitely rivals the climbs up Mount Washburn and Mount Holmes for scenery.

The trail starts out through some large meadows before going into burned lodgepole and a series of large switchbacks. The switchbacks soon give way to a steeper, winding trail up the north ridge of the mountain. This is the steepest part of the climb. At the 2-mile mark, the trail breaks out above the timberline, and the slope gets more gradual as the trail loops around to the west side of the mountain. But "more gradual" does not imply "gradual."

Be sure to bring water because you won't find any on the mountain unless you go early enough to catch a few snowbanks before they disappear. To avoid deep snow, don't try this hike until mid-July.

Plan on spending an hour or so at the lookout at the summit to identify all the mountains and lakes you can see such as the nice view of Grand Teton to the south and the seldom-seen Delusion Lake to the north, not to mention a stunning aerial view of Heart Lake. Even from up here, Heart Lake looks big, and you can see way down at the Continental Divide, which comes through the area just north and east of Heart Lake.

Exploring thermal areas near Heart Lake.

Last pitch to the top of Mount Sheridan.

Camping: These designated campsites are on the Yellowstone Lake Trails Illustrated map. Stock-party-only or boater-access sites are not included.

8C5 (4★) is a mixed site along the trail, just west of the junction with the Heart River Trail. Great view, good tent sites and water source. Closed until July.

8C6 (3★) is a semiprivate, mixed site on the west of the ford of the Snake River about 50 yards from the trail. Exposed site with lots of good tent sites and a good view of the Snake River. Far enough to water to be inconvenient.

8C9 (3★) is a mixed site near the confluence of Crooked Creek and the Snake River. Heavily used by stock parties. Limited view, good tent site, and water source.

Notes on Heart Lake campsites: All six campsites (8H6, 8H5, 8H4, 8H3, 8H2, 8H1) on the west side of the lake are hiker-only and closed until July. Only 8H2 and 8H3 allow campfires. With the exception of 8H1, these campsites are close to the lake. All sites have their own toilets or share with a nearby site. All six campsites are suited for small groups with no more than two tents.

8H6 (4★), *8H5* (4★) and *8H4* (4★) are clumped together near the Mount Sheridan Trail with limited privacy. Avoid old tent sites too close to the bear poles. *8H3* (4★) and *8H2* (4★) have the best views and are the most private, but each has a marshy trail leading to it. 8H2 and 8H3 are close together—a good choice for two parties who know each other. *8H1* (2★) is at the far end of the lake, located 200 yards from the lake in a narrow gully with no view and marginal tent sites. All sites closed until July.

8J1 (5★) is a private, hiker-only site on the lakeshore with a great view and pit toilet. Closed until July.

8J3 (3★) is a hiker-only site right along the trail less than a half mile from the Heart River Trail Junction. Good water source. Minimal view and marginal tent sites. Closed until July.

8J4 (3★) is a not-so-private, hiker-only site at the junction with the Trail Lake Trail and the confluence of the Heart River and Outlet Creek. Limited tent sites, marginal view, but good water source. Closed until July.

8J6 (4★) is a private, hiker-only site about a quarter mile from the trail on the shore of Heart Lake with a super view of the lake and Mount Sheridan. Good water source, but limited tent sites. Pit toilet. Closed until July.

8B1 (3★) is a semiprivate, hiker-only site on your right (west) along a small tributary to Basin Creek. Good water source and a fair view out into a big meadow along Basin Creek. Watch for the sign immediately south of the stream. Closed until July.

8B2 (3★) is a mixed site on your right (west) just north of Basin Creek Lake. If the signs are down (as they were when I was there), the site is difficult to find. It's in a grove of trees about 150 yards from the lake (the water source). It's private with decent tent sites, but has no view. Closed until July.

8B5 (3★) is a hiker-only site right along the trail, but still fairly private since very few people use this trail. Good water source, plenty of good tent sites, but no view. Closed until July.

Fishing: Heart Lake has good populations of both cutthroat and lake trout, usually averaging 18 to 20 inches. When conditions are right, fishing can be very good. You can also catch a few cutthroats in Beaver Creek and the Heart River.

13

The Gallatin Skyline

General description: A long adventure through the best high country of the northeastern corner of Yellowstone

Special attractions: Remoteness and perhaps the best scenery in Yellowstone

Type of trip: A long, strenuous shuttle

Total distance: 40.3 miles (64.9 kilometers)

Difficulty: Difficult

Traffic: Light

Maps: Trails Illustrated map of Mammoth Hot Springs; Mammoth, Quadrant Mountain, Joseph Peak, Sportsman Lake Electric Peak, and Big Horn Peak USGS quads

Starting point: Glen Creek Trailhead (1K3)

Finding the trailhead: Drive 5 miles south of Mammoth to just past the Golden Gate and park at the Glen Creek Trailhead parking lot on the east side of the road.

Parking and trailhead facilities: Ample parking; no facilities; limited parking and no facilities at the exit point at Daly Creek Trailhead.

Recommended itinerary: This trip requires a minimum of six days, but I recommend taking seven, adding an extra day to climb Electric Peak.

First night:	Preferred—1G4; alternate—1G3
Second night:	Same campsite
Third night:	Preferred—WD3; alternate—WD2
Fourth night:	Preferred—WD4; alternate—WD5
Fifth night:	Preferred—WE5; alternate—WE7
Sixth night:	Outside park on Sky Rim

The hike: Regardless of how experienced or well-conditioned you are (and you must be both to attempt this trip!), this hike is a true adventure. This is not a hike you decide to do a few days in advance. Instead, it's a hike you plan months ahead, going over every detail to keep your pack as light as possible but still to be prepared for all types of

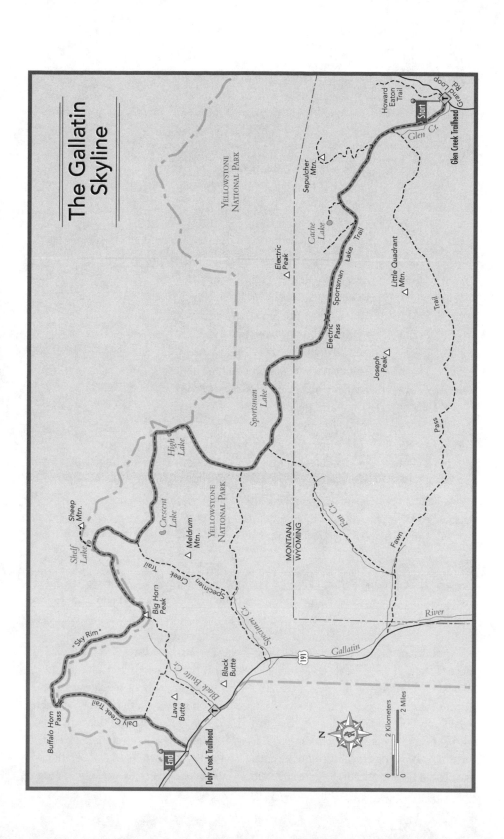

The Gallatin Skyline

YELLOWSTONE NATIONAL PARK

Howard Eaton Trail

Glen Cr.

Start

Glen Creek Trailhead

Grand Loop Rd.

Sepulcher Mtn.

Electric Peak

Cache Lake

Sportsman Lake Trail

Little Quadrant Mtn.

Electric Pass

Joseph Peak

Fan Cr.

Sportsman Lake

Trail

High Lake

Pass

MONTANA
WYOMING

Crescent Lake

Meldrum Mtn.

YELLOWSTONE NATIONAL PARK

Fawn

Sheep Mtn.

Shelf Lake

Creek Trail

Specimen Cr.

River

Big Horn Peak

"Sky Rim"

Black Butte Cr.

Black Butte

Gallatin

191

Buffalo Horn Pass

Daly Creek Trail

Lava Butte

Daly Creek Trailhead

End

2 Kilometers

2 Miles

N

0

0

0.2 m. (0.3 k)	Junction with Howard Eaton Trail to Mammoth; turn left
2.1 (3.4)	Fawn Pass Trail junction, go straight
2.9 (4.7)	Sepulcher Mountain Trail junction; turn left
3.7 (5.9)	Cache Lake Trail junction; turn left
5.7 (9.1)	Electric Peak Spur Trail junction; turn left
5.8 (9.2)	1G3 (3★)
5.9 (9.3)	1G4 (4★)
9.9 (15.9)	Electric Pass
12.7 (20.4)	Sportsman Lake; 4D3 (5★) and 4D4 (3★)
15.7 (25.3)	Sportsman Lake Creek Cutoff Trail
16.8 (27.0)	High Lake Trail
19.7 (31.7)	Fan Creek Trail junction; turn right
20.2 (32.5)	High Lake, WD4 (5★) and WD5 (2★)
24.7 (39.7)	Crescent Lake, WE6 (4★)
25.3 (40.7)	Junction with Specimen Creek and Shelf Lake Trails; turn right
27.1 (43.6)	Shelf Lake; WE5 (5★) and WE7 (5★)
27.3 (43.9)	Gallatin Divide
30.1 (48.4)	Big Horn Peak
30.3 (48.7)	Junction with Black Butte Trail; turn right
35.8 (57.6)	Junction with trail to Buffalo Horn Pass; turn left
36.6 (58.9)	Daly Pass
38.9 (62.6)	Teepee Creek Trail junction; WF2 (3★); turn left
39.6 (63.7)	Black Butte Cutoff Trail junction
41.4 (66.6)	Daly Creek Trailhead

weather. If you're looking for a "get high" backpacking trip to really experience the essence of the Yellowstone high country, this is how you'll want to spend your summer vacation.

You hike above treeline much of the way, backpacking right over the top of one mountain (Big Horn Peak), and you'll probably want to take side trips to the top of two more (Electric Peak and Sheep Mountain). You visit five gorgeous high-altitude mountain lakes, camping at three of them. You'll probably see lots of wildlife, and you'll definitely view some of the most outstanding mountain scenery in the northern Rockies. When you finish, you'll definitely have that "hard body" feeling. And finally, for those who like an extra dose of wildness, you'll live with Yellowstone's most famous resident, the grizzly bear, for a week or more since this route goes through some of the park's best bear habitat. (This means no off-trail hiking on some sections of the route to minimize the impact of human behavior on bear behavior.)

The view from Electric Peak.

Planning is the key to making this trip a success. Since it's a shuttle (and a long one at that), you'll have to leave a vehicle or arrange for a pick up at the Daly Creek Trailhead.

Waiting until August maximizes your chances of getting a week of good weather. Bad weather can really take the fun out of this trip (and make it dangerous) because you're often exposed at high altitude. (Fortunately, you can safely "bail out" if you get in trouble by hiking back to the Glen Creek Trailhead on the first two days or out to U.S. 191 down Fan, Specimen, or Black Butte Creeks after you cross Electric Pass.)

It might be tempting to wait for the wonderful weather that often hits this area in September, but this is also the time the early big game seasons opens in Montana. You'll run into hordes of hunters on the divide, which is mostly devoid of people the rest of the year.

The first 2.1 miles of trail to the Fawn Pass Trail Junction go through sagebrush-carpeted flats on a double-wide trail along the south edge of Terrace Mountain. At the Fawn Pass Trail Junction, go straight (west) and head into a small valley, through a short section of burned forest along Glen Creek and past the Sepulcher Mountain Trail Junction, where you go left (west). At the 3.7-mile mark, you can hang your pack and take a short side trip up to Cache Creek.

After the Cache Lake Trail Junction, the trail gradually climbs through open, unburned timber. Just after the Electric Peak Spur Trail, the trail drops into the Upper Gardner River valley for a quarter mile or so to 1G3 or 1G4 (just after an easy ford of the stream). These campsites serve as base camps for a day trip up Electric Peak.

Even though the trail up to Electric Pass barely qualifies as a Category 2 climb, it doesn't seem that difficult. About halfway up you break out of the unburned timber and stay in open terrain the rest of the way to the pass.

Studying the map on Electric Pass.

After resting awhile on the pass, head down to Sportsman Lake. After about 1 mile of treeless landscape (where the trail gets faint and cairns mark the route), the trail heads into deep timber and stays there until Sportsman Lake.

Sportsman Lake could be called "Hidden Lake" because even though you're standing in the open meadow at the foot of the lake you can't see it, nor can you see it coming down from the pass. A trail sign in the huge meadow below the lake marks a four-way crossroads. Eventually, you'll go straight, but if you're staying at WD3, take a right. The spur trail used to go up Mol Heron Creek into the Gallatin National Forest (now essentially abandoned), but now it only goes to WD3.

When you leave Sportsman Lake, you climb for almost 1 mile through a heavily burned forest. When you reach the top of the ridge, you drop into unburned timber and stay there until you reach the cutoff trail to Specimen Creek and the High Lake Trail.

Turn right (north) here, and follow the cutoff trail through open timber and one large meadow before joining the trail to High Lake. Turn right (east), and tackle the Category 2 climb to High Lake, which sits in a open, high-elevation bowl. It also hosts a hardy, self-sustaining cutthroat population. If you plan on fishing (catch-and-release), don't forget your park fishing license.

When leaving High Lake, you face a 400-foot hill to get up to the Gallatin Divide. Once on the divide, plan on soaking in the serious scenery and watching for elk along this section of trail. To the right (east) is the Cinnabar Basin in the Gallatin National Forest with the mighty Absaroka Range in the background. To the left (west) look into the expansive Gallatin Valley and its main artery, the Gallatin River. Don't get too wrapped up in the scenery, however, and get off the trail. It gets faint in places, especially after you veer left and head down to Crescent Lake. You can easily get diverted onto one of the many game trails in the area, which are often more distinct than the official trail. The main trail gets especially difficult to follow in the fall.

After Crescent Lake the trail switchbacks down to the junction with the Specimen Creek Trail. Turn right (north) here, and start the 2.1-mile, Category 1 climb up to Shelf Lake. This is a very tough hill, and you'll probably be worn out after three days of backpacking—and you'll likely be hiking this section in the hot midday sun. It goes straight up, and whoever built it forgot the switchbacks.

When you get to Shelf Lake, however, your effort will be well rewarded. This is an enchanting, if ominous, place just below the Gallatin Divide and Sheep Mountain. Both campsites at this lake are among the best in the park. If you spend two nights here, use part of the rest of the day to scramble up to the top of 10,095-foot Sheep Mountain, the highest peak in this section of the park. It has a big, metal reflector telecommunications screen on the summit.

From Shelf Lake stay on the Gallatin Divide for the next 8.5 miles. Start early because this is your toughest day, and before leaving the lake, load up on all the water you can carry. With the exception of late-season snowbanks (which you usually can find as late as early August), you won't find any water on the ridgeline.

This section makes this trip one of the most unusual and scenic backpacks found anywhere. From Shelf Lake to Big Horn Peak and the Black Butte Trail junction, the going is fairly easy. After the junction, however, you face the toughest part of the trip. The trail more or less disappears for about a half mile after the junction, but the official route stays on the ridgeline, and the walking is fairly easy but essentially off-trail. At this point you can rejoice that you aren't lugging your pack up this pitch, a Category H hill from the north.

The trail goes up and down over two smaller summits on the ridge. Between each summit is a flat saddle where you can spend your last night out. The park boundary goes right on the ridgeline and is marked in many places. Be sure that you're camped outside of the park. These are all marginal campsites with no water sources, but the night on this high divide is a special treat. (The NPS may put an official campsite along this stretch, so check on this before you leave on this trip.)

From this last camp it's downhill to Daly Pass. You pass two junctions with trails going off to the right (northeast) into the Gallatin National Forest. You stay left at both junctions.

The trip down from the pass may be difficult on your knees, but once you break out into the openness of Daly Creek, it's easy walking the last 4 miles to the trailhead.

Options: You can trim one day off this trip by skipping the climb to Electric Peak. You could lengthen the trip by staying an extra night at Shelf Lake or staying at Crescent Lake instead of going all the way from High Lake to Shelf Lake in one day. You could also tack one more day on the trip by staying at WF2 in Daly Creek. You could start at the Daly Creek Trailhead, but this might mean a more difficult trip.

You can also shorten this hike in several places by taking feeder trails down to U.S. 191, such as trails down the Upper Gallatin River, Fan Creek, and Black Butte Creek.

Sportsman Lake.

Side trips: The Cache Lake and Electric Peak side trips are both worth it, and the side trip up Sheep Mountain is an easy scramble.

Camping: These designated campsites are on the Mammoth Hot Springs Trails Illustrated map. Stock-party-only or boater-access sites are not included.

1G3 (3★) would have a great view if the food area was moved slightly to the west. Here you could sit in camp and look out over a beautiful meadow, split by the Upper Gardner River, and see Electric Peak in the background. But the present food area offers no view. This private (300 yards off the trail), hiker-only site has adequate tent sites and a fairly accessible water source (the Gardner River, about 100 yards from camp). One of the traditionally used tent sites is too close to the bear pole, so don't camp there.

1G4 (4★) is similar to 1G3 (private, hiker-only) but has a better view (although you still can't see Electric Peak). Good tent sites and water source (about 25 feet to the Gardner River).

WD2 (3★) is a poor cousin to WD3, the other campsite at Sportsman Lake. This is a mixed site that gets heavy use from stock parties, and the view isn't nearly as nice as that from WD3. Good water source and lots of tent sites. No off-trail travel from campsite.

WD3 (5★) is an excellent, but difficult to find, campsite. It's on the northeast side of the big meadow below Sportsman Lake. (Right after you cross the stream, you might see an old campsite—that's not WD3) From this private, hiker-only site you get a great view of the lake and the massive mountain meadow where you're likely to see moose. Good water sources and plenty of tent sites safely removed from the food area.

WD4 (5★) is a hiker-only site near the outlet of High Lake. It has limited tent sites and marginal privacy, but the view is so fabulous that staying here is a rare delight. You can sit in the food area and watch the cutthroats nail flies on the surface of the lake. Good water source. No campfires.

WD5 (2★) is a difficult-to-find, mixed site on the west end of High Lake about 300 yards from the trail. There is no discernible trail to the site, so go to the west end of the lake and head across the marshy inlet area and up the steep slope on the other side of the lake. It's in a flat area on the other side of the hill. No view of the lake. A long walk to water. Private. Good tent sites. No campfires.

(Note: If you can't get WD4 or WD5, you can camp outside the park in the Gallatin National Forest along a short section of trail just south of High Lake. You'll have to haul water from the lake, but you can have a campfire.)

WE6 (4★) is between Crescent Lake and the trail (and close to both) at the west end of the lake near the outlet. This hiker-only site has a great view of the lake (where you can easily get water). Limited tent sites; one commonly used tent site is too close to the food area and bear pole. It's better to use one of the tent sites above the trail.

WDI (2★) is not in the big meadow along the East Fork of Specimen Creek Trail as shown on some maps. In 1995 it was moved. Now it's on the north side of the trail and tucked back in the trees just west of the East Fork of Specimen Creek. Private (about 200 yards off the trail), hiker-only site, good water source (East Fork), but no view.

WE4 (3★) isn't in the location shown on some maps. It's 0.75 mile west of the Shelf Lake Trail Junction on the north side of the trail—and only 20 feet from the trail. No privacy. Good water source. Plenty of tent sites. A fair view of a small meadow along the North Fork of Specimen Creek with Meldrum Mountain as a backdrop.

If you decide to camp at Shelf Lake, you'll be treated with two extraordinary hiker-only campsites. **WE5** (5★) is on the northeast side of the lake on a little bench overlooking the lake about 300 yards of the trail. It's in a little grove of subalpine fir and whitebark pine to protect your camp from the elements which can be a big issue here since you're camping at 9,200 feet. As the case with all campsites above or near treeline, it's quite damaging to have a campfire, and the NPS rightfully disallows them at Shelf Lake.

WE7 (5★) is on the northwest side of Shelf Lake and is similar to WE5 but less protected from weather. Both Shelf Lake campsites have limited tent sites and outstanding views, but be prepared for high altitude weather. The lake serves as an easy water source for both campsites.

WF2 (3★) is a mixed site right along the Daly Creek Trail with little privacy. Be alert because it's easy to walk right by this seldom used campsite without noticing the sign on a tree away from the trail. Look for this site just east of the Teepee Creek Junction, not west of it as shown on some maps. Good water source (Daly Creek) and tent sites. A fair view of the meadows along Daly Creek. Firewood is sparse.

The Sky Rim section of this route follows the park boundary and the Gallatin Divide.

Fishing information: This hike is not a great choice for avid anglers. With the exception of the marginal fishing in the Upper Gardner River on the first day of the hike and a lively cutthroat population in High Lake, the route offers no fishing opportunities.

14

The Thorofare

General description: Perhaps the best, long backpacking trip in Yellowstone

Special attractions: Possibly the only place in the lower forty-eight states where you can hike 30 miles on a flat trail and then be 30 miles (by trail) in all four directions from the nearest road.

Type of trip: A long shuttle

Total distance: 68.5 miles (110.3 kilometers)

Difficulty: Difficult because of length

Traffic: Light with the exception of large stock parties common in the Thorofare

Maps: Trails Illustrated map of Yellowstone Lake; Lake Butte, Frank Island, Sylvan Lake, Trail Lake, Eagle Peak, The Trident, Badger Creek, Crooked Creek, Mount Hancock, Snake Hot Springs and Lewis Canyon USGS quads

Starting point: Nine Mile Trailhead (5K5)

Finding the trailhead: Drive 9 miles east of Fishing Bridge to the east shore of Yellowstone Lake and park at the Nine Mile Trailhead parking area on the south side of the road.

Parking and trailhead facilities: Limited parking, so be careful not to take more than your share; no facilities; plenty of parking and modern toilets (just north of the entrance station) at the South Boundary Trailhead where you exit.

Recommended itinerary: This trip requires at least seven days, and you could spend as long as two weeks, but I recommend a nine-day trip averaging about 8.5 miles per day. This includes one rest day and extra time for fishing.

First night:	Preferred—5E9 or 5E8; alternate—5E7
Second night:	Preferred—5E1; alternative—5E3
Third night:	Preferred—6D2; alternative—6D1
Fourth night:	Preferred—6T2; alternative—6T1
Fifth night:	Rest day, same campsite
Sixth night:	Preferred—6M2; alternative—6M4
Seventh night:	Outside park
Eighth night:	Preferred—8C2; alternative—8C1

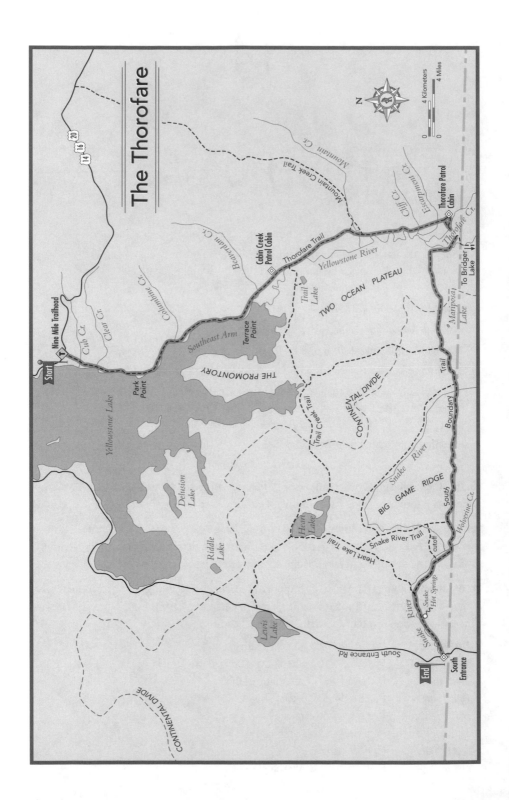

The Thorofare

Cub Cr.
Clear Cr.
Columbine Cr.
Beaverdam Cr.

14 16 20

Nine Mile Trailhead
Start

Yellowstone Lake

Park Point

Southeast Arm

Cabin Creek
Patrol Cabin

Thorofare Trail

Mountain Creek Trail

Mountain Cr.

Cliff Cr.

Escarpment Cr.

Thorofare Patrol
Cabin

Thorofare Cr.

To Bridger
Lake

Terrace
Point

THE PROMONTORY

Trail
Lake

Yellowstone River

TWO OCEAN PLATEAU

Mariposa
Lake

Delusion
Lake

Trail Creek Trail

CONTINENTAL DIVIDE

Snake River

Boundary

Trail

Riddle
Lake

Heart
Lake

BIG GAME RIDGE

South

Wolverine Cr.

Lewis
Lake

Heart Lake Trail

Snake River Trail

cutoff

Snake
Hot Springs

Snake
River

South Entrance Rd.

End
South
Entrance

CONTINENTAL DIVIDE

N

0   4 Kilometers
0   4 Miles

1.3 m. (2.1 k)	Cub Creek
3.0 (4.8)	Clear Creek
6.3 (10.1)	Park Point and 5E9 (5★)
6.5 (10.4)	5E7 (1★) and 5E8 (5★)
9.2 (14.8)	5E6 (4★) and 5E5 (4★)
9.4 (15.1)	Columbine Creek
12.3 (19.8)	5E4 (5★)
14.7 (23.6)	5E3 (3★)
15.5 (24.9	Terrace Point
17.3 (27.8)	Beaverdam Creek and spur trail to 5E1 (4★)
19.3 (31.0)	Cabin Creek patrol cabin
19.7 (31.6)	Trail Creek junction (lower ford); turn left
20.5 (33.0)	Junction with Trail Creek Trail (upper ford); turn left
21.5 (34.6)	6C1 (1★)
22.3 (35.9)	Spur trail to 6C2 (5★)
22.5 (36.2)	Spur trail to 6C3 (3★)
24.7 (39.7)	Junction with Mountain Creek Trail (north); turn right
25.5 (41.0)	Ford of Mountain Creek
25.6 (41.2)	6D2 (3★)
26.2 (42.2)	Junction with Mountain Creek Trail (south); turn right
26.3 (42.3)	Spur trail to 6D1 (4★)
28.5 (45.8)	6Y6 (4★)
29.5 (47.5)	Cliff Creek and spur trail to 6Y5 (3★)
30.6 (49.2)	Escarpment Creek
31.0 (49.9)	Junction with trail to Thorofare Ranger Station, Bridger Lake and the South Boundary Trail; turn right
32.0 (51.8)	Spur trail to 6Y4 (3★)
32.2 (51.8)	Junction with cutoff trail to Thorofare Ranger Station; turn right
32.5 (52.3)	Spur trail to 6T2 (5★)
32.6 (52.4)	Ford of Thorofare Creek and 6T1 (4★)
33.1 (53.3)	Junction with trail to Bridger Lake; turn right
34.0 (54.7)	6Y2 (4★) and ford of Yellowstone River
35.2 (56.6)	Lynx Creek
39.5 (63.6)	Continental Divide on Two Ocean Plateau
41.0 (66.0)	Mariposa Lake and 6B3 (2★)
41.2 (66.3)	6M2 (4★)
42.0 (67.6)	Junction with Two Ocean Plateau Trail and 6M4 (3★); turn left
45.0 (72.4)	6M7 (3★) and Fox Creek patrol cabin

45.2 (72.7)	Trail heading south out of park; turn right
45.6 (73.4)	Ford of Snake River
45.7 (73.5)	Junction with Snake River Trail; go straight
49.0 (78.9)	Big Game Ridge
56.5 (90.9)	Harebell Patrol Cabin and trail heading north to Heart Lake; turn left
57.9 (93.2)	Trail heading south out of park; turn right
59.0 (94.9)	8C2 (5★)
59.5 (95.8)	Junction with Snake River Cutoff Trail; turn left
62.0 (99.8)	Junction with Heart Lake Trail; turn left
62.5 (100.6)	Snake Hot Springs and 8C1 (3★)
68.2 (109.8)	Ford of Snake River
68.5 (110.3)	South Boundary Trailhead and entrance station

The hike: Like the Gallatin Skyline hike, this hike offers hardy backpackers the opportunity to savor the wild essence of Yellowstone. Yet, these two major backpacking trips are strikingly different. The Gallatin Skyline transverses the highest ridgelines with easy escape routes, while this trip captures the uniqueness of Yellowstone Lake and the Thorofare with the added attractions of world-famous fishing and the allure of extreme remoteness with no easy way out.

Regardless of how you slice up this trip, it's still 68 miles long, which means ultra-cautious and tedious preparation. Unlike the case with most trips in Yellowstone, you really can't bail out on this one if something goes wrong. When you get to the confluence of the Yellowstone River and Thorofare Creek, it's approximately 30 miles by trail in any direction to the nearest road. Therefore, more so than for any other trip in this book, make triple sure you're physically ready and packed as lightly as possible. Also, don't forget key equipment and carefully check all gear before leaving the trailhead. Plan for extreme weather and take a back-up stove and filter. Other essential pieces of equipment are waterproof bags to keep the contents of your backpack dry during several serious fords. Before you leave on your trip, check with rangers at the Lake Ranger Station for current conditions of the fords. Because of the fords, don't try this trip until late-July.

The scenery along this region rivals anything in the Rocky Mountains. You spend the first two days hiking along the "matchless mountain lake" of John Colter's journals. Yellowstone Lake, one of the world's largest freshwater lakes, is like an inland ocean. It covers 136 square miles (20 miles long, 14 miles wide) and is at least 320 feet deep in spots (139-foot average depth!). Regardless of how hot it gets on an August afternoon, the lake stays cold enough to bring on hypothermia in a few minutes. The level of the lake would probably drop several feet if the enormous population of cutthroat trout was removed. These native fish support the food chain in this area, so watch for all the fish-eaters—

pelicans, cormorants, mergansers, otters, mink, eagles, ospreys, and, of course, the-biggest-fish-eater-of-them-all, the grizzly.

After the lake, you go into the famous Thorofare, a wide, flat valley through which the upper Yellowstone River meanders. Because of the gentle terrain, trappers commonly used this route in and out of the Yellowstone Plateau and called it the "Throughfare," later shortened to Thorofare. The Two Ocean Plateau looms over the Thorofare from the west, and some of the highest peaks in the park (Colter Peak, Table Mountain, and the massive Trident) dominate the eastern horizon.

You also get to see a special jewel of the wildflower world, the Mariposa lily, which grows in the southern reaches of the Thorofare.

Anglers dream of this place and, if they take this hike, their dreams come true. The fishing in the lake, river, and several tributaries is fantastic. Most fish caught range in the 16- to 18-inch range, and it's actually hard to catch a legal-sized, 13-inch cutthroat.

You can hike four days on a perfectly flat trail, and then you get the rare experience of fording major rivers and climbing over the Continental Divide in the same day. You ford the Snake River, struggle up the precipitous Big Game Ridge, and then ford the Snake River again.

Simply put, this is a truly incredible trip. When you get to the South Boundary Trailhead, you'll want to give each other high-fives because you'll really have done something! And your jeans will definitely be easier to get on after this trip.

Since this is such a major backpacking trip, it only seems appropriate that it would have an especially difficult vehicle shuttle. If you can't arrange to be picked up at the end of the hike, plan on a half-day to shuffle vehicles around, leaving one at the South Boundary Trailhead just outside the park at the South Entrance Station. This makes it a wise decision to plan a fairly easy first day since you probably won't hit the trail until noon, and you don't want to wear yourself down on the first day when your pack is its heaviest.

Perhaps the only negative comment one could make about this trip is the condition of the trail. Although distinct and easy to follow, the trail suffers from extra-heavy horse traffic and has been pounded into dust. In some places you have to hike 20 feet from your fellow hikers to see through the dust cloud your partner kicks up.

The first 6-mile leg to Park Point is strikingly flat and somewhat monotonous as you hike over Cub and Clear Creeks and through unburned lodgepole, with no view of the lake until you reach Meadow Creek and Park Point, where you probably want to spend your first night out. The trail is wide and dusty, but the view from Park Point makes 5E9 and 5E8 two of the truly spectacular campsites in the park.

From Park Point to Beaverdam Creek at the end of the Southeast Arm, the trail opens up and passes through several open meadows, crosses Columbine Creek, and often goes right on the lakeshore with views of the Promontory. The meadows are carpeted with balsamroot and lupine in July.

After fording Beaverdam Creek you go through the first section of burned trees. Even though most hikers prefer unburned forest, keep in mind that if you hiked through here a hundred years ago, it would probably look similar, including the burned forest. Fire has been a vital part of the ecology of Yellowstone Park for centuries.

A fat cutthroat from Thorofare Creek.

The trail continues flat and dusty through open, intermittently burned forests and huge, marshy meadows (the trademark of the Thorofare) all the way to the South Boundary Trail. At Trail Creek you'll see two trails going off to the right (west) to ford the Yellowstone River and continue on to Heart Lake. You go straight (south). Some older maps show three trail junctions at Trail Creek, but the middle ford has been abandoned.

At Mountain Creek two trails head off to the left (east), joining and heading out of the park and up Eagle Pass in the South Absaroka Mountains. You ford Mountain Creek (a difficult ford early in the year) between the two junctions.

As you walk through and camp in the Thorofare, you discover that, along with all the great scenery, it has a huge wildlife population, including several bazillion mosquitoes. You commonly see elk, deer, and moose, but no bison. And it can be a noisy place, with the incessant honking of Canada geese accompanied by sandhill cranes calling, coyotes howling, elk bugling, and squirrels chattering—all on the background buzzzzzz of mosquitoes. It's a regular concerto—a guy can't even get a good night's sleep!

When you reach the major junction with the South Boundary Trail, go right (west). The trail going straight (south) leads to the Thorofare Ranger Station (where you can usually find a ranger if you need one) and into Bridger Lake in the Bridger-Teton National Forest. About a quarter mile later, a cutoff trail goes east to the ranger station. You go right (west) to Thorofare Creek.

Most people would consider Thorofare Creek a river. It's a very large tributary to the Yellowstone and can be hazardous to ford early in the year. Depending on the place you choose to ford, it can be more difficult to cross than the Yellowstone. Shortly after this ford, another trail heads off to the left (south) to Bridger Lake. Go right (west) and in less than 1 mile, ford the Yellowstone River. Here, take a moment to look back into the Thorofare because you're leaving a very special place.

Both of these fords can be deep enough early in the year to get your adrenaline level up and backpack wet (especially for vertically challenged hikers), so be sure to pack your clothes and sleeping bag in waterproof bags.

After the Yellowstone ford you hike along the river for about a half mile in mostly burned timber, crossing Lynx Creek and heading up this valley toward Two Ocean Pass. This is a Category 2 climb, and the trail worsens slightly from what you've hiked on so far. And don't be surprised by frequent downed trees over the trail. The forest opens up into high-altitude meadows just before the Continental Divide at about 9,400 feet in elevation and stays in the open terrain of the Two Ocean Plateau all the way to Mariposa Lake.

Not many people see Mariposa Lake, which is too bad for them. It's a charming but small (twelve acres) mountain lake in a lush, greenish swale with a small population of hard-to-catch cutthroat-rainbow hybrids.

From the lake the trail drops sharply down through unburned forest to the junction with the Two Ocean Plateau Trail. At this junction go left (west) and hike along Plateau Creek to the Fox Creek patrol cabin. Just after the cabin, you might see a trail heading south out of the park and shortly thereafter the headwaters of the Snake River. The map may indicate that the junction with the trail up the Snake River to Heart Lake is on the east side of the river, but it's actually on the west side.

After hiking through the meadow on the west side of the Snake, head up the 2,000-foot, Category 1 climb to the top of Big Game Ridge. About halfway up the ridge, you'll see signs indicating the park boundary. For the next few miles, the trail goes in and out of the park. Unless you're up to 18 miles with a heavy pack (including this monster hill), you should spend the night in an undesignated site outside the park. There is no designated campsite in the park anywhere over this 18-mile stretch of trail.

Hope for a clear day when you go over Big Game Ridge (which was not the case when we did it). You should get some great views of the Grand Teton. Also, be alert for grizzly bears. We saw more bear sign on Big Game Ridge than anywhere in Yellowstone.

After enjoying a well-deserved rest on the ridge, drop into the headwaters of Harebell Creek where you stay all the way to the Harebell patrol cabin. This section of trail goes through burned forest most of the way, and if you're unlucky enough to get caught in a big rain (as we did) the trail gets extremely slick.

At the junction at the Harebell Patrol Cabin, the Snake River Trail goes off to the right (north). Go straight (west) and drop down into Wolverine Creek, where you go right (northwest) at the junction with the Wolverine Creek Trail, which goes left (south) out of the park.

Shortly thereafter, you see the Snake River again, although this is the real Snake River—swollen with the infusion of many tributaries and quite the departure from the little stream you waded across on the other side of Big Game Ridge. You might see the Snake River Cutoff Trail going off to the right about 2 miles later. Even though the first part is marked, this trail is far down on the maintenance priority list and difficult to follow.

Hiking over the Continental Divide east of Mariposa Lake.

At the junction with the Heart Lake Trail, take a left (south) and continue to hike along the Snake River. Shortly after this junction, you see the Snake Hot Springs, several hot pools and streams over a half-mile stretch of river. Near Snake Hot Springs, you might think you see a small prairie dog town, but this is actually the burrows dug by yellow-bellied marmots. Interestingly, this local population tends to build burrows in the open meadow along the trail instead of the rocky hillsides. Also, they tend to delay hibernation later than usual because of the extra warmth the hot springs area provides.

After the hot springs the trail goes through unburned forest with minimal views until a big meadow just before the trailhead. When you see the trail register, don't think you're done. It's still another mile to the trailhead. Also, watch for several unmarked spur trails. Right after the register, you see an unmarked split in the trail. Take the left fork. Later, at another unmarked split, take the right fork.

The trip finishes with a grand finale, a serious ford over the Snake River, swollen with the recent inclusion of the Lewis River. You can see the entrance station and the highway, but you still need to cross the river. After mid-July, this ford is safe, but earlier in the summer, or after a big thunderstorm, it can be dangerous. We forded just north of the marked ford and found it to be significantly easier than the designated route. (If the ford looks too dangerous, you can follow an unofficial but well-maintained trail along the east side of the river for 3 miles to the Shelfield Creek Trailhead, which comes out at the highway just south of the Flagg Ranch.)

After the ford it's less than a quarter mile and a small hill up to the bench above the river where you will find your vehicle—and where you can give each other those high-fives you richly deserve.

Options: You can do this trip in reverse with no significant difference in difficulty, but you start out with a big ford of the Snake River instead of finishing with it. Also, you can skip the first one or two days by taking a boat to Park Point or Beaverdam Creek.

Side trips: If you decide to spend more than eight days in this area, try side trips to Trail Lake or Bridger Lake.

Camping: These designated campsites are on the Yellowstone Lake Trails Illustrated map. Stock-party-only or boater-access sites are not included.

5E7 (1★) is a mixed site right along Meadow Creek. In a swampy area close to the trail with a minimal view over a small meadow. Poor tent sites. Pit Toilet. Closed until July 15.

Both 5E9 (5★) and 5E8 (5★) rank among the best campsites in the park, with postcard views of Yellowstone Lake and Frank Island from the food areas. Both hiker-only campsites have good tent sites, and the lake serves as an easy water source. 5E8 is more difficult to reach (not a good access trail), but it's more private than 5E9. Pit toilet. Closed until July 15.

6A2 (5★) is a secluded, hiker-only site on a little point in the Southeast Arm, about a third-mile off the main trail. Great view, good water source, but limited tent sites. Also used by boaters. Closed until July 15.

6A3 (5★) is a secluded, hiker-only site requiring a half-mile off-trail bushwhack from the main trail. Hard to get to but worth the effort. Most often used by boaters (nonmotorized only). Located on Trail Point, which juts out into the Southeast Arm providing a terrific view from camp. Good water source and tent sites. Closed until July 15.

6A4 (4★) is a hiker-only site right along the trail and on the lakeshore near the Trail Creek Patrol Cabin. Great view of the Yellowstone River. Good tent sites and water source. Stays mildly boggy until late in the year. This site has a history of bear problems. Closed until July 15.

5E3 (3★) is similar to 5E4, a hiker-only site about 200 yards off the trail for privacy. Again, a great view from camp of the lake with Chicken Ridge, Channel Mountain, and the Two Ocean Plateau as a backdrop. Closed until July 15.

5E4 (5★) is a private, hiker-only site right on the lakeshore about 200 yards from the trail. Great view of the Promontory from the food area. Closed until July 15.

5E5 (4★) is not on most maps, but you might be able to stay there if you ask about it. It's about 200 yards south of 5E6, and has the same amenities. Great view and adequate tent sites. More private than 5E6. Use pit toilet at 5E6. Closed until July 15.

5E6 (4★) is a semiprivate, mixed site near the start of the Southeast Arm with a great view of the Promontory from the food area. Good tent sites and pit toilet. Closed until July 15.

5E1 (4★) would be an ideal campsite (especially for anglers) if it wasn't so difficult to get water. The hiker-only campsite is on a high bench above Beaverdam Creek, and it's difficult to get up the steep trail with water. It's private (about a quarter mile east of the main trail) and has a great view across Beaverdam Creek and of Colter Peak. Closed until July 15.

Fording the Snake River at the end of the trip, just before the trailhead.

6B2 (5★) is a rarely used, hiker-only site on the Yellowstone River near the upper ford. Good view and water source and plenty of tent sites. Closed until July 15.

6C1 (1★) is a mixed site right along the trail with a poor water supply and a minimal view, but lots of good tent sites.

6C2 (5★) is a very private, mixed site on the bank of the Yellowstone River. It's about 1 mile west of the main trail, but it's worth the walk and would be a good destination camp for a two- or three-day stay.

6C3 (3★) is a hiker-only site about 150 yards east of the main trail on the edge of a big meadow below Turret Mountain. It's private and has a decent view, but you need to hike about 75 yards to water.

6D1 (4★) a private, mixed site at the confluence of Mountain Creek and the Yellowstone River. A fair view of Mountain Creek. Good water source and tent sites. A mile-long bushwhack (something you might not want at the end of a hard day) to the site. On the way back, we hiked along the stream instead of the "trail" and found it easier. This would be a good destination camp where you could stay two or three days. It's interesting to note from this site how the river stopped the advance of the 1988 fires.

6D2 (3★) is a not-so-private, hiker-only site on your left (east) just after you ford Mountain Creek. It has room for lots of tents, a good view over the stream wash of Mountain Creek and Turret Mountain, and an easily accessible water source.

6Y4 (3★) is a private, mixed site near the confluence of Thorofare Creek and the Yellowstone River. The food area is regrettably located in a stand of live timber that blocks the view. Lots of good tent sites and a good water source. When coming from the north, it's tempting to look at the topo map and bushwhack across the marshy meadow to the site. But it's better to wait until you get past the South Boundary Trail junction, where you find a good trail leading to this campsite.

6Y5 (3★) is a private, hiker-only site about 150 yards west (on a marginal trail) of the main trail. Watch for the sign just after you cross Cliff Creek. Good water source and a fair view out into the meadows along the river.

6Y6 (4★) is a semiprivate, mixed site on the Three Mile Bend of the Yellowstone River. A good view of the meadows south down the Thorofare and Hawks Rest, which overlooks Bridger Lake. Good water source and tent sites.

6T1 (4★) is a not-so-private, mixed site on the left just west of Thorofare Creek. Good tent sites and water source, but exposed to the weather. Both 6T1 and 6T2 make good destination sites and are each close to the ranger station if you need help.

6T2 (5★) is an ideal campsite on the banks of Thorofare Creek just north of the ford on the east side of the stream. This private, hiker-only site has a great view, good tent sites, and an easy water source.

6Y2 (4★) is a not-so-private, hiker-only site right along the trail and just east of the ford of the Yellowstone River. Good water source and a great view.

You can also camp south of the park around Bridger Lake.

6M2 (4★) is a private, mixed site at the west end of the lake. It's nicer than 6M3, with a better view and tent sites and a good water source. You have to cross the outlet stream to get to the campsite. Off-trail travel between July 15 and August 21 by permit only.

6B3 (2★) is a lightly used, mixed site on the east end of Mariposa Lake. Private and so infrequently used that it's difficult to find. Good location and a nice view, but only one tent site (and a marginal one at that). No trailside sign when we were there. Off-trail travel between July 15 and August 21 by permit only.

6M4 (3★) is a semiprivate, mixed site at the junction of the South Boundary and Two Ocean Plateau trails. Good tent sites and water source. Decent view out into a big meadow. Off-trail travel between July 15 and August 21 by permit only.

6M7 (3★) is a hiker-only site about 300 yards off the trail just before reaching the Fox Creek patrol cabin. Rarely used campsite. Marginal tent sites and a minimal view, but a good water source.

You can also camp outside the park up Wolverine Creek, on Big Game Ridge, and near the Harebell patrol cabin.

8C1 (3★) is a not-so-private, hiker-only site right along the trail near the Snake Hot Springs. Limited tent sites, but a good water source (the river) and a terrific view up the Snake River Valley.

8C2 (5★) is a private, mixed site on the banks of the Snake River. Great view of the Snake River, plenty of excellent tent sites, an easy water source, and the spur trail is easy to follow. Firewood is sparse.

8C6 (3★) is a semiprivate, mixed site on the west of the ford of the Snake River about 50 yards from the trail. Exposed site with lots of good tent sites and a good view of the Snake River. Far enough from water to be inconvenient.

Fishing: Both Yellowstone Lake and the Upper Yellowstone River are fantastic fisheries for nice-sized cutthroat trout, ranging from 15 to 20 inches. Fish from the lake spawn in the spring, so if you can catch the spawners in the river in mid- to late July, you can enjoy some great fishing. The spawn varies from year to year, depending on weather and runoff conditions, but the spawners usually return to Yellowstone Lake before the end of August, and often earlier. There are also resident cutthroats, of course, but they are hard to find and smaller. Many of the streams flowing into the Upper Yellowstone River can offer as good if not better fishing than the river if you can get there before the spawners leave. Mariposa Lake has a few cutthroats, but they are wary. And you can plan on catching some 10 to 14 inch cutthroats in the Upper Snake River and perhaps a few browns below Red Creek.

15

Two Ocean Plateau

General description: A long loop requiring a boat to get to the trailhead

Special attraction: Remoteness

Type of trip: Loop with an out-and-back boat ride

Total distance: 40 miles (64.4 kilometers)

Difficulty: Difficult

Traffic: Light

Maps: Trails Illustrated map of Yellowstone Lake; Trail Lake, Alder Lake, Crooked Creek, Badger Creek, The Trident, and Eagle Peak USGS quads

Starting point: Trail Creek patrol cabin at the southernmost tip of the Southeast Arm of Yellowstone Lake *after* a boat ride across the lake

Finding the trailhead: This is the only hike in this book that requires a boat to reach the trailhead, which is at the southernmost tip of the Southeast Arm. Consult with rangers at the Lake Ranger Station for advice on the best routes and for special boating regulations in the Southeast Arm.

Parking and trailhead facilities: You can park your boat at the trailhead; no toilet facilities.

Recommended itinerary: If you take one day to paddle to the starting point (and another to return to your vehicle), this turns into a nine-day trip, including the two days spent paddling, with no rest day in the Thorofare.

First night:	Preferred—6A3; alternate—6A2 or 6A4
Second night:	Preferred—6M5
Third night:	Preferred—6M2; alternate—6M3
Fourth night:	Preferred—6T2; alternate—6T1 or 6Y2
Fifth night:	Preferred—6D2; alternate—6D1
Sixth night:	Preferred—6B2; alternate—6B1
Seventh night:	Preferred—6A3; alternate—6A4 or 6A2

The hike: This hike is like no other in Yellowstone. It combines the pleasures of paddling the shoreline of Yellowstone Lake with some of the best backpacking in the park. It skips

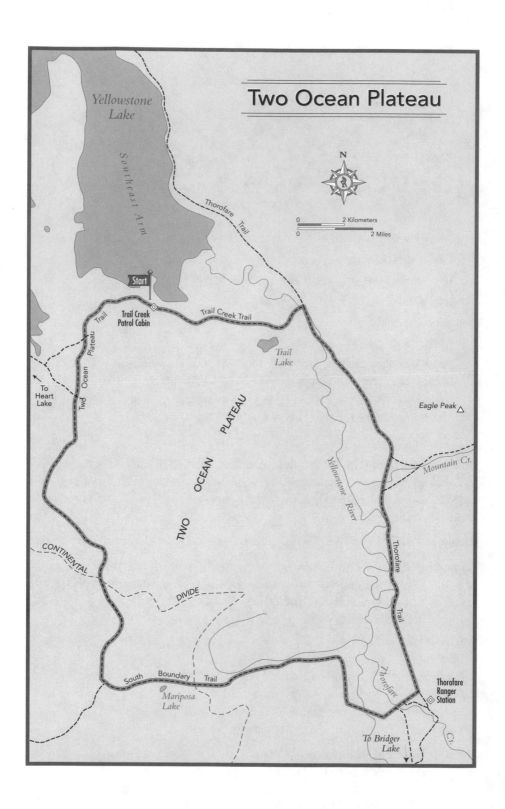

Two Ocean Plateau

Yellowstone Lake

Southeast Arm

Thorofare Trail

N

0   2 Kilometers
0   2 Miles

Start

Trail Creek Patrol Cabin

Trail Creek Trail

Trail Lake

Two Ocean Plateau Trail

To Heart Lake

TWO OCEAN PLATEAU

Eagle Peak △

Yellowstone River

Mountain Cr.

CONTINENTAL

DIVIDE

Thorofare Trail

South Boundary Trail

Mariposa Lake

Thorofare

Thorofare Ranger Station

To Bridger Lake

Cr.

0.6 m. (0.9 k)	Spur trail to 6A2
1.5 (2.4)	Junction with Two Ocean Plateau Trail; turn left
4.0 (6.4)	Junction with cutoff trail to Heart Lake; turn left
9.5 (10.4)	6M5 (3★)
13.5 (21.7)	6M4 (3★) and junction with South Boundary Trail; turn left
14.5 (23.3)	6M2 (4★) and Mariposa Lake
14.8 (23.8)	6M3 (2★)
16.3 (26.2)	Continental Divide
21.8 (35.1)	Ford the Yellowstone River and 6Y2
22.7 (36.6)	Junction with trail to Bridger Lake; turn left
22.9 (36.8)	6T1 (4★) and ford Thorofare Creek
23.0 (37.0)	Spur trail to 6T2 (5★)
23.3 (37.5)	Junction with cutoff trail to Thorofare Ranger Station; turn left
23.5 (37.8)	Spur Trail to 6Y4 (3★)
24.5 (39.4)	Junction with trail to Thorofare Ranger Station and Bridger Lake; turn left
26.0 (41.8)	Cliff Creek and 6Y5 (3★)
27.0 (43.4)	6Y6 (4★)
29.2 (47.0)	Spur trail to 6D1 (4★)
29.3 (47.1)	First junction with trail to Eagle Pass; turn left
29.9 (48.1)	6D2 (3★) and ford Mountain Creek
30.8 (49.5)	Second junction with trail to Eagle Pass; turn left
33.0 (53.1)	6C3 (3★)
33.2 (53.4)	Spur trail to 6C2 (5★)
34.0 (54.7)	6C1 (1★)
35.0 (56.3)	Junction with trail to upper ford; turn right
35.4 (57.0)	Junction with trail to lower ford and 6B2 (5★); turn left
36.9 (59.4)	Junction with off-trail route to Trail Lake; turn right
39.2 (63.1)	Southeast Arm and 6A4
40.0 (64.4)	Trail Creek patrol cabin

the heavily used sections of trails near the highways by taking a 20-mile paddle across Yellowstone Lake, which leaves 40 miles of remote and scenic hiking. A ranger stays at Trail Creek Cabin for most of the summer, so this is a good place to safely store your canoe or kayak.

After spending your first night at one of the three campsites (6A2, 6A3, 6A4) on the shoreline of the Southeast Arm, start the loop by heading west toward the South Arm. When you reach the junction with the Two Ocean Plateau Trail, go left (south) and head

Yellowstone Lake from the end of the Southeast Arm.

for the highlands of Two Ocean Plateau. This high-altitude ridge gets its name from Two Ocean Pass just south of the park where the waters of Pacific Creek and Atlantic Creek mingle before they start their long journeys to their respective oceans. This may be the only place where fish can actually swim over the Continental Divide.

You spend the first half of your first day hiking through mostly burned forest, as the trail goes along Chipmunk Creek and then Passage Creek, until you get up to the high country, which escaped the 1988 fires. The last pitches up to the plateau get steep. Most of the rest of the trip down to the South Boundary Trail goes through open terrain with great scenery.

At the junction with the South Boundary Trail, turn left (east) and climb the mile-long hill up to Mariposa Lake. The lake sits in a gentle, lush meadow and hosts a small population of cutthroat-rainbow hybrids.

From the lake it's a short 1.5 miles up to the Continental Divide through open terrain and more superb mountain scenery. After another mile of high-altitude hiking near the treeline, you drop into Lynx Creek and go through burned forest most of the way to the Yellowstone River. Expect to climb over some downfall on this leg.

Before fording the river, make sure your sleeping bag and clothes are in waterproof bags. This ford can be deep enough to get your pack wet.

After the ford the trail goes through a big meadow and past the junction with the trail to Bridger Lake where you go left (east). Immediately after the junction, you ford Thorofare Creek, which can be almost as deep as the Yellowstone. After the ford you pass by two trails going off to the right (east) to the Thorofare Ranger Station. If you need help, take the short trip over to see the ranger who stays there most of the summer.

From here its a flat, dusty hike through the scenic openness of the Thorofare all the way to the upper ford where you cross the Yellowstone again. After the ford follow the trail along the south edge of the Southeast Arm back to the patrol cabin where you stashed your boat. Spend the night at one of the nearby campsites before paddling back to your vehicle fresh with the memories of a classic backpacking vacation.

The trail is well-defined and in generally great shape the entire way with the exception of Lynx Creek (prone to heavy downfall) and a few stretches of the Thorofare, where extra-heavy horse traffic has pounded the trail into dust.

Options: If you take the counterclockwise route (as described here) you don't have to start the trip with a ford of the Yellowstone River. If you want to spend more time on the lake before hitting the trail, you can paddle over to the tip of the South Arm and start the loop there. You can also start at Beaverdam Creek in the Southeast Arm, but this requires retracing your steps from the lower ford to Beaverdam Creek. You might want to extend your trip by one day by taking a rest day in the Thorofare. If you don't like paddling, you can arrange a motorboat ride to Columbine Creek on the east side of the Southeast Arm and start your hike from there.

Side trips: If you take a rest day in the Thorofare, you could use it for a nice loop around Bridger Lake. If you don't mind bushwhacking, take the short off-trail route to Trail Lake.

Camping: These designated campsites are on the Yellowstone Lake Trails Illustrated map. Stock-party-only or boater-access sites are not included.

6A2 (5★) is a secluded, hiker-only site on a little point in the Southeast Arm, about a third-mile off the main trail. Great view, good water source, but limited tent sites. Also used by boaters.

6A4 (4★) is a hiker-only site right along the trail and on the lakeshore near the Trail Creek patrol cabin. Great view of the Yellowstone River. Good tent sites and water source. Stays mildly boggy until late in the year. This site has a history of bear problems.

6B2 (5★) is a rarely used, hiker-only site on the Yellowstone River near the upper ford. Good view and water source and plenty of tent sites. Closed until July 15.

6C1 (1★) is a mixed site right along the trail with a poor water supply and a minimal view, but lots of good tent sites.

Part of Lynx Creek was severely burned in 1988, so be ready for a few trees over the trail.

6C2 (5★) is a very private, mixed site on the bank of the Yellowstone River. It's about 1 mile west of the main trail, but it's worth the walk and would be a good destination camp for a two- or three-day stay.

6C3 (3★) is a hiker-only site about 150 yards east of the main trail on the edge of a big meadow below Turret Mountain. It's private and has a decent view, but you need to hike about 75 yards to water.

6D1 (4★) is a private, mixed site at the confluence of Mountain Creek and the Yellowstone River. A fair view of Mountain Creek. Good water source and tent sites. A mile-long bushwhack (something you might not want at the end of a hard day) to the site. On the way back, we hiked along the stream instead of the "trail" and found it easier. This would be a good destination camp where you could stay two or three days. It's interesting to note from this site how the river stopped the advance of the 1988 fires.

6D2 (3★) is a not-so-private, hiker-only site on your left (east) just after you ford Mountain Creek. It has room for lots of tents, a good view over the stream wash of Mountain Creek and Turret Mountain, and an easily accessible water source.

6Y4 (3★) is a private, mixed site near the confluence of Thorofare Creek and the Yellowstone River. The food area is regrettably located in a stand of live timber that blocks the view. Lots of good tent sites and a good water source. When coming from the north, it's tempting to look at the topo map and bushwhack across the marshy meadow to the site.

But it's better to wait until you get past the South Boundary Trail junction, where you find a good trail leading to this campsite.

6Y5 (3★) is a private, hiker-only site about 150 yards west (on a marginal trail) of the main trail. Watch for the sign just after you cross Cliff Creek. Good water source and a fair view out into the meadows along the river.

6Y6 (4★) is a semiprivate, mixed site on the Three Mile Bend of the Yellowstone River. A good view of the meadows south down the Thorofare and Hawks Rest, which overlooks Bridger Lake. Good water source and tent sites.

6T1 (4★) is a not-so-private, mixed site just west of Thorofare Creek. Good tent sites and water source, but exposed to the weather. Both 6T1 and 6T2 make good destination sites and are close to the ranger station if you need help.

6T2 (5★) is an ideal campsite on the banks of Thorofare Creek just north of the ford on the east side of the stream. This private, hiker-only site has a great view, good tent sites, and an easy water source.

6Y2 (4★) is a not-so-private, hiker-only site right along the trail and just east of the ford of the Yellowstone River. Good water source and a great view.

You can also camp south of the park around Bridger Lake.

6M2 (4★) is a private, mixed site at the west end of the lake. It's nicer than 6M3 with a better view and tent sites and a good water source. You have to cross the outlet stream to get to the campsite. Off-trail travel between July 15 and August 21 by permit only.

6M3 (2★) is a lightly used, mixed site on the east end of Mariposa Lake. Private and so infrequently used that it's difficult to find. Good location and a nice view, but only one tent site (and a marginal one at that). No trailside sign when we were there. Off-trail travel between July 15 and August 21 by permit only.

6M5 (3★) is a private, mixed site on Two Ocean Plateau. Good tent sites and water source. Off-trail travel allowed between July 15 and August 21 by permit only.

6M4 (3★) is a semiprivate, mixed site at the junction of the South Boundary and Two Ocean Plateau trails. Good tent sites and water source. Decent view out into a big meadow. Off-trail travel between July 15 and August 21 by permit only.

Fishing: Refer to the Thorofare fishing information (p. 144).

ABSAROKA-BEARTOOTH WILDERNESS

The Absaroka-Beartooth Wilderness isn't a national park. It's a national treasure.

Straddling the Montana-Wyoming border, the 943,377-acre Absaroka-Beartooth Wilderness is one of the most visited wilderness areas in the United States. This is surprising considering snow covers the area until July and often comes again in early September. Although the political line drawn on the map includes both the Absaroka and Beartooth ranges, that's about where the similarity ends.

The Beartooth Mountains are a high-elevation, lake-shrewn uplift, locally called the Beartooth Plateau, or more simply, the Beartooths. Even though the Beartooths attract lots of visitors, the area can absorb this use in a way that gives almost all visitors the feeling that they have the wilderness to themselves. Instead of competing for designated campsites or huts, backcountry travelers can camp anywhere. And anywhere is a big place in the Beartooths.

Most hikers go to the Beartooths during a six-week period from mid-July through August. While this narrow window of opportunity may conjure up images of crowded trails and overused campsites, in reality this rarely happens in the Beartooths. With 944 lakes the Beartooths have an amazingly large number of destinations for backpackers, and the open plateau invites off-trail use, reducing the congestion on the trails.

Most people admire the Beartooths for their sheer, unbridled beauty. But many geologists marvel at this range for a different reason. A band of igneous rock rich in rare minerals lies along the northern edge of these mountains. The uplifted granite that comprises most of the range dates back more than three billion years and contains some of the oldest rocks on earth.

The Beartooths boast the highest mountain in Montana, Granite Peak, at 12,799 feet. From the top of Granite Peak or many others in the range, the view is dizzying.

Anglers also like the Beartooths. Rainbow, cutthroat, brook, golden, and lake trout thrive in the waterways of the plateau. Though the area is extremely popular, a persistent angler can usually find an unoccupied lake or stream to call his or her own for a day or two.

Much of the Beartooth Plateau rests at more than 10,000 feet and is covered with delicate alpine tundra. Because of the high use, zero-impact camping practices are essential to the preservation of this fragile ecosystem. Actually, most people visiting the Beartooths nowadays take great care to leave no trace of their visit. This is, of course, one reason this great masterpiece of the national forest system still seems pristine and uncrowded.

In contrast to the Bearthooth's high-altitude grandeur, the Absaroka Range to the west is what could be called a more "typical" mountain range—lower elevation and more forested with fewer lakes and higher wildlife populations. Hiking in the Absarokas is more difficult, because you can't start out at a 10,000-foot trailhead on the Beartooth Highway. To get to 10,000 feet in the Absaroka, you have to climb, not drive.

Granite Peak, Montana's highest point and a popular destination in the Beartooths.
PHOTO: MICHAEL S. SAMPLE

All this means, of course, that the Absaroka is much less populated with hikers. The more well-known Beartooths and Yellowstone National Park on the south boundary of the Absarokas tend to attract most hikers, so you can get lonely on the trails in the Absaroka.

In September, however, you won't be isolated in the Absaroka. Hordes of big game hunters swarm into the area with long pack trains to set up spike camps. Trailheads are choked with horse trailers. In other words, avoid the Absaroka in September.

The Absaroka is like a second child who has put up with the first-born getting all the fanfare, friends, fame, and fortune while the second-born sulks in the background. The Absaroka is just as pretty and magnificent, but almost forgotten next to its big sister, the Beartooths and the world-famous Yellowstone National Park. Consequently, the Absaroka has some terrific backpacking opportunities begging for attention. So when you get tired of crowded national parks or the Beartooths, try the mighty Absaroka.

GETTING TO THE ABSAROKA-BEARTOOTH WILDERNESS

This wilderness is not exactly in the backyard of any major urban area, so be prepared for some extra time in getting there.

Perhaps the best destination airport is Billings, Montana. You can also fly into Bozeman, Montana, but it's a slightly longer drive to most trailheads. The closest major airport is in Salt Lake City, Utah.

SPECIAL REGULATIONS

The Forest Service has special regulations for hikers and backcountry horsemen. In some cases the regulations apply throughout the wilderness and in other cases, they apply to specific trails or ranger districts. For example, campfires are prohibited in some alpine areas. Check with the FS before you leave on your trip, and be sure to read and follow any special regulations posted at the trailhead. The FS doesn't come up with these regulations to inconvenience users. Instead, they create them to promote sharing and preservation of the Wilderness and to make your trip as safe as possible.

FINDING MAPS

For trips into the Absaroka-Beartooth Wilderness, you have three good choices for maps. Most backpackers choose to take the USGS quads for the route (specific maps are listed with each trip). In addition the USDA-Forest Service publishes an excellent Absaroka-Beartooth Wilderness map, and Rocky Mountain Survey (RMS), a private company in Billings, Montana, publishes a series of six terrific topo maps covering the entire wilderness. You can get Forest Service maps at any of the ranger district offices or at local sporting goods stores where you can also get the RMS maps.

FOR MORE INFORMATION

The Absaroka-Beartooth Wilderness is managed by three national forests—Custer, Gallatin, and Shoshone. This can be confusing to say the least, which is a good reason to make sure you have the USDA-Forest Service Absaroka-Beartooth Wilderness map. This helps you see which national forest manages the route you've chosen so you can contact the appropriate ranger district.

Driving the Beartooth Highway can be as exciting as backpacking the trails of the Absaroka-Beartooth Wilderness. PHOTO: MICHAEL S. SAMPLE

For more information, contact these national forests or the respective ranger districts:

Custer National Forest, 1310 Main Street, P.O. Box 50760, Billings, MT 59105; (406) 657–6200, fax: (406) 657–6222.

Custer National Forest, Beartooth Ranger District, HC 49, Box 3420, Highway 212 S of Red Lodge, Red Lodge, MT 59068; (406) 446–2103, fax: (406) 446–3918.

Gallatin National Forest, 10 East Babcock Avenue, P.O. Box 130, Bozeman, MT 59771; (406) 587–6702, fax: (406) 587–6758.

Gallatin National Forest, Big Timber Ranger District, Highway 10 East, P.O. Box 1130, Big Timber, MT 59011; (406) 932–5155, fax: (406) 932–5777.

Gallatin National Forest, Gardiner Ranger District, Highway 89, P.O. Box 5, Gardiner, MT 59030; (406) 848–7375, fax: (406) 848–7485.

Shoshone National Forest, Forest Supervisor's Office, 808 Meadow Lane Avenue, P.O. Box 2140, Cody, WY 82414; (307) 527–6241.

Shoshone National Forest, Clarks Fork Ranger District, 203 A Yellowstone Avenue, Cody, WY 82414; (307) 527–6921.

16

Aero Lakes

General description: A short but strenuous base-camp trip into the heart of the Beartooth's alpine country

Special attractions: The stark beauty of this high plateau area and a wide diversity of potential side trips

Type of trip: Out-and-back base camp

Total distance: 12 miles, not counting side trips

Difficulty: Difficult

Traffic: Moderate

Maps: Forest Service—Absaroka-Beartooth Wilderness Map; USGS quads—Cooke City, Fossil Lake, and Granite Peak; Rocky Mountain Survey—Cooke-City-Cutoff Mountain

Starting point: Fisher Creek Trailhead

Finding the trailhead: To reach the trailhead from Cooke City, drive east on U.S. Highway 212 for 3.2 miles to a turnoff marked with a large Forest Service sign as the Goose Lake Jeep Road, just before the Colter Campground. Turn north off U.S. Highway 212 and drive northeast about 2 miles up this gravel road to a cluster of old buildings. An inconspicuous trailhead on the right shoulder of the road has an old Forest Service sign for Lady of the Lake. The 2 miles of road to the trailhead are passable with any vehicle, but to continue up the road past the trailhead for any reason a high-clearance vehicle is essential.

Parking and trailhead facilities: Limited parking; no facilities; undeveloped campground at the trailhead.

Recommended itinerary: You could hike into Aero Lakes and out the same day, but this would be a shame. Instead, plan on a long day hike to get to the lakes and spend the time to find an idyllic campsite. Then, spend two or three days exploring this incredible high country.

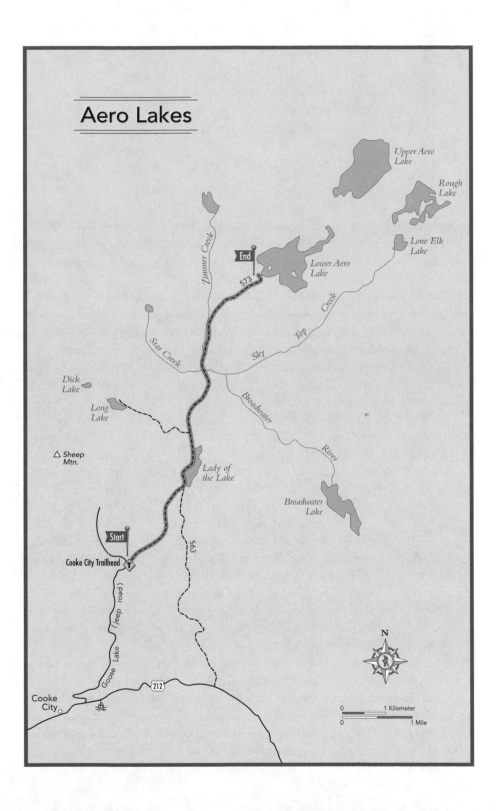

Aero Lakes

Upper Aero Lake

Rough Lake

Lone Elk Lake

Lower Aero Lake

End

573

Zimmer Creek

Star Creek

Sky Top Creek

Broadwater

Dick Lake

Long Lake

△ Sheep Mtn.

Lady of the Lake

Broadwater River

Broadwater Lake

Start

Cooke City Trailhead

563

Goose Lake (jeep road)

212

Cooke City

N

0   1 Kilometer
0   1 Mile

1.5 m.	Lady of the Lake and junction with trail 563; turn left
2.5	Junction with trail to Long Lake; turn right
2.8	Stream coming in from Long Lake
3.6	Star Creek
4.8	Start of climb to Aero Lakes
5.7	Base of Lower Aero Lake

The hike: This trailhead is slightly harder to locate than most others in the Beartooths, but this hasn't lessened its popularity. The area has lots to offer, and it receives heavy use both by locals and those who travel from afar for a chance to experience this spectacular wild area.

The trailhead lies on the eastern fringe of the section of the Beartooths that has been extensively mined, logged, and roaded. Even in the 2 miles of gravel road to the trailhead, the contrast between this area and the pristine wilderness is clearly evident. To get an early start, camp at the undeveloped campground at the trailhead.

At Aero Lakes you're many miles from the nearest machine. At night no city lights nor smog block the view of the stars. Nearly one million acres of pristine land surrounds you here, more than enough for a lifetime of wandering.

At this altitude, the summer season is very short. Ice may not free the lakes until mid-July. The moist tundra tends to produce a prodigious number of mosquitoes when the wind isn't blowing. Bring lots of bug dope.

The first leg of the trip takes you to Lady of the Lake, an ideal choice for an easy day hike or overnighter with small children. Unfortunately, they might get their feet wet immediately upon starting this trip. The bridge over Fisher Creek washed out years ago, and until late in the year, the stream carries too much water to ford without wading.

After Fisher Creek the trail goes by a small private inholding with a cabin, and then heads down a well-maintained, forest-lined trail to Lady of the Lake. The Forest Service sign says 1 mile to the lake, but it's probably more like 1.5 miles.

The trail breaks out of the trees in the large marshy meadow at the foot of the lake Just before the lake, Trail 563 heads off to the right (south) to Chief Joseph Campground on US 212. (Trail 563 also offers fairly easy access to Lady of the Lake, but the route described here is much shorter and faster.)

Once at Lady of the Lake follow the trail along the west side of the lake. At the far end of the lake, the trail heads off to the left for about a quarter mile to a meadow on the north side of the lake where two trails depart. The left trail heads northwest to Long Lake. Take the right trail, which leads almost due north less than a half mile to the confluence of Star and Zimmer Creeks. Ford the stream here and continue north along Zimmer Creek another mile or so until you see Trail 573 switchbacking up the steep right side of the cirque. If you see a major stream coming in from the left, you have gone too far up the drainage.

160   *Absaroka-Beartooth Wilderness*

Upper Aero Lake.

The scramble up the switchbacks is short but steep and requires good physical conditioning. Locals call this "Cardiac Hill," and for good reason. It climbs almost 900 feet in about a mile, close to a Category H on our hill rating chart.

At the top of Cardiac Hill, the trail suddenly emerges from the timber and pauses above Lower Aero Lake. Be sure to notice the dramatic contrast between the treeless plateau here and the timbered country below.

The shoreline around Lower Aero is rocky and punctuated with snowbanks. There are a number of places to camp. They all have great scenery, and the air conditioning is always on. Those planning to stay here for two or three nights should spend some extra time searching for that five-star campsite. Drop the packs and look around for an hour or so. Don't expect to have a campfire on this treeless plateau.

To proceed to Upper Aero Lake, follow the stream that connects the two lakes. Another good camping spot is just below the outlet of the upper lake. This provides a good view of the lake and prominent Mount Villard with its spiny ridges. It also makes a good base camp for fishing both lakes and for exploring east to Rough Lake and then north up the Sky Top Lakes chain.

Although most people visit Rough Lake or Lone Elk Lake on side trips, there's also good camping there. Both are large, deep lakes similar to Aero Lakes. Sky Top Lakes might look inviting on the map, but camping is very limited in this rocky basin.

After a day or two of exploring the high country, retrace your steps down Cardiac Hill to Zimmer Creek—and then, back to civilization.

An alternate route back to the trailhead down Sky Top Creek, for experienced hikers only.

Options: This trip could turn into a long (four or five days) shuttle for experts only by continuing east from Aero Lakes through the "top of the world" and exiting the Beartooths at the East Rosebud or Clarks Fork trailheads.

You could also make a loop out of your trip by exiting on an off-trail route down Sky Top Creek, but be careful on the steep upper section of the stream where it tumbles off the plateau from Lone Elk Lake. Be forewarned: This route is only for the fit, agile, and adventuresome. It requires carrying your pack cross-country over to Rough Lake (probably named for how hard it is to reach) and then down to Lone Elk Lake. From Lone Elk Lake, it's a scramble down a steep route with no trail to a meadow where the stream from Splinter Lake slips into Sky Top Creek. This is a long, slow mile, and it can be hazardous, so be careful and patient. But it's also very beautiful, especially the falls where Sky Top Creek leaves Lone Elk Lake. At the meadow, there is an unofficial trail along Sky Top Creek all the way to the main trail. Follow cascading Sky Top Creek all the way until near the end when it veers off to the left to join up with Star Creek to form the Broadwater River. The track comes out into the same meadow (where Star and Zimmer Creeks join) you passed through on the way up Zimmer Creek on Trail 573. From here, retrace your steps back to Lady of the Lake and the trailhead.

Side trips: Aero Lakes perimeter (moderate), Upper Aero Lake (easy), Leaky Raft Lake (easy), Rough Lake (moderate), Lone Elk Lake (moderate), Sky Top Lakes (difficult), Zimmer Lake (difficult), Iceberg Peak/Grasshopper Glacier (difficult), Mount Villard (difficult), and Glacier Peak (difficult).

Camping: There are no designated campsites in this area, but there are numerous possibilities. Please use zero-impact camping principles to preserve this fragile landscape.

Fishing: Lady of the Lake is a favorite place to take kids for their first wilderness camping experience. The hike is easy, and the brook trout are always willing. For those with some wilderness experience, there are four small lakes nestled in the trees to the southeast. They're a bit tough to find, but they promise solitude. Grayling are stocked in Mosquito Lake when available, while the other lakes are scheduled for stocking with cutthroats.

Don't bother to fish Fisher Creek. Acid effluent from mines abandoned before environmental protection laws were in place keeps this stream pretty sterile.

Fishing is generally slow in both Upper and Lower Aero Lakes, but the rewards can be worth it. Lower Aero has brookies that are large, occasionally approaching a pound or more. They are supplemented with cutthroats that have migrated down from Upper Aero and seem to be reproducing. Cutts can be seen trying to spawn between the lakes through most of July. Upper Aero is stocked with cutts, but a change in its current six-year cycle is being discussed. Fishing is tough here as the cutthroats tend to school, and they can be hard to find in a lake of this size.

Sky Top Lakes were once stocked with grayling, and these worked down into Rough and Lone Elk Lakes, but all seem to have disappeared, leaving just brook trout in Lone Elk and Rough. The Sky Tops will probably be stocked once again to maintain a fishery in this chain originating on the slopes of Granite Peak.

To the east of Sky Top Creek are a number of lakes, supporting mostly brook trout, although Weasel, Stash, and Surprise Lakes are stocked with cutts. For hearty souls Recruitment Lake holds a few extremely large brookies, but the chances of getting skunked are pretty good. Nevertheless, just one hefty fish from this lake would be the high point of a summer vacation.

17

The Beaten Path

General description: The most popular trans-Beartooth route

Special attractions: Perhaps the best opportunity to really experience the breadth and diversity of the Beartooths

Type of trip: Shuttle

Total distance: 26 miles, not counting side trips

Difficulty: Long and strenuous, but not technically difficult or dangerous

Traffic: Heavy

Maps: Forest Service—Absaroka-Beartooth Wilderness Map; USGS quads—Alpine, Castle Mountain, and Fossil Lake; Rocky Mountain Survey—Alpine-Mount Maurice and Cooke City-Cutoff Mountain

Starting point: East Rosebud Trailhead

Finding the trailhead: From Interstate 90 at Columbus, drive south 29 miles on Montana Highway 78 to Roscoe. Drive into this small ranching community, being careful not to stop at the Grizzly Bar—until the return trip of course, when you'll really be ready for the famous "Grizzly Burger." At the north end of Roscoe the road turns to gravel and goes about 14.5 miles to the East Rosebud Trailhead. About 7 miles from Roscoe the road crosses East Rosebud Creek and forks. Take a sharp right and continue south along the creek. The road is mostly gravel except a 4-mile paved section near the end.

Actually, there are three trailheads at East Rosebud Lake. Phantom Creek Trail 17 begins on the right (west) side of the road 0.3 mile before the lake. This is a popular route to Froze-to-Death Plateau and Granite Peak. About a half mile farther, as the road swings by Alpine and around the east side of the lake, turn left into East Rosebud Campground to reach the trailhead for Trail 13 to Sylvan Lake. Finally, Trail 15 up the East Rosebud (The Beaten Path) begins at the end of the road about a quarter mile past the campground.

Parking and trailhead facilities: Huge parking lot; rest rooms; nearby developed campground.

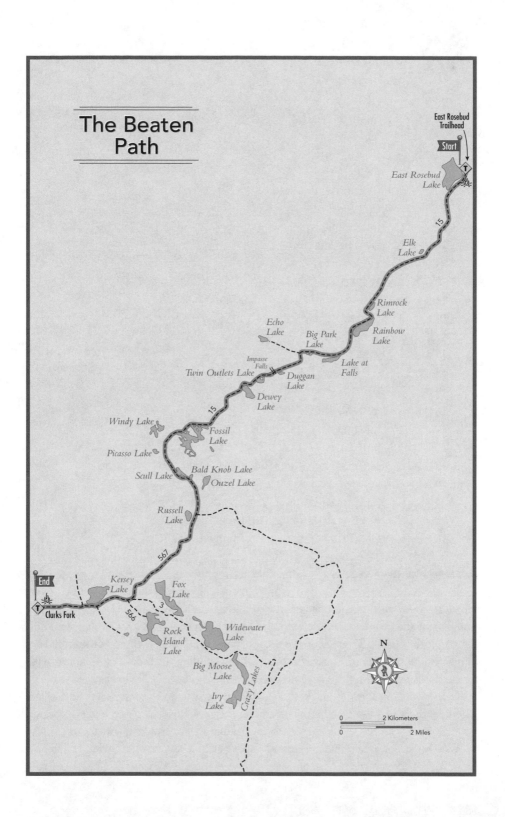

The Beaten Path

East Rosebud
Trailhead

Start

East Rosebud
Lake

15

Elk
Lake

Rimrock
Lake

Rainbow
Lake

Echo
Lake

Big Park
Lake

Lake at
Falls

Impasse
Falls

Twin Outlets Lake

Duggan
Lake

15

Dewey
Lake

Windy Lake

Fossil
Lake

Picasso Lake

Bald Knob Lake

Scull Lake

Ouzel Lake

Russell
Lake

567

Kersey
Lake

Fox
Lake

End

3

Clarks Fork

566

Rock
Island
Lake

Widewater
Lake

Big Moose
Lake

Ivy
Lake

Crazy Lakes

N

0   2 Kilometers

0   2 Miles

3.0 m.	Elk Lake
6.0	Rimrock Lake
7.0	Rainbow Lake
9.0	Lake at Falls
9.9	Big Park Lake
10.2	Junction with trail to Echo Lake; turn left
11.8	Duggan Lake
12.0	Impasse Falls
12.8	Twin Outlets Lake
14.0	Dewey Lake
16.0	Fossil Lake
16.8	East Rosebud/Clarks Fork Divide
16.8	Gallatin/Custer National Forest boundary
17.1	Windy Lake
17.8	Skull Lake
18.4	Bald Knob Lake
18.8	Ouzel Lake
20.0	Russell Lake
22.0	Junction with trail to Fox Lake; turn right
22.2	Junction with Crazy Lakes Trail No. 3; turn right
23.0	Junction with Trail 566 to Rock Island Lake; turn right
24.5	Kersey Lake
24.7	Junction with trail to Vernon Lake; turn right
25.2	Junction with trail to Curl Lake; turn left
26.0	Clarks Fork Trailhead, U.S. Highway 212

Recommended itinerary: Twenty-six miles is not a bragging distance, and a strong hiker could do the entire trip in a day. However, to really make this a best backpacking vacation, you should plan on taking at least four days. If you get a late start, you might want to stay the first night at little Elk Lake, but most hikers go at least as far as Rainbow Lake before pitching a tent. For the second night, you have a choice of hundreds of campsites. Pick a good one and stay two nights, spending the second day experiencing the heart of the Beartooth Plateau around Fossil Lake. You can hike all the way out to the Clarks Fork Trailhead from Fossil Lake in one day, but if you prefer a less demanding schedule, there are also many campsites along the way. Russell Lake is a logical choice, but everybody else has that idea, too, so this lake is always crowded and shows signs of overuse. Strive for an alternate campsite. Many backpackers search for that idyllic base camp somewhere on the plateau and stay several nights before leaving paradise. Be sure to read the most current Forest Service camping regulations at an information board at the trailhead.

First night:	Rainbow Lake
Second night:	Somewhere around Fossil Lake
Third night:	Same campsite
Fourth night:	Russell, Fox, or Rock Island Lakes

The hike: Many people who know the Beartooths say the East Rosebud is the most scenic valley of all. It's filled with lakes and waterfalls that would be major tourism attractions anywhere else. Here, there are so many, most don't even have names. The cutthroat-filled lakes bring a smile to any angler's face, and climbers love the place because of the endless array of rock faces. Families and friends frequently choose the Beaten Path for that long-planned wilderness adventure. Consequently, the East Rosebud Trailhead is probably the largest and most heavily used in the Beartooths. Adding even more use to the area is the small community of summer homes called Alpine right at the trailhead. The summer homes extend up both sides of the lower sections of East Rosebud Lake, closing off much of the lake to public use.

This backpacking trip showcases all the beauty, austerity, emptiness, and majesty of the Beartooths. It's a great introduction to the region's richness, diversity, and starkness, traveling through the lowest bottomlands and the highest plateaus. Along the way the route skirts dozens of trout-filled lakes and stunning waterfalls. It penetrates rich forests and wanders the treeless, lichen-covered Beartooth Plateau. This trail touches the true essence of the Beartooths.

This is the land of rushing water. Waterfalls and frothy, cascading streams are everywhere. There's no such scenery in Yellowstone National Park. Nonetheless, we should all be elated to have the park so near, because it sucks up most of the visitors and leaves places like the East Rosebud for us.

Still, this trail receives relatively heavy use compared to other routes in the Beartooths. Amazingly, however, the Beaten Path does not seem crowded. Even though hundreds of people may be somewhere along the 26-mile trail at any given time, most hikers would never know it. It's always a surprise to meet another party on the trail, and quiet spots to camp abound.

For uninterrupted solitude, and to really enjoy and experience the Beartooths, do make an effort to get off the Beaten Path. This trail has dozens of options for off-trail adventures—which is one reason the Beartooths can swallow up hundreds of people and leave the trail seemingly abandoned.

Don't take this trip lightly. It requires a minimum of four nights out, but avid explorers could stay two weeks and not see anything twice. This trail description assumes a minimum of four nights out.

It's also hard to make good time on this trail. There are simply too many distractions—too many scenic vistas, too many hungry trout, too many fields of juicy berries. Plan on traveling about a mile per hour slower than normal.

Lake at Falls.

Also, be sure to plan this trip carefully. The first big issue is transportation. The best option is to arrange with another group of hikers to do the trip at the same time. Each party starts at opposite ends of the trail, meeting at a campsite midway along the trail. Spend a day or two together, then head out and drive each other's vehicles home. Or leave a vehicle at one end of the trip and drive around to the other trailhead, or arrange to be picked up.

The entire 26 miles of trail is well maintained and easy to follow, so even a beginning backpacker can master it with ease. However, getting off the beaten path requires advanced wilderness skills.

The first 3 miles into Elk Lake are well-traveled and go by quickly. Expect to see lots of people on this popular stretch of trail. But every step of the way beyond Elk Lake is a step deeper and deeper into the wilderness, and it really seems like it. Elk Lake has a few campsites, but Rainbow Lake (7 miles in) is a better choice for the first night out if there's enough daylight left to get there.

Just after Elk Lake, the trail passes through an area where wild berries are as abundant as anywhere in the Beartooths, so browsers beware. Progress can slow to glacial speed. For about a mile a kaleidoscope of berries beckons from trailside, with huge crops of most species found in the Beartooths in abundance, especially huckleberries, thimbleberries, and wild raspberries, all nicely ripe in mid-August.

From berry heaven the trail breaks out of the forest and climbs about 800 feet through a monstrous rock field to Rimrock Lake. For a mile or so below the lake, East Rosebud Creek is little more than a long set of rapids. Apparently a big rockslide formed a natural dam and backed up Rimrock Lake. Take a rest on the rock field and look

East Rosebud Creek below Rimrock Lake.

Rainbow Lake.

around at the trail to marvel at how it was constructed. Building a trail here was no small feat, especially negotiating the steep slopes around Rimrock Lake.

The trail crosses East Rosebud Creek on a sturdy wooden bridge at the outlet. Then it skirts above the west side of the lake, the tread expertly etched out of the rock face. After the climb to get here, camping at Rimrock Lake might seem like a good idea. But campsites are limited here, so it's better to drag on for another mile to Rainbow Lake for the first night out.

Both Rimrock and Rainbow Lakes display a beautiful blue-green color (often called "glacier milk") indicative of a glacier-fed lake. Camping at Rainbow Lake affords a great view of Whirlpool Creek as it falls into the lake after tumbling down from Sundance Glacier on 12,408-foot Castle Rock Mountain.

The terrain at the upper end of Rainbow Lake flattens out and offers plenty of good campsites. Other parties probably will be camped here, but the area is big enough to provide ample solitude for all campers. Horse campers use this place heavily, but the Forest Service has required horses to stay above the trail, leaving several excellent campsites below the trail for backpackers only.

After the great scenery at Rimrock and Rainbow Lakes, you might think that it can't get much better. Guess again. Plan on lots of camera stops on the trip from Rainbow Lake to Fossil Lake. Also watch for the mountain goats that inhabit this section of the East Rosebud drainage.

If the falls on Whirlpool Creek were impressive, the two falls from Martin Lake that drop into well-named Lake at Falls are awe inspiring. Yet another mile or so up the trail be prepared for perhaps the most astounding sight of the trip, massive Impasse Falls, which plunge about 100 feet into Duggan Lake. Travelers get great views of the torrent from both below and above as the trail switchbacks beside the falls.

From Impasse Falls, the trail goes by two more large, unnamed waterfalls before arriving at Twin Outlets Lake. And the short stretch between Twin Outlets Lake and Dewey Lake features another series of waterfalls.

With all this scenery (and all the film you'll put through your camera) on the second day of this trip, it's hard to hold a steady pace. Each person's mileage and time on the trail will vary widely. It's 9 miles from Rainbow Lake to Fossil Lake. Figuring four nights from trailhead to trailhead, there are two options for the second night's camp. Either camp somewhere along the trail or push on to Fossil Lake and stay two nights there.

From the standpoint of available campsites, it's slightly better to forge on to Fossil Lake. Even though the scenery is great along this stretch, it lacks a good selection of campsites. The most serviceable sites are at Big Park Lake, Twin Outlets Lake, or Dewey Lake, and along the stream above Big Park Lake. Lake at Falls and Duggan Lake offer virtually no campsites.

Twin Outlets Lake is just below timberline, and it's the last place the Forest Service allows campfires. Campfires are prohibited in the Fossil Lake area too, which is at about 10,000 feet in elevation, but this should take nothing away from the grand experience of spending a few nights in the absolute core of the Beartooths.

One more choice for the second campsite is Echo Lake, which entails a 1-mile side trip. The trail breaks off to the west from the main trail above Big Park Lake and just before the bridge across Granite Creek. This isn't an official trail, but it's easy to follow. Watch for mountain goats on the slopes on the south side of Echo Lake.

Count on spending at least one night in the Fossil Lake area. Arriving fairly early on the third day allows extra time to search for that flawless, dream campsite. If you can't find that ideal campsite at Fossil, try nearby Windy, Bald Knob, or Mermaid Lakes.

The Fossil Lake area is the beating heart of a great wilderness, and much of the spirit of this top-of-the-world environment seems to flow from it, just as East Rosebud Creek does. You'll really be missing something if you just pass through it.

From a five-star base camp here, a multitude of remarkable day trips await. Always keep a close eye on the weather, and head back to camp if a storm rolls in—as they often do in this high-elevation paradise. Try to rise early and cruise around in the mornings instead of the afternoons, which is when thunderstorms rip through the Beartooths on an almost daily basis. Figure on spending a full day just to walk the perimeter of Fossil Lake.

About halfway along the trail around octopus-like Fossil Lake, a huge cairn marks the divide between two drainages (East Rosebud Creek and the Clarks Fork of the Yellowstone River) and the boundary between Custer and Gallatin National Forests. Fossil Lake drains into the East Rosebud, and Windy Lake empties into the Clarks Fork. On the Forest Service maps, the trail numbers change from Trail 15 to Trail 567. This is also the place for cross-country hikers to break off the main trail and head over to Windy Lake, which can be seen off to the west. Windy Lake might be called Fizzle Lake on some maps, just as several other lakes in this area have different names on different maps. That's reason enough to bring along a complete selection of maps.

Fossil Lake, deep into the Beartooth Plateau and commonly called the Top of the World.

Leaving Fossil Lake, the trail goes by Skull, Bald Knob, and Ouzel Lakes before dipping below timberline on the way to Russell Lake. Russell is nicely located for the last night out. Camp at either the upper or lower end of Russell Lake. To reach the campsite at the lower end, ford the stream, which gets seriously large as it slowly leaves the lake. Unfortunately, Russell Lake receives heavy use and shows it, so you might want to camp elsewhere. Other choices for the last night out would be Fox or Rock Island Lakes. The trail to Fox isn't an official trail, but it's well-marked.

The trail from Russell Lake is probably the least attractive stretch of the trip, but most people would still rate it fairly high. For 6 miles, it passes through a dense lodgepole forest. The 1988 fires burned the section around Kersey Lake.

With luck you'll come out on a hot day. Besides being the most scenic trailhead in the Beartooths, the Clarks Fork Trailhead offers the best swimming hole. Wearing a five-day accumulation of sweat and grime, most hikers feel an overpowering temptation to jump in. Don't fight it; just do it.

Options: Less elevation is gained by starting this trip at the south end at the Clarks Fork Trailhead, at 8,036 feet. However, since the north end is more accessible and scenic, more parties start from the East Rosebud Trailhead at 6,208 feet. Either way, the uphill climb really isn't severe; it's more of a gradual ascent most of the way. Perhaps the steepest section is between Elk Lake and Rimrock Lake.

Many backpackers choose the base camp option and stay several nights on the plateau around Fossil Lake, sometimes called the "top of the world," before leaving the area.

Side trips: The Beaten Path offers a nearly endless selection of side trips, mostly off-trail and difficult. Note that some lakes have different names depending on which map you're using. Here are a few possibilities: Snow Lakes (difficult), Arch Lakes (difficult), Echo Lake (easy), Martin Lake (difficult), Medicine Lake (difficult), Fossil Lake perimeter (easy), Cairn Lake (moderate), Fizzle (Windy) Lake (easy), Basin (Picasso) Lake (easy), Fulcrum (Mermaid) Lake (easy), Lake of the Clouds (moderate), Nymph (Leo) Lake (moderate), Looking Glass (Stephanie) Lake (moderate), Rough Lake/Aero Lakes (difficult), Sky Top Lakes (difficult), Gallery Lake (moderate), Mariane Lake (easy), Lake of the Winds (moderate), Fox Lake (easy), Rock Island Lake (easy), Vernon Lake (easy), Curl Lake (easy), and Aquarius Lake (difficult).

Camping: There are no designated campsites along this route, so use zero-impact principles to find appropriate campsites each night.

Fishing: The Montana Department of Fish, Wildlife & Parks (DFWP) knows this is the most popular trail in the Beartooths and tries hard to complement this popularity with a great fishery.

East Rosebud Lake houses a mixed bag of brown trout, brookies, rainbows, and cutthroat trout. The steep terrain keeps the browns from moving far upstream, but brookies, rainbows, and cutthroats, and even a few goldens survive in various places upstream in East Rosebud Creek. Goldens were stocked in several lakes along this trail in the 1950s, but they have readily cross-bred with both rainbows and cutthroats. Unless you really know trout, the golden trout characteristics are difficult to see.

With the exception of Cairn and Billy Lakes there are no brook trout above Elk Lake in this drainage. Rainbows dominate in Rimrock and Rainbow Lakes, and cutthroat trout dominate in the lakes above Rainbow Lake. Because of its popularity, Fossil Lake is stocked frequently with cutts to keep the fishing hot, although they can be hard to find because they tend to school.

If you camp at Elk Lake, you might have time for a side trip up to Snow Lakes. These lakes hold some nice rainbows, but the tough climb up the east side of Snow Creek keeps all but the most determined anglers away.

Anglers who camp near Big Park Lake might want to reserve an entire day for climbing (and it truly is a climb) into and out of Scat and Martin Lakes. DFWP is trying to establish a pure golden trout fishery there, and it may be worth the climb.

Cairn Lake would also provide a worthwhile side trip for those camping near Dewey Lake. Cairn and Billy Lakes both have brook trout well above average in size. The trout don't reproduce well here, allowing those remaining to grow larger. DFWP closely monitors these lakes—a downstream migration of brook trout would seriously harm the cutthroat/rainbow fishery down below. If you catch brookies below Billy Lake, notify DFWP.

A sturdy bridge over the Clarks Fork just down the trail from the Clarks Fork Trailhead.

Entering the Clarks Fork side of the pass near Fossil Lake, the fishing gets even better. There are a great many lakes in the Clarks Fork drainage, and this trail goes through the heart of this incredible fishery. Because of the easy access for horses, most of the lakes along the trail were stocked with brook trout in the first half of the twentieth century. The brookies tend to be on the smaller side but provide some great fishing, and an easy meal.

Just off the trail, Leo Lake, Lake of the Winds, and Lake of the Clouds host cutthroat trout, while Gallery Lake also has rainbows. Fox Lake is one of those places that few people stop at, but many more should. It sports larger than average brookies, nice rainbows, and an occasional grayling that works its way down from Cliff Lake.

As an experiment DFWP has stocked lake trout in Kersey Lake to prey on the brook trout population. It is hoped that by reducing the number of brookies, the remaining ones will grow larger. At last check, this seems to be working.

18

Green Lake

General description: A long loop on the southwest edge of the Beartooth Plateau, best suited for at least two nights out, with one short off-trail section. A short section is impassable for horses.

Special attractions: The short, easy, off-trail section can be a confidence builder, and unlike some trips, there are plenty of opportunities to get your feet wet.

Type of trip: Loop

Total distance: 19.4 miles

Difficulty: Difficult

Traffic: Heavy near the Martin Lake Basin and Granite Lake, but light along the rest of the route

Maps: Forest Service Absaroka-Beartooth Wilderness Map; USGS quads—Muddy Creek, Beartooth Butte, Castle Mountain, and Silver Run Peak; Rocky Mountain Survey—Wyoming Beartooths and Alpine-Mount Maurice

Starting point: Clay Butte Trailhead on the Beartooth Highway

Finding the trailhead: The well-marked Clay Butte Road 142 turns north off the Beartooth Highway 20 miles east of Cooke City or 43 miles west of Red Lodge. Any passenger car can make it up the moderately steep, well-maintained gravel road to Clay Butte Lookout, but it's not recommended for vehicles pulling trailers. The road to the trailhead turns off to the left about 1.5 miles from the Beartooth Highway.

Parking and trailhead facilities: Limited parking; no room for large horse trailers; no facilities; several developed campgrounds nearby.

Recommended itinerary: This is one of those hikes that you don't have to plan extensively. There are so many places to see and camp, that you can sort of "play it by ear" and when you get ready to camp, you can usually find a good spot in an hour or two. You should take at least three days to do this loop, but you can spend much longer by setting up base camps at several points such as around Native Lake, Martin Lake, Green Lake, or Lake Elaine.

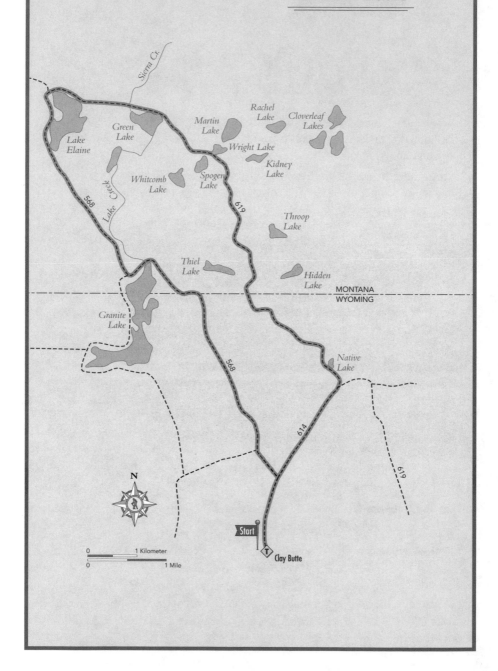

Green Lake

1.2 m.	Junction with Trail 568 to Granite Lake; turn right
2.9	Junction with Trail 619 from Beartooth Lake Trailhead; turn left
3.1	Native Lake
4.3	Mule Lake
4.6	Thiel Lake
6.5	Martin Lake Basin
7.8	Green Lake
8.8	Sierra Creek
10.1	Upper Lake Elaine and junction with Trail 568 to Farley Lake; turn left
10.9	Lower Lake Elaine
13.7	Upper Granite Lake and junction with Trail 618; turn left
14.9	Junction with trail to Thiel Lake; turn right
17.9	Junction with trail to Muddy Creek; turn left
18.2	Junction with Trail 614; turn left
19.4	Clay Butte Trailhead

The hike: Clay Butte is one of those rare trailheads that allow backpackers to go downhill instead of up at the beginning of a trip. In fact, the trailhead, at 9,600 feet, is almost the highest point on any trail leaving from it. The trail edges a few feet over 10,000 just before reaching Martin Lake, but most of the trip is at a lower elevation than the trailhead.

Clay Butte and neighboring Beartooth Butte to the east and Table Mountain to the south are the only outcrops on the entire Beartooth Plateau still covered with sedimentary rock. Erosion removed the sedimentary rock from the rest of the area, but for some reason, still somewhat unclear to geologists, these three remnants survived.

Most people are in a big hurry to hit the trail when they get to the trailhead, but here it's worth taking an extra fifteen minutes to drive to the top of Clay Butte for the view. It's only another mile drive to the lookout, where (at 9,811 feet) a splendid view is had of the Beartooth Plateau. From this vista, much of the terrain covered on this hike can be seen. As at other trailheads along the Beartooth Highway, anglers need to know which state they are in, so they can be sure to have the appropriate fishing license(s) and regulations.

Trail 614 starts out downhill but turns uphill after 1 mile at the junction of Trail 568 to Upper Granite Lake. Turn right and stay on Trail 614. For the first 2.5 miles, the trail travels through an enormous, high-altitude meadow carpeted with wildflowers. At one point the trail fades away into a string of cairns, so watch carefully for the next trail marker.

About a quarter mile before Native Lake the trail meets Trail 619 coming from Beartooth Lake. Turn left (west) onto Trail 619. Native Lake is the beginning of a long string of lakes. Native, Box, Mule, and Thiel Lakes all boast excellent campsites. Thiel

Hiking through the high meadows around the Clay Butte Trailhead.

Lake is a frequent overnight stay for backcountry horsemen; be careful not to miss it. Thiel Lake is off to the left (south) at the bottom of the hill after Mule Lake, just after the trail breaks out into a lush meadow.

Regardless of where you spend your first night, continue along Trail 619 the next morning. Just after Thiel Lake, start a long, strenuous climb into the Martin Lake Basin. It's a fairly tough, Category 3 grind, but the reward at the end is well worth it. Martin Lake Basin is one of the most alluring spots in the Beartooths. Four major lakes (Martin, Wright, Spogen, and Whitcomb) stair-step through this magnificent basin, and there's a spectacular, high-altitude waterfall between Wright and Spogen Lakes. The waterfall seems larger and more majestic here at 9,600 feet.

You can camp almost anywhere in the basin, especially around Wright and Martin Lakes. This is like a five-star hotel; every room with a view—nature's penthouse. Firewood, however, is in short supply and essential to the extraordinary charm of this basin, so resist the temptation to have a campfire.

As is obvious with a quick look at the topo map, this is lake country. Dozens of lakes lie within a day's trek from this basin. Even avid explorers could spend a week here and not see the same lake twice. Don't forget to spend one of those days simply hiking around the four lakes in the basin to fully appreciate a place that would put most national parks to shame.

Since this is one of the most spectacular spots in the Beartooths, plan to spend the night in this basin. For those who hiked all the way in on their first day, this area is worth a two-night stay. There are plenty of enticing day trips you can take from Martin Lake Basin.

The creek between Wright and Spogen Lakes must be forded. When selecting a campsite consider whether you want wet feet that night or first thing the next morning.

After spending a night in the Martin Lake Basin you might have to force yourself to hit the trail the next morning. After a small hill to get out of the basin, the route skirts Trail Lake before heading down a steep hill into the gorgeous Green Lake valley. Going down this grade is all the argument needed against doing this trip in reverse. This hill makes the climb from Thiel Lake to Martin Lake Basin seem mild.

At Green Lake do not continue around the lake to the south, even though the trail appears to head in that direction. Instead, turn north, cross the inlet stream, and head around the north side of Green Lake on a less defined trail. This isn't an official Forest Service trail, nor is it on the national forest map or topo map, but it's an easily followed pathway around the lake to Sierra Creek. If you decide not to camp in the Martin Lake Basin, camp instead at the head of Green Lake or after crossing Sierra Creek.

The Sierra Creek ford can be fairly difficult early in the season, so be careful. After the ford the trail leaves the Green Lake shoreline and heads straight west to Lake Elaine. Again, this isn't an official trail and it is not maintained or marked, but it's still fairly easy to navigate. The trail through this section fades away in several wet meadows. Stay on the south edge of these meadows.

At Lake Elaine traverse the north shoreline—including a short boulder field—until you hit well-used Trail 568. Be careful in the boulder field; it can be dangerous, especially if you're carrying a big pack or if the rocks are wet. Turn left (south) on Trail 568, which hugs the west shore of Lake Elaine for about 1 mile.

Shortly after leaving Lake Elaine, the trail heads down a steep hill, another good reason not to do this trip in reverse. This downhill grade receives heavy horse traffic, which has ground up the rock into a fine dust that can make footing precarious, so watch your step. From the bottom of this climb, it's a pleasant 2 miles to upper Granite Lake.

Granite Lake is a huge mountain lake fed by massive Lake Creek, which splinters into six channels just before tumbling into Granite Lake. Some folks moan and groan about having to cross six streams, but imagine how difficult the crossing would be if Lake Creek stayed in one channel.

The first view of Granite Lake is all the enticement most people need to stay, so why not? Choose from any of the numerous campsites at the upper end of the lake.

From Granite Lake, the trail gradually climbs all the way to the Clay Butte Trailhead. This final stretch can become fairly muddy in frequent boggy sections. The hardest part of the trip, it seems, is the last uphill mile, which seemed so pleasant three or four days ago.

Options: This loop can be done in reverse, but that route would require a steep climb just south of Lake Elaine and another up from Green Lake. This trip is also a good choice for backpackers who like to set up base camps and explore some of the surrounding terrain without a big pack.

Actually, this trip can be done as a shuttle by leaving a vehicle at the Muddy Creek Trailhead. This avoids the uphill grind back to the Clay Butte Trailhead. The trail along the west side of Granite Lake leads out of Muddy Creek. Another option is to continue toward Clay Butte, but then turn off on a trail that heads west about 1 mile before the

Upper end of Lake Elaine.

trailhead and drops steeply down to Muddy Creek. If you go around Granite Lake, you must make a difficult ford of Lake Creek as it leaves Granite Lake.

Side trips: If you take time for side trips, this trip offers a full menu, including: Box Lakes (easy), Surprise Lake (easy), Mule Lake (easy), Thiel Lake (easy), around the Martin Lake Basin (easy), Hidden Lake (moderate), Swede Lake (moderate), Cloverleaf Lakes (difficult), Kidney Lake (easy), Marmot Lake (moderate), Sierra Creek (moderate), and Jorden Lake (easy).

Camping: There are no designated campsites, but there are delightful places to camp everywhere along this route, with the possible exception of Lake Elaine where campsites are marginal. Be sure to set up a zero-impact camp.

Fishing: Most of the lakes in this area were stocked with brook trout, and the chain of lakes in Martin Lake Basin is named after the men who hauled the brook trout in. The brookies here are average for the Beartooths with Whitcomb Lake having slightly larger fish.

For variation Trail Lake (appropriately named) has cutthroats that are stocked, but which also reproduce. Head upstream from Martin Lake to reach the cutthroat hotbed found in the Cloverleaf Lakes.

Earlier along the route in, a side trip to Swede and Hidden Lakes is worthwhile for the cutthroats found there. Goldens were once found in Hidden Lake, and a few may still remain.

Green Lake contains oodles of pan-sized brookies. Take some of these brook trout with you—those remaining will thank you.

From Green Lake try a nice side trip up Sierra Creek to Crystal or Flat Rock Lakes. The cutthroats stocked here provide a nice contrast to the brook trout found in surrounding lakes. Both Crystal and Flat Rock have eight-year stocking cycles.

From camp near Lake Creek at Granite Lake, a side trip can be made to Skeeter and Spaghetti Lakes for grayling. When grayling are available, DFWP stocks these lakes. It's a tough, off-trail trip that should be attempted only by those proficient in reading a topo map and compass.

19

Lake Plateau

General description: A week-long backpacking vacation into a popular hiking area with a myriad of side trip opportunities. Nicely suited to backpackers who like to set up a base camp

Special attractions: A gorgeous, lake-dotted, high-altitude plateau, plus the equally spectacular Columbine Pass

Type of trip: Loop, but can be done as a shuttle or out-and-back base camp

Total distance: 34.3 miles, not counting side trips

Difficulty: Moderate

Traffic: Moderate to heavy; plan on seeing a few stock parties

Maps: Forest Service Absaroka-Beartooth Wilderness map; USGS quads—Mount Douglas, Tumble Mountain, Pinnacle Mountain, and Haystack Peak; Rocky Mountain Survey—Mount Douglas–Mount Wood and Cooke City–Cutoff Mountain

Starting point: Box Canyon Trailhead

Finding the trailhead: To find the trailhead take County Road 298 (locally referred to as the Boulder River Road) south from Big Timber. The road doesn't take off from either of the two exits off Interstate 90. Instead, go into Big Timber and watch for signs for County 298, which heads south and passes over the freeway from the middle of town between the two exits.

It's 48 miles from Big Timber to the Box Canyon Trailhead, so make sure to top off the gas tank. It's 16 miles to the small community of McLeod and another 8 miles until the pavement ends—which means 24 miles of bumpy gravel road are still ahead. There are two major trailheads with parking areas (Upsidedown Creek and Box Canyon) providing access to the Lake Plateau and Slough Creek. Upsidedown Creek is about 1.5 miles before Box Canyon. Both trailheads are well signed.

A jeep road continues on to the Independence Peak area, where signs of early 1900s mining operations still remain. But almost all of the trails in this region can be accessed without bumping and grinding up this very rough road. At best it is passable only with four-wheel-drive or all-terrain vehicles.

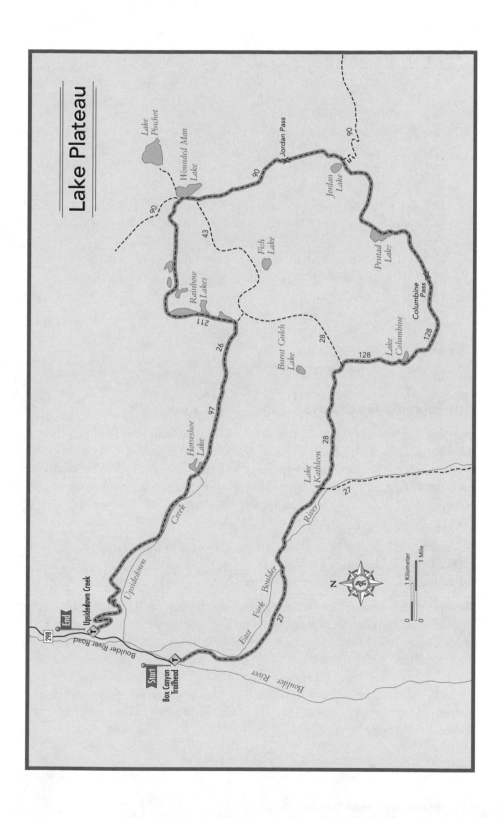

Lake Plateau

3.5 m.	East Fork Boulder River
5.2	Junction with Trail 28; turn left
5.4	Lake Kathleen
7.9	Junction with Trail 128; turn right
9.3	Columbine Lake
11.1	Columbine Pass
12.5	Pentad Lake
14.5	Jordan Lake and junction with Trail 90; turn left
15.9	Jordan Pass
18.7	Wounded Man Lake and junction with Trail 43; turn left
18.9	Junction with Trail 211; turn left after trip to Lake Pinchot
19.5	Lake Pinchot
21.0	Rainbow Lakes
22.5	Junction with Trail 26; turn right
25.9	Horseshoe Lake
34.3	Upsidedown Creek Trailhead

Parking and trailhead facilities: Large parking lot; no facilities.

Recommended itinerary: This trip works best if you get an early start from Box Canyon, but since the drive is long, it might be difficult to hit the trail early. If you start later in the day, try East Fork Boulder River for the first night out. This may lengthen the trip by one day—not a bad price to pay for sleeping late. The following recommended itinerary lays out a five-day trip, but you could easily spend more time on Lake Plateau.

First night:	Columbine Lake
Second night:	Lake Pinchot, Wounded Man, Owl, or other nearby lakes
Third night:	Same campsite
Fourth night:	Diamond or Horseshoe Lakes

The hike: Most locals consider the Boulder River the dividing line between the Beartooths to the east and the Absaroka Range to the west. Boulder River Road ends 48 miles south of Big Timber at Box Canyon Campground. In the 1970s there was a proposal to punch the road all the way through to Cooke City, splitting the Absaroka-Beartooth Wilderness into two smaller wild areas. Look at a topo map and the feasibility (or lack of it) of such a road becomes obvious. After a hard fight by wilderness advocates, the two spectacular mountain ranges were permanently joined into one wilderness, and the controversial road proposal was dropped.

The Boulder River is a popular place. The road is lined with dude ranches and church camps in addition to numerous summer homes. During the early hunting season in September dozens of horse trailers may be parked at Box Canyon Trailhead.

The Lake Plateau region of the Beartooths is as popular as any spot in the entire wilderness. The Boulder River trailheads (Box Canyon and Upsidedown Creek) attract many backpackers. Few backcountry horsemen use Upsidedown Creek, but many hunters and outfitters use the Box Canyon trailhead to access the Slough Creek Divide area.

The Lake Plateau is a unique and spectacular part of the Beartooths accessed by four major trails. Two of these trailheads (Box Canyon and Upsidedown Creek) originate along the Boulder River. Others leave from the West Stillwater and the main Stillwater. This creates a variety of options for hiking into the Lake Plateau, but this route is special because there aren't many opportunities like this one to see so much wild country without working out a burdensome shuttle or retracing your steps for half of the trip.

From the Box Canyon Trailhead, Trail 27 climbs gradually through timber and open parks along the East Fork Boulder River for about 3.5 miles before crossing a sturdy bridge. If you started late, you may wish to stay the first night in one of several excellent campsites located just before the bridge.

It would be wise to get up early on the first day, drive to Box Canyon Trailhead, and cover at least the first 3.5 miles to a series of excellent campsites just before the bridge over the East Fork Boulder River. This area can accommodate a large party or several parties, as long as Forest Service limits for group size aren't exceeded.

Base camp on the Lake Plateau.

After crossing the East Fork, the trail follows the river for a half mile before climbing away through heavy timber. Several trout-filled pools beckon along the riverside stretch, so be prepared to fight off temptations to stop and rig up the fly casting gear.

In less than 2 miles you reach the junction with Trail 28. Trail 27 goes straight and eventually ends up in Yellowstone National Park. Turn left here onto Trail 28. In about a quarter mile, watch for tranquil little Lake Kathleen off to the left. This is also a possible first-night campsite.

About 2 miles from Lake Kathleen the trail joins Trail 128 to Columbine Pass. Turn right onto this trail, which climbs a big hill and breaks out of the forest into a subalpine panorama. From the junction it's about 1.5 miles to Lake Columbine. With an early start on the first day, this would also make a good first campsite. If it's your second day out, consider pushing on to Pentad or Jordan Lakes for the second night's camp.

From Lake Columbine continue another scenic 2 miles up to 9,850-foot Columbine Pass. In a good snow year snowbanks cover the trail on Columbine Pass well into July. The trail fades away twice between Lake Columbine and the pass, so watch the topo map carefully to stay on track. A few well-placed cairns make navigation here easier.

After the Category 2 climb to Columbine Pass, take a break and enjoy a snack and the vistas, including 10,685-foot Pinnacle Mountain to the south. From here the trail leaves the Boulder River drainage behind and heads into the Stillwater River drainage. Hereafter, the trip leapfrogs from one lake to another for the next 14 miles.

Those who camped at Lake Columbine can make it all the way into the Lake Plateau for the next night's campsite. Otherwise, plan to pitch a tent at Pentad or Jordan Lakes. Pentad is more scenic, but Jordan offers better fishing (and suffers more from overuse). There are also several smaller lakes near Pentad—Mouse, Favonius, Sundown, and several unnamed lakes. Many great campsites can be found in the area, and they won't be as crowded as Jordan Lake probably will be. Don't rush to take the first campsite. Look around for a while and you'll find a better one. It might be wise to stop at the south end of Pentad anyway, as the trail is difficult to follow because of all the tangent trails created by backcountry horsemen to various campsites. To untangle the maze check the topo map. The trail skirts the east shore of Pentad Lake heading north.

Jordan Lake, another 2 miles down the trail from Pentad, has limited camping with one campsite at the foot of the lake. The campsite is, however, large enough to serve a large party or several parties—although it may be too heavily impacted to be used by parties with stock animals.

At Jordan Lake the trail meets Trail 90, coming out of Lake Plateau and dropping east down into the Middle Fork of Wounded Man Creek. Turn left (north) here onto Trail 90, which climbs gradually 1.5 miles over Jordan Pass and drops into the Lake Plateau. This isn't much of a pass, but it's a great spot to take fifteen minutes to marvel at the mountainous horizons in every direction.

If you camped last at Jordan or Pentad Lakes, you have lots of options for the next night out or for a base camp. The closest site is at Wounded Man Lake, but this is a busy place. The best campsite is along the North Fork of Wounded Man Creek just southwest of the lake. But consider hiking the short mile northeast from Wounded Man Lake to Lake Pinchot to stay at the crown jewel of the Lake Plateau. The third option is to turn

Taking a break during a day hike from base camp on the Lake Plateau.

left onto Trail 211 at the junction on the west side of Wounded Man Lake and stay at Owl Lake or one of the Rainbow Lakes that follow shortly thereafter. These offer some of the best base camps in the area because there are innumerable sights to see all within a short walk.

After a night or two on the plateau, follow Trail 211 along the west shore of Rainbow Lakes down to the junction with Trail 26 at the south end of Lower Rainbow Lake. Turn right (west) here, and spend the last night out at Diamond or Horseshoe Lakes (sometimes called Upper and Lower Horseshoe Lakes). Horseshoe Lake is probably better because it has more campsites and it leaves the shortest possible distance along Upsidedown Creek the last day. And that's still about 8.5 miles, plus the 1.5 miles some lucky volunteer has to walk or try to catch a ride up to the Box Canyon Trailhead to get the vehicle. Sorry—there are no real campsites anywhere from Horseshoe Lake to the Boulder River Road.

Options: If you can arrange transportation for a shuttle, you can hike out the West Stillwater or the main Stillwater. You might need a four-wheel-drive vehicle to get to the West Stillwater Trailhead, depending on the condition of the road. You can also make this an out-and-back trip from either the Box Canyon or Upsidedown Creek Trailheads.

Side trips: You could spend weeks exploring the Lake Plateau, and these are only a few of the dozens of great side trips in the area. Lake Pinchot (easy), Flood Creek Lakes (moderate), Asteriod Lake Basin (difficult), Chalice Peak (difficult), Lightning Lake (difficult), Lake Diaphanous (easy), Fish Lake (easy), Barrier Lake (difficult), Mirror

Lake (moderate), Chickadee Lake (difficult), Squeeze Lake (difficult), Mount Douglas (difficult), Martes Lake (moderate), Sundown Lake (moderate), Pentad and Favonius Lakes (easy), and Burnt Gulch Lake (difficult).

Camping: The Lake Plateau has hundreds of terrific campsites, all undesignated. Find one for your base camp, and please make it a zero-impact camp.

Fishing: Anglers who want to fish the first day of the trip should camp near the East Fork Boulder River or Rainbow Creek, as most of the lakes along this route—including Lake Columbine—are barren. Burnt Gulch Lake is an exception, sporting dinner-sized cutthroat trout. Cutthroats dominate the fishery along this route until the Lake Plateau is reached. Cutthroats are fairly easy to catch and are frequently found along rocky shorelines on the downwind sides of lakes. Anglers often fish "past the fish" by casting out into the lake.

Once the Lake Plateau is reached there are a variety of fishing opportunities easily available, and Lake Pinchot would certainly make the desirable list, as would the entire Flood Creek chain of lakes.

20

Sundance Pass

General description: A fairly rugged, two- or three-day hike for experienced hikers

Special attractions: Spectacular mountain scenery, especially the view from Sundance Pass

Type of trip: Shuttle

Total distance: 21 miles, not counting side trips

Difficulty: Difficult

Traffic: Heavy

Maps: Forest Service—Absaroka-Beartooth Wilderness Map; USGS quads—Black Pyramid Mountain, Silver Run Peak, and Sylvan Peak; Rocky Mountain Survey—Alpine–Mount Maurice

Starting point: Lake Fork of Rock Creek Trailhead

Finding the trailhead: From Red Lodge drive southwest for about 10 miles on U.S. Highway 212. Turn west at the well-marked road up the Lake Fork of Rock Creek. A short, paved road leads to a turnaround and the trailhead. Leave a vehicle or arrange for a pick up at the trailhead parking lot at the end of the West Fork of Rock Creek Road. To find this trailhead take West Fork of Rock Creek Road (FR 71), which leaves U.S. Highway 12 on the south edge of Red Lodge. Drive 2.7 miles to where the road forks. Take the left fork and drive another 11.3 miles until the road ends at the trailhead.

Parking and trailhead facilities: Large parking lot; rest rooms; several developed campgrounds nearby.

Recommended itinerary: A three-day trip staying one night in the Lake Fork of Rock Creek and another in the West Fork of Rock Creek.

The hike: This well-maintained and heavily used trail is not only one of the most scenic in the Beartooths, but it's only a short drive from the Billings area.

This trail offers absolutely spectacular scenery. From Sundance Pass, for example, vistas include 12,000-foot mountains such as 12,548-foot Whitetail Peak, and the Beartooth Plateau, a huge mass of contiguous land above 10,000 feet. Hikers are also

Sundance Pass

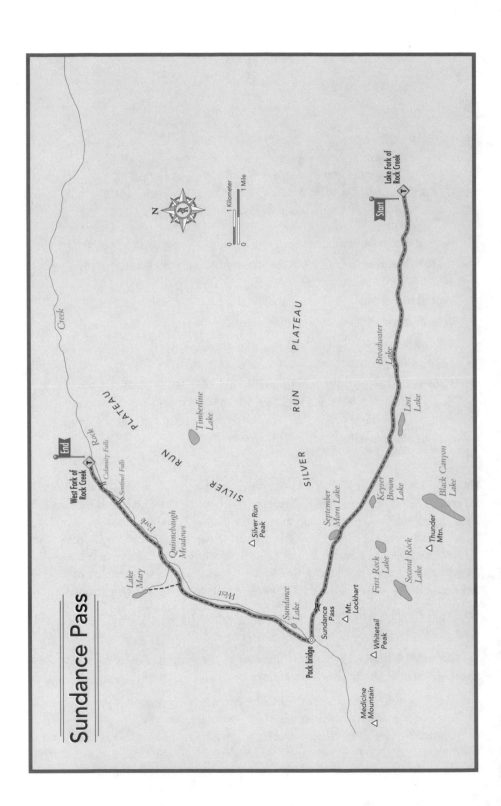

N

0   1 Kilometer
0   1 Mile

Creek

Rock

PLATEAU

Calamity Falls

Sentinel Falls

End

West Fork of
Rock Creek

Fork

Quinnebaugh
Meadows

Lake
Mary

West

Medicine
△ Mountain

Sundance
Lake

Rock bridge

Sundance Pass

△ Whitetail
Peak

△ Mt.
Lockhart

First Rock
Lake

Second Rock
Lake

△ Thunder
Mtn.

Black Canyon
Lake

Keyser
Brown
Lake

September
Morn Lake

SILVER

SILVER

RUN

RUN

PLATEAU

Silver Run
△ Peak

Timberline
Lake

PLATEAU

Lost
Lake

Broadwater
Lake

Start

Lake Fork of
Rock Creek

3.5 m.	Broadwater Lake
5.0	Spur trail to Lost Lake
5.2	Spur trail to Black Canyon Lake
6.5	Turn to Keyser Brown Lake
8.5	September Morn Lake
11.3	Sundance Pass
13.0	West Fork of Rock Creek
13.5	Sundance Lake
15.9	Junction with trail to Lake Mary; turn right
16.0	Quinnebaugh Meadows
21.0	West Fork of Rock Creek Trailhead

treated to views of glaciers and obvious results of glaciation, exposed Precambrian rock, and waterfalls. And watch for mountain goats, deer, golden eagles, and gyrfalcons. Goats are frequently seen from First and Second Rock Lakes.

This is a fairly difficult, 21-mile shuttle trip that ends on the West Fork of Rock Creek just south of Red Lodge. Arrange to be picked up at the trailhead at the end of the West Fork of Rock Creek Road (Forest Road 71) or leave a vehicle there. An alternative is to have another party start at the other end of the trail, meet up on Sundance Pass and trade keys.

Plan to do this trip no earlier in the year than July 15. Sundance Pass usually isn't snow-free until then. This delay also avoids the peak season for mosquitoes and no-see-ums, which can be quite bad in this area, especially on the West Fork side.

Although nicely suited to a three-day/two-night trip, the route also offers many scenic side trips. Plan an extra day or two in the backcountry for exploring these.

The main route passes by three lakes—Keyser Brown, September Morn, and Sundance—but several others can be reached with short side trips. One of these is Lost Lake, which is a quarter-mile climb from the main trail. This is a very heavily used lake, and it shows it. There are campsites here, but consider staying somewhere else that hasn't been trampled so much. The trail to Lost Lake leaves the main trail on the left, 5 miles from the trailhead or about 200 yards before the bridge over the Lake Fork of Rock Creek.

Another lake-bound trail departs from the main trail immediately before the same bridge. The unofficial trail to Black Canyon Lake scrambles uphill to the left also. Black Canyon Lake lies just below Grasshopper Glacier. The undeveloped trail to Black Canyon Lake is a rough but short hike of about 1.5 miles. Part of the route traverses rock talus with no trail, and there is a steep climb near the lake. The hike to Black Canyon is probably too tough for small children or poorly conditioned hikers. There is almost no place to camp at this high, rugged lake, and it's usually very windy at Black Canyon during midday.

Medicine Mountain and the headwaters of the West Fork of Rock Creek.

The main trail continues west along the Lake Fork another mile to Keyser Brown Lake, about 7 miles from the trailhead. To do this trip in three days and two nights, plan to start early and spend the first night at Keyser Brown. Although the wood supply is ample enough around Keyser Brown, this is one of the most heavily used campsites in the Beartooths. Please consider doing without a campfire here.

The lake is about a quarter mile to the left (southwest), so watch carefully for the side trail. It is an official trail, and it's signed. The lake itself comes into view from the main trail, but if you can see it you've missed the junction and need to backtrack about 200 yards to the trail to the lake. An angler's trail leads south from the far end of Keyser Brown to First and Second Rock Lakes. This side trip involves some difficult boulder-hopping.

For another campsite option, continue 1.5 miles up the main trail to September Morn Lake. The campsite selection is much more limited here than at Keyser Brown, but it is closer to Sundance Pass.

Get a good night's sleep and a hearty breakfast before starting the second day. From Keyser Brown it's a 1,660-foot, Category 2 climb to the top of Sundance Pass. The scenery is so incredible, however, that hikers might not notice how much work it is getting to the top. To the north and east stretch the twin lobes of the Silver Run Plateau, rising to their apex at 12,500-foot Silver Run Peak. Directly south of the pass, 11,647-foot Mount Lockhart partially shields the pyramid of 12,548-foot Whitetail Peak.

Coming down from Sundance Pass into the West Fork won't take long. A series of switchbacks drops about 1,000 feet in 1 mile or so to a bridge over the headwaters of the West Fork. Remember to carry extra water on this stretch—it is scarce on the pass.

Although there are campsites in a meadow about a quarter mile down the trail from the Sundance Bridge, Quinnebaugh Meadows is probably the best choice for the second night out. It offers plenty of excellent campsites, and there's enough downed wood for a campfire. It's a long 8 miles from Keyser Brown to Quinnebaugh Meadows, but there aren't many good campsites between September Morn Lake and Quinnebaugh Meadows. Camping at the meadows leaves an easy 5 miles for the last day out. It might also allow enough time for a side trip up to Lake Mary or Dude Lake. Dude Lake is 1 mile west via a rough, steep trail from Quinnebaugh Meadows. And there's a steep but good trail from Quinnebaugh Meadows to Lake Mary. Some people use the saddle to the north of Lake Mary as a cross-country route to Crow, Sylvan, and East Rosebud Lakes.

The final day of hiking follows the trail along the north bank of the West Fork all the way to the trailhead. Sentinel and Calamity Falls both offer good places to drop the pack and relax.

Both the Lake Fork and the West Fork are probably used as heavily as any wild area in Montana. Consequently, the Forest Service has rangers out enforcing several protective regulations. These special regulations are listed at a sign on the trailhead. Be sure to read them carefully, and then, of course, obey them. They are necessary to protect these fragile environs.

This trip also works well in reverse. In fact, starting from the West Fork results in about 600 feet less overall elevation gain. However, Sundance Pass is tougher to climb from the West Fork side.

Options: This trip can be done from either trailhead with no noticeable difference. Climbing Sundance Pass is a lung-buster from either side.

Quinnebaugh Meadows on the West Fork of Rock Creek.

Fishing at Black Canyon Lake.

Side trips: This hike offers an abundant variety of side trips, including: Lost Lake (easy), Black Canyon Lake (difficult), Rock Lakes (moderate), Whitetail Peak (difficult), Sundance Mountain (difficult), Sundance Lake (easy), Marker Lake (difficult), Ship Lake Basin (difficult), Kookoo Lake (difficult), Shadow Lake (easy), Dude Lake (difficult), Lake Mary (moderate), and Crow Lake (difficult).

Camping: There are no designated campsites in this area. Since this area gets heavy use, please make sure you have zero-impact campsites.

Fishing: The lakes found along the Lake Fork provide some of the easiest fishing in the Beartooths. Anglers will find plenty of hungry brookies in September Morn, Keyser Brown, and First and Second Rock Lakes. Overnight campers can count on these lakes to supply dinner. Keyser Brown and Second Rock Lakes also support healthy cutthroat fisheries.

For those with something other than brook trout on their mind, Lost Lake supports a few cutthroat trout of surprising size. Grayling also have been planted in Lost Lake, and they grow large as well.

The scramble up to Black Canyon Lake rewards anglers with plenty of cutthroats near the glacial moraine that blocks the outlet. While this lake once grew exceptionally large fish, a probable change in food organisms, caused by the fish themselves, now keeps them in the slightly above-average range. This lake offers the best chance for catching a 15-inch or larger trout in the Lake Fork drainage.

From the crest of Sundance Pass, look to the lakes in the high basin across the West Fork to the northwest. Ship Lake is the largest of these. There are plenty of fish in these waters for hikers who don't mind climbing up the other side of the valley after coming down Sundance Pass.

21

The Hellroaring

General description: A trip starting inside Yellowstone National Park, hiking through the open terrain of northern Yellowstone and into the lush upper Hellroaring Country in the Absaroka-Beartooth Wilderness in Gallatin National Forest

Special attractions: Open remoteness and abundant wildlife

Type of trip: Loop

Total distance: 20 miles (32.2 kilometers)

Difficulty: Moderate

Traffic: Heavy in first and last 2 miles; light for rest of the trip

Maps: Trails Illustrated Mammoth Hot Springs and Tower Junction and Specimen Creek USGS quads

Starting point: Hellroaring Trailhead (2K8)

Finding the trailhead: Drive 14.5 miles east from Mammoth or 3.5 miles west from Tower and pull into the Hellroaring Trailhead. The actual trailhead is about a half-mile down an unpaved service road.

Parking and trailhead facilities: Ample parking; no facilities.

Recommended itinerary: Try a three-day trip staying two nights somewhere near the Hellroaring Guard Station, spending the second day of the hike day-hiking and fishing. This might be the most efficient way to do this trip, but it means long days with the overnight pack coming in and going out, so you could opt for a five-day trip by spending the first night at 2C1 or 2C2, the second and third nights near the Guard Station, and the fourth night in one of the many campsites along Hellroaring Creek.

The hike: This is not the most spectacular hike in this book, but it offers some special features not found on most other backpacking vacations.

The hike penetrates the uncrowded remoteness of the southern Absaroka Mountains. Such privacy is rare in today's popular hiking areas—even though about half of the trip lies within famous Yellowstone National Park.

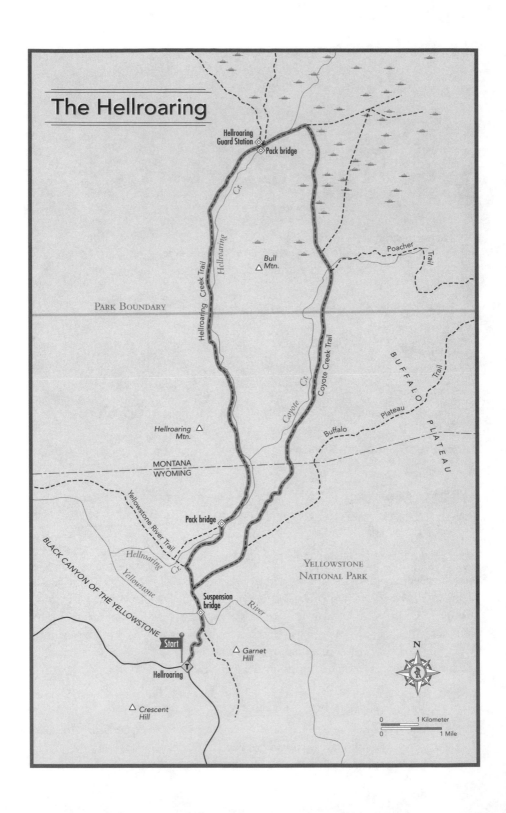

The Hellroaring

Hellroaring
Guard Station
Pack bridge

Hellroaring Creek Trail

Hellroaring Cr.

Bull
Mtn.

Poacher
Trail

PARK BOUNDARY

Coyote Creek Trail

Coyote Cr.

BUFFALO

Plateau

PLATEAU

Trail

Buffalo

Hellroaring △
Mtn.

MONTANA
WYOMING

Yellowstone River Trail

Pack bridge

Hellroaring Cr.

Yellowstone

YELLOWSTONE
NATIONAL PARK

BLACK CANYON OF THE YELLOWSTONE

Suspension
bridge

River

Start

Garnet
Hill

T

Hellroaring

△ Crescent
Hill

N

0   1 Kilometer
0   1 Mile

0.8 m.	Junction with trail to Tower; turn left
1.0	Suspension bridge over Yellowstone River
1.6	Junction with Coyote Creek/Buffalo Plateau Trail; turn right
2.1	Junction with trail to Buffalo Plateau Trail; turn left
6.0	2C1 (4★)
6.4	2C2 (4★)
6.7	Park boundary
7.2	FS Poacher Trail No. 98; turn left
9.5	FS Coyote Creek Trail No. 97; turn left
9.8	Hellroaring Bridge
10.2	Hellroaring Guard Station and Horse Creek Bridge
10.4	Junction with FS trail to Jardine; turn left
13.0	Park boundary
15.8	8H9 (3★)
16.3	Junction with trail to 8H8 (4★); trail down west side to creek and to 8H5 (4★), 8H3 (5★), and 8H1 (5★); a foot bridge; and trail down the east side of Hellroaring Creek; turn left and cross creek on bridge
17.8	8H6 (4★)
18.1	Junction with Yellowstone River Trail and spur trail to 8H4 (4★) and 8H2 (5★); turn left
18.4	Junction with trail to Coyote Creek and Buffalo Plateau; turn right
19.0	Suspension Bridge over Yellowstone River
19.2	Junction with trail to Tower; turn right
20.0	Hellroaring Trailhead

Also, expect to see large wildlife. Elk, moose, bison, and bears, including the mighty grizzly, are abundant in the area.

This trip makes a nice loop thanks to two trails (Hellroaring and Coyote Creeks) that head north out of the park, looping around a grassy butte called Bull Mountain, which is easily viewed from the Coyote Creek Trail.

In Yellowstone the trails go through low-altitude, dry, open terrain where you can hike in June on most years with no snowbanks. Hit the trail early to see wildlife that often retreats to shady day beds as the landscape heats up in late morning.

In September hundreds of big game hunters crowd into the area just north of the park boundary, most using horses and staying in large outfitter camps. In summer months however, the area is amazingly devoid of people.

The trail starts out with a steep drop through mostly open hillside to the suspension bridge over the Yellowstone River. From here, go another 0.6 mile to the junction with the Coyote Creek and Buffalo Plateau Trails. (Some maps for this area may have not been updated. The outdated maps show the Coyote Creek Trail coming up from Hellroaring Creek instead of branching out from the Buffalo Plateau Trail 0.5 mile after taking a right [north] at this junction.)

You can do this loop in either direction with little extra effort, but we took the coutnerclockwise route, so go right (north) at the Coyote Creek/Buffalo Plateau junction.

About a half mile after leaving the Yellowstone River Trail, the Buffalo Plateau Trail goes off to the right. You go left (north) on the Coyote Creek Trail. In another half-mile or so, you might see the abandoned trail coming up from Hellroaring Creek (abandoned but still visible on the ground and shown on many maps).

Before and after the park boundary, the trail goes into a partially burned forest and stays there for about a mile. I couldn't help notice that during this forested leg of the trip, the trail seemed to serve as a fire line with the trees on the west side of the trail green and unburnt and those on the east side victims of the 1988 fires.

After you go left (north) at the junction with the Poacher Trail (about a half mile north of the park), the trail breaks out on the east edge of a huge, marshy meadow. This is a very easy place to get on the wrong trail. Note on the map that the trail crosses this meadow and goes up the west side even though an excellent trail (not on most maps) continues up the east side of the meadow, tempting you to follow it. If you do, you won't be completely lost, but you'll add about a mile to your trip. Both trails intersect with the FS Coyote Creek Trail No. 97, about a half mile apart. Whichever trail you follow, turn left (west) when you reach the Coyote Creek Trail.

This section of the trip goes through a more lush forest than the lower stretches of Coyote and Hellroaring Creeks. Just before crossing Hellroaring Creek, the trail drops steeply for about a half-mile, making you happy you didn't do the trip in reverse.

Hellroaring is a huge stream even this far from its eventual merger with the Yellowstone, and the Forest Service has constructed a great bridge to handle the heavy horse traffic this area gets during the hunting season.

After the bridge, you pass through a large meadow and by the Hellroaring Guard Station. If you're staying overnight outside of the park, pick from the many nice campsites in this area. Four FS trails take off to the north and west from this area, but you keep turning left at all the junctions and follow Hellroaring Creek back to the park. After the guard station, the trail stays out-of-sight of the creek up on the west hillside and passes through mature lodgepole.

After the park boundary until just after 2H9, the trail stays away from the creek in timber. However, when we hiked this trail, we came through a live forest fire burning on both sides of the trail, including 2H9. Later, this fire burned north up to Hellroaring Guard Station. Since this lightning-caused fire was a natural part of the Yellowstone ecosystem (just like rain and wind), the NPS rightfully let it burn.

After breaking out into a series of large meadows, you reach the junction with the stock bridge over Hellroaring Creek. Unless you want to ford Hellroaring Creek, take a left (east) here. On the other side of the bridge, a spur trail to 2H8 goes off to the left and

Massive bridge over Hellroaring Creek near the guard station.

you go right (south), following the stream for 1.5 miles back to the Yellowstone River Trail where you go left (east) and retrace your steps back to the trailhead.

The trail is in excellent shape the entire way, but the many trail junctions (some not on maps) can be confusing, especially when you're outside of the park.

Options: You can do this loop in reverse, but it might be slightly more difficult because of the hill east of the Hellroaring Guard Station. You can also skip the loop option and go out-and-back into either Coyote or Hellroaring Creeks.

Side trips: Several trails juncture at the Hellroaring Guard Station, so you have plenty of options for side trips. We only had one extra day, so we took the Carpenter Lake loop. It's about 13 miles around the loop, including some confusing spots on the little-used Carpenter Lake Trail. The 1988 fires burned the Carpenter Lake area, including the lakeshore.

Camping: This route has designated campsites within Yellowstone National Park and undesignated camping areas outside the park. The designated campsites are indicated on the Tower/Canyon Trails Illustrated map. Stock-party-only sites are not included.

Coyote Creek: 2C1 (4★) a private, hiker-only site right along Coyote Creek. Good water source and tent sites. Protected from the elements. Marginal view.

2C2 (4★) is similar to 2C1 with a slightly better view but less privacy (only about 50 yards off trail).

Camping just north of Hellroaring guard station.

Hellroaring Creek: All nine campsites along Hellroaring Creek (described below) are excellent hiker-only sites. On the Trails Illustrated map it's difficult to see this, but the odd-numbered campsites are on the west side of the stream and the even-numbered on the east side. All of the sites are close to Hellroaring Creek with the stream serving as a readily accessible water source. None of the campsites allow campfires, but these campsites (as well as others farther down the river) prove that you can have a five-star camping experience without a campfire.

2H1 (5★) is at the confluence of Hellroaring Creek and the Yellowstone and has all the elements of a great campsite.

2H2 (5★) is also right at the confluence and even has a beach for lounging on a hot day. Tent sites are somewhat limited, so you might be tempted to pitch your tent on the beach, which would be a bad idea if it rained up in the headwaters of Hellroaring Creek.

2H3 (4★) is about a quarter-mile from the main trail and has a great view from the food area under a spreading spruce tree. Even though there is a trail going around the campsite, hikers going to 2H1 might pass through your camp.

2H4 (4★) is on your left as you approach Hellroaring Creek. In fact, the trail naturally goes downstream toward 2H4 and 2H2 so you might accidentally see this site when you're looking for the ford. It's a private site except for people going to 2H2 who come right through your camp.

2H5 (4★) is similar to 2H6, but it doesn't have quite as nice of a food area or view, and you have to labor down a very steep slope to get there.

2H6 (4★) is on your right about a half mile up Hellroaring Creek. It's private, and the food area and the view are slightly better than 2H5, which is just upstream on the other side of the creek.

2H7 (4★) is not quite as private as other campsites along Hellroaring Creek (about 100 yards off trail), but it is similar to the other sites in most respects. It lacks a well-defined food area.

2H8 (4★) is a private, hiker-only site about a half-mile north of the Hellroaring footbridge on a good spur trail right at the confluence of Hellroaring and Coyote Creeks. Good water source. No campfires allowed.

2H9 (3★) was closed when we hiked Hellroaring Creek because a lightning fire had burned right through the campsite. However, the NPS plans to keep it open. It's a hiker-only site about 50 feet off the trail on the west bank of Hellroaring Creek. Good water source and fair view, but a little too close to the trail.

Outside Yellowstone you'll find an abundance of excellent campsites around the Hellroaring Guard Station.

Fishing: Cutthroat abound throughout Hellroaring Creek and in lower Coyote Creek. If you have time, hike a mile or two down to the Yellowstone River for some superb cutthroat fishing. Carpenter Lake is loaded with cutthroats, but the tree-lined shoreline makes fly casting difficult.

22

Three Passes in the Absaroka

General description: A demanding route through the remote and uncrowded heart of the Absaroka Range

Special attractions: Three major passes in one trip and the chance to be alone in the wilderness

Type of trip: Loop

Total distance: 42.5 miles

Difficulty: Difficult, especially Speculator Pass

Traffic: Light

Maps: Forest Service—Absaroka-Beartooth Wilderness; Rocky Mountain Survey— Mt. Cowan Area; The Pyramid, West Boulder Plateau, Chrone Mountain, The Needles, Mount Cowan, Mount Rae USDA quads

Starting point: Fourmile Trailhead

Finding the trailhead: Take County Road 298 (locally called the Boulder River Road) south from Big Timber, Montana. The road does not turn off from either of the two Big Timber exits off Interstate 90. Instead, go into Big Timber and watch for signs to County Road 298, which heads south out of town and over the freeway about halfway between the two exits. From Big Timber, drive 42 miles to the Fourmile Trailhead on your right (west). You might want to top off your gas tank before leaving Big Timber. The first 24 miles of the road are paved. From the end of the pavement, the road is passable with two-wheel-drive vehicles, but it can be slow, dusty and full of giant potholes. Leave a vehicle or bicycle at the Speculator Trailhead four miles north of the Fourmile Trailhead, also on the right (west) side of the road. If you don't have an extra vehicle or a bicycle or can't arrange a pick up, you'll face a four-mile walk on the Boulder River Road at the end of the trip.

Parking and trailhead facilities: Minimal parking at both trailheads; no facilities.

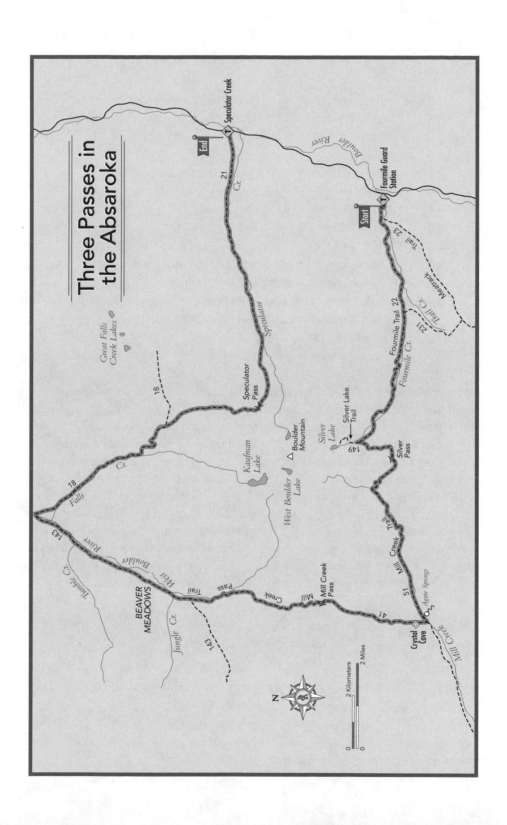

Three Passes in the Absaroka

Speculator Creek

End

Boulder River

Fourmile Guard Station

Start

Trail 23

Meadneck

Trail 231

Speculator Cr.

21

Fourmile Trail 22

Fourmile Cr.

Great Falls Creek Lakes

18

Speculator Pass

Silver Lake Trail

Silver Lake

Kaufman Lake

149

Silver Pass

18

Falls Cr.

△ Boulder Mountain

West Boulder Lake

143

West Boulder River

Mill Creek Trail

Mill Creek Pass

51

Tumble Cr.

BEAVER MEADOWS

Jungle Cr.

West Boulder Trail Pass

1A3

Mill Creek

41

Crystal Cove

Agate Springs

Mill Creek

N

0   2 Kilometers

0   2 Miles

1.0 m.	Junction with Meatrack Creek Trail 23; turn right
3.5	Junction with Trail Creek Trail 231; turn right
6.0	Junction with Silver Lake Trail 149; turn right
8.5	Silver Lake
11.5	Back to Fourmile Trail 22; turn right to Silver Pass
14.0	Silver Pass and start of Mill Creek Trail 51
18.0	Agate Springs and junction with Mill Creek Pass Trail 41; turn right
18.3	Crystal Cave
22.0	Mill Creek Pass
24.5	Junction with West Boulder Trail 143; turn right
25.5	Jungle Creek and start of Beaver Meadows
28.0	Falls Creek and junction with Falls Creek Trail 18; turn right
31.5	Junction with Speculator Creek Trail 21; turn right
33.5	Speculator Pass
42.5	Speculator Creek Trailhead and Boulder River Road

Recommended itinerary: We did this route in four days, but I wish we had taken five. It would have been a more enjoyable (though still difficult) trip. Even though it's 8.5 miles uphill (most of it gradual), I suggest trying to make it to Silver Lake, a delightful place, for the first night out. The next best option for the first campsite would be the junction of the Silver Lake and Fourmile Trails, which means a shorter day but a less spectacular campsite. Spend the second night along Mill Creek somewhere near the junction of the Mill Creek Pass Trail and Agate Springs, and the third night along the West Boulder or first part of Falls Creek. The last night out probably won't be your best, with the best choice probably being somewhere in the open meadows just over Speculator Pass. Once you get out of the meadows and into the thick lodgepole forest of Speculator Creek, good campsites are scarce. When we did this trip, we hiked from Silver Lake to Falls Creek in one day, which was too much, but we didn't have the extra day we needed.

First night: Silver Lake, 8.5 miles
Second night: Agate Springs, 9.5 miles
Third night: Falls Creek Junction, 10 miles
Fourth night: Upper Speculator Creek, 8 miles

The hike: As you do for many long backpacking trips, you have to get away from the trailheads for the best hiking. In this case, both the first few miles and the last few miles could be described as slightly boring as you hike through mature lodgepole forests without much topography. However, after breaking out of the lower elevation timberland, it doesn't get much better than this.

One note of caution: This is not a national park or a popular wilderness area. One disadvantage (or advantage?) of this is getting exact distances from maps or signs. Consequently, I had to estimate mileage more than I did for any other trip in this book.

This trip is for well-conditioned backpackers. After getting to the top of Speculator Pass you won't need to hit the Stairmaster machine for a while. But if you want to get ready for this trip, you should spend three hours a day on it.

Fourmile Trail 22 starts right at the Forest Service guard station and climbs steeply for about a mile before settling into a gradual ascent through lodgepole all of the way to the junction with the Silver Lake Trail 149, 6 miles from the trailhead. Two trails veer off to the left (south)—Meatrack Creek 23 (1 mile) and Trail Creek 231 (3.5 miles). You stay right (west) at both junctions. Just after the junction with the Meatrack Creek Trail, a major social trail goes off to the right. You stay left on the Fourmile Trail.

Along the way to the Silver Lake Trail junction, you pass through two large meadows. Finding water is not a problem as several small feeder streams come in from the north on their way to Fourmile Creek. The trail is in great shape all the way to the Silver Lake junction, kept that way by horse traffic, primarily during the fall hunting season. There definitely is not enough backpacker traffic to keep the trail distinct through the meadows. We did not, however, see a single stock party during our August trip.

At the Silver Lake junction, you have a decision. You've hiked 6 miles and might be ready to pitch the tent. There are some campsites in this area, but you probably will enjoy staying at Silver Lake much more than along Fourmile Creek. Plan to start early enough in the day to leave enough time and energy for the climb up to Silver Lake. You follow Fourmile Creek to its source, Silver Lake, and the last mile to the lake is quite steep. You'll be ready to stop when you get there.

Silver Lake.

Silver Lake is a truly beautiful place. Boulder Mountain and an awesome, serrated ridge extending from it provide a gorgeous backdrop. The horseshoe of mountain ridges rising up from three sides of the lake keeps the sun out of camp in early morning and evening. There are three or four good campsites, but this is a most fragile place, so please use the strictest zero-impact camping techniques. The lake has a healthy population of rainbows, but they are smart and skittish. One fly line on the water sends them to the other end of the lake.

After a wonderful night in the five-star hotel called Silver Lake, retrace your steps back to the Silver Lake junction and turn right. You might get your feet wet, depending on how high the water is, when you cross Fourmile Creek.

It's about 1,700 feet in about 2.5 miles to 9,673-foot Silver Pass, a demanding Category 1 climb. However, the trail has a nice grade with well-designed switchbacks that make it seem moderately easy. The steepest parts are right after Fourmile Creek and the last quarter mile to the pass.

Unfortunately, we did this section in a pouring rain and fog, so I didn't see what surely was some spectacular scenery. The trail is well-defined up to about a half mile from the pass where it can get confusing. In fact, there is one place where it is easy to get off the main trail and onto a major social trail veering to the right (north). If you start going downhill on a trail marked with cairns, hit the brakes and backtrack to the main trail.

Silver Pass is an austere, knife-edged ridge. You can see an old "silvery" sign marking the pass from a half-mile below. When we did this, it was so wet that we couldn't keep our footing and had to virtually crawl up the last hundred yards, which is very steep. Once on top, though, we experienced the exhilaration of unbridled remoteness. I loved the old, weathered sign on Silver Pass—oh, the stories it could tell!

Silver Pass.

But keep in mind that this is only the first of three major passes on this trip—and definitely not the most difficult.

Silver Pass is part of the major east-west divide that forms the backbone of the Absaroka Range. On the pass, Fourmile Trail 22 becomes Mill Creek Trail 51. After enjoying Silver Pass, head down toward Mill Creek on switchbacks for about a mile before the trails enters a fairly open forest. On the way to Agate Springs, you cross Mill Creek two more times than those crossings shown on the topo maps for the area. Sorry, no bridges. This is the wilderness, not a national park. When we hiked Upper Mill Creek, heavy rain had turned Mill Creek into a brown, silt-laden torrent, and we actually had a hard time finding clean water to drink. There were, however, lots of huckleberries to eat.

After spending a night along Mill Creek somewhere near the junction (no trail sign when I was there), go right (north) on Mill Creek Pass Trail No. 41, heading toward Mill Creek Pass. About a quarter mile up the trail from Mill Creek, stop briefly to see Crystal Cave. As you'll note, this isn't much of a cave, but there are several major caves in this area. Local cavers spend lots of time around here exploring and mapping the caves, but they carefully conceal the locations of the caves to preserve them from overuse and notoriety.

The trail climbs steeply for the first 1.5 miles but switchbacks make the climb easier. Then, the switchbacks end, the trail straightens out, and the grade gets gradual for about a mile before heading up another series of switchbacks all the way to the pass. The well-defined trail stays in the timber until just before the pass and gains 2,400 feet in 4 miles from Mill Creek, another Category 1 climb (but easier than Silver Pass) to another spot on the Absaroka Divide.

From Mill Creek Pass you get a spectacular view to the north down the West Boulder River Valley, The Pyramid and Crow Mountain to the south, and a sweeping panorama of wild country in all directions.

As the trail descends into the West Boulder from the pass, it fades away twice. You can stay on track, however, by following a series of well-placed cairns. After a short, steep section on top, the well-defined trail gradually descends all the way to Falls Creek. The West Boulder Valley is more open with lots of beautiful meadows and is arguably more scenic than Fourmile Creek or Mill Creek. The West Boulder River is also a much larger stream especially after Tumble Creek and Falls Creek join in.

You can go all the way to Falls Creek to camp, or you can pick one of many campsites along the way. It would be challenging to find a bad campsite in this scenic valley. If you have any extra time, you can exercise members of the abundant cutthroat population in the river.

So far on this trip, you have had many stream crossings, but crossing the West Boulder at Falls Creek might qualify as a ford, so be careful, especially early in July when the river will be close to maximum levels. When you get across Falls Creek and start heading toward Speculator Pass, you are entering one of the wildest drainages in the Absaroka Range. The trail is less-defined and brushy, as it follows cascading (and well-named) Falls Creek. The scenery is amazing in this, the fourth of five mountain valleys you hike through on this trip. As you hike up Falls Creek, you are treated with views of Boulder Mountain, the Needles, and, in the distance, The Pyramid.

About 3.5 miles up from the West Boulder, you see the junction with Speculator Trail 21. Trail 18 goes left (east) to Great Falls Creek Lakes and out to the Boulder River Road. You can take this route, but you'll be a long way from your vehicle, and you'll miss Speculator Pass, so go right (south) toward the pass.

At this point the trail significantly worsens and becomes difficult to follow. This is not a popular route, so you might have to use some route-finding skills and even get the compass out here and there. However, the route to the pass is fairly obvious even if you get off the trail momentarily.

The scenery is incredible and rugged, climbing 3,300 feet in 5.5 miles from the West Boulder River. Actually, the last 2 miles up to Speculator Pass, a rare Category H hill, is the steepest designated trail I have ever hiked. Your lungs will feel it, and your calves will get stretched out.

On top of the pass we had fun speculating on why it was named Speculator Pass. One theory was that there was speculation whether you could make it at all or have a heart attack trying to get up there. Another theory was that some mountain man couldn't spell spectacular, so he jotted down speculator. In any regard, you won't forget Speculator Pass.

On the south side of Speculator Pass, the trail goes through open Upper Speculator Creek and disappears in several places. This section will test your route-finding skills. While trying to stay on the trail, keep you eye open for a good campsite.

After spending your last night in the extreme wildness of Upper Speculator Creek, you hike through a lodgepole forest similar to Fourmile Creek all the way to the Boulder River Road. This stretch of trail seems to go on forever. We were wasted after climbing three passes, and I couldn't stop thinking about that big steak I planned to attack aggressively as soon as I could find a restaurant.

At the trailhead you need to hang your packs and take an easy 4-mile stroll up to the Fourmile Trailhead where you left your vehicle. When we did this trip, I stashed an old bicycle at the Speculator Trailhead and rode back to my vehicle.

Options: If you aren't quite ready for the wildness of the Speculator Pass area, you can hike out to the Boulder River Road by going out Great Falls Creek, which is, oddly, only a mile or two shorter than going out Speculator Creek. You need two vehicles to do this route because it's 11 miles up the Boulder River Road to get back to the Fourmile Trailhead.

You could also skip Falls Creek and keep going out the West Boulder for 8 gradually descending miles to the West Boulder Trailhead and a vehicle campground. This is a nice hike with a long shuttle.

And for a really, really long shuttle, you could keep going down Mill Creek and come out at the Mill Creek Trailhead in the Paradise Valley near Pray, Montana. It's an easy 7 miles from Agate Springs to the Mill Creek Trailhead.

Side trips: Silver Lake could be a side trip instead of the first campsite. Depending on how early you hit the trail, you can pitch your tent somewhere around the junction with the Silver Lake Trail and day hike up to the lake. Great Falls Creek lakes might look like a nice side trip, but make sure you have plenty of daylight left to get over the intensely demanding Speculator Pass.

Photo op on Speculator Pass.

Camping: Regulations allow you to set up a zero-impact campsite anywhere along this route. Be especially careful not to leave your mark in the nearly untouched meadows at the head of Upper Speculator Creek.

Fishing: Silver Lake has some nice rainbows, but they've seen a few flies, so be stealthy. Mill Creek has some nice cutthroats, as well as a few rainbows and browns, but fishing is fairly lean at the upper stretches of the creek along the route of this hike. The upper stretches of the West Boulder are great fishing for small cutthroat, and as you get farther downstream, you might snag a brown or rainbow.

Hiking among Grand Teton, Mount Moran, and the other famous peaks of the Teton Range can put things in perspective. It's easy to feel unimportant and Lilliputian in the shadow of such grandeur.

Grand Teton National Park probably has the most famous wilderness skyline in the country. It shows up on millions of postcards, calendars, magazine and book covers, and television ads every year. But to appreciate this amazing place, just looking at it is not enough. You really need to go there and hike through the deep canyons gouged out by glaciers and over the big divides to feel the true essence of these mountains.

On some trails you have lots of company, but on others you can be alone. In either case, however, you can feel it.

For outstanding mountain scenery, Grand Teton is, quite simply, the best.

WHAT IT'S REALLY LIKE

Here are a few things you might want to know about hiking in Grand Teton National Park.

Prime season. The best time to hike Grand Teton is August and September. Snow buries the high peaks each winter, and it takes until mid-July to melt off, sometimes even later on the high trails like Hurricane Pass, Paintbrush Divide, and Moose Basin Divide.

Weather. It can snow any day of the year in Grand Teton, so always be prepared for cold weather. Normal weather patterns (if there are such things) in the summer create clear mornings with thundershowers in the mid-afternoons, followed by clear, coolish evenings. This means early morning hikers usually enjoy better weather, and they more often get their tents set up before it rains. And June can frequently (but not always) be a fairly wet month in Grand Teton.

Moose country. This is definitely moose country. In fact, it's difficult to go hiking all day in Grand Teton without seeing moose. Enjoying watching them, but stay out of the way. Moose do not yield to hikers.

Bears. Grand Teton has bears, both the common black bear and its larger, more cantankerous cousin, the grizzly. You probably won't see the latter, but as the population in the greater Yellowstone area grows, the number of grizzlies in Grand Teton will gradually increase. Already, grizzlies are more common in the northern and less frequently used sections of the park, but all of the Grand Teton should be considered grizzly country. And all bears—black and grizzly—are dangerous, so take all the standard precautions. Refer to the Bear Aware section on pages 19–28.

The canyons. Many hikes in Grand Teton leave the valley floor and penetrate the Teton Range via deep, glacier-scoured canyons. The canyons serve as pathways into the high peaks. They are usually steep in the first few miles and then they level out and you're surrounded by steep-walled majesty on your way up a spectacular pass or divide.

Bugs. Perhaps the two summers I hiked Grand Teton were off years for the mosquito populations, but I have to say that there seem to be fewer of these pesky insects here than in most places in the Rocky Mountains. In the Beartooths or Yellowstone, the mosquitoes can block out the sun on a clear day, but in Grand Teton, I only took out the repellent once (in Glade Creek), which is unusual to say the least.

Large furry things on the road. When hurrying to get to the trailhead in the early morning hours or anxiously driving home in the evening, be especially watchful for large wildlife on the roadways. Hitting a moose or antelope will certainly ruin your day, and it's even harder on the animal.

Hiker friendly. In some national parks, it's easy to feel over-regulated. However, Grand Teton National Park has made special efforts to provide the freedom of choice and to limit the number of regulations. For example, most camping zones in this park have "indicated" campsites where you can camp, but you are allowed to set up camp anywhere in the zone. Most parks have designated sites where you are required to camp.

Research pays. It's amazing how pleasant and stress free your hiking trip to Grand Teton National Park can be when it's well planned. The following information should help you plan your trip.

GETTING TO GRAND TETON NATIONAL PARK

Grand Teton National Park is in northwestern Wyoming, just south of Yellowstone National Park. You can drive to the park from Salt Lake City on Interstate 15 north to Logan, Utah, connecting to U.S. Highway 89 through Idaho and Wyoming to Jackson, Wyoming, and Grand Teton National Park. You can also take U.S. Highway 26 east from Idaho Falls, Idaho, to Jackson or west from Dubois or Casper, Wyoming. From Montana, you can drive through Yellowstone National Park (a slow but scenic route) or take U.S. Highway 20 south of West Yellowstone, Montana, and turning off onto Idaho Highway 32 and 33 over Teton Pass to Jackson, Wyoming.

Since federal highways pass through the park, you can see parts of Grand Teton without paying an entrance fee. Entrance stations are located on the Teton Park Road just west of the Moose Visitor Center, at the Moran Junction, and on the Moose-Wilson Road just south of the Granite Canyon Trailhead. Expect to pay a fee to enter the park at these stations.

The roads to the park are well maintained, but only two-lanes, and often crowded with traffic, including slow-moving vehicles. If you drive during midday, don't be in a hurry. Unlike roads in neighboring Yellowstone Park, the roads within Grand Teton are generally in good shape.

You can also fly to a small Jackson Hole airport with limited jet service just north of Jackson, Wyoming. The airport is actually within the boundaries of the park.

GETTING A BACKCOUNTRY PERMIT

In Grand Teton National Park, you must have a permit for all overnight use of the backcountry. Get these permits at visitor centers at Moose and Colter Bay and at the Jenny Lake Ranger Station. Be sure to ask the National Park Service for a backcountry camping brochure that includes most of the basic information you need to get a permit. Get a copy by contacting:

Backcountry Office, Grand Teton National Park, P.O. Drawer 170, Moose, WY 83012-0170; (307) 739–3602, fax: (307) 739–3438.

Grand Teton has a backcountry permit reservation system, but only for designated sites such as Marion Lake and Holly Lake. No reservations are available for open camping areas. Designated sites can be reserved from January 1 through May 15 for $15 per trip, regardless of the number of people or the length on the trip. The NPS allows up to one-third of the designated sites to be reserved. Permits requested at park visitor centers and ranger stations are free but must be given out within twenty-four hours before the start of your trip.

Reservations must be sent in by mail or fax to the backcountry office or can be applied for in person at the Moose Visitor Center, open daily from 8:00 A.M. to 5:00 P.M. Include the following information: name, address, daytime phone number, number of people in your party, preferred campsites, and preferred dates. If possible, include alternate campsites and dates. The NPS will send out a written confirmation. Telephone reservations are not accepted, but you can get information by calling (307) 739–3309 or (307) 739–3397. Include a check with your permit request.

Your reservation holds your permit, but you still need to pick up your permit no later than 10:00 A.M. the day your trip starts. If you fail to pick it up by then, it will become available to others. If you're running a little late, you can call ahead and the NPS will hold your permit.

If you have a reservation but are unable to take the trip, be sure to notify the NPS and cancel your reservation so the campsites can be made available to others. No refunds are given for canceled reservations.

BACKCOUNTRY CAMPING POLICY

Some national parks have policies that can hardly be described as "hiker friendly," and consequently, it's easy to feel overregulated. However, Grand Teton has a hiker-friendly backcountry policy. For example, consider these long-range goals, which come from the park's backcountry management plan:

- Provide visitors to the backcountry with a high-quality experience.
- Provide for a range of levels of solitude.

- Provide for visitor use of the backcountry with a minimum level of restrictions.

- Provide hikers in pristine areas with the opportunity to have the same type of wilderness experience that people would have had before Europeans arrived in this area.

To allow more people to enjoy the backcountry, the NPS limits campsite use to no more than two nights in the same site and to ten nights per summer.

Quotas are set to prevent overuse, and party size is limited to six people. If you have a larger party (up to twelve allowed), you must camp at a designated group site.

In 1973 the NPS banned all campfires in the park above 7,000 feet elevation. Only designated, low-elevation sites have fire grills where campfires can be built.

Backcountry camping is allowed at designated sites at backcountry lakes like Marion or Holly Lakes or in camping zones. The camping zones have indicated sites, which are usually convenient and well-placed. However, you can set up a zero-impact camp anywhere in the camping zone. You do not have to camp at the indicated sites. In some cases, the NPS also allows off-trail camping.

BACKCOUNTRY-USE REGULATIONS

Backcountry-use regulations aren't intended to complicate your life, but rather to help preserve the natural landscape and protect park visitors. The following backcountry-use regulations are distributed to hikers when they get their permits.

In Grand Teton, you must:
- Have a permit for all overnight stays in the backcountry.
- Carefully follow the instructions on the permit.
- Build campfires only in designated fire pits at certain low-elevation campsites. Use only collected dead and down wood. Keep fires small, and do not leave them unattended. Backpacking stoves are encouraged.
- Use food storage poles or boxes or suspend food at least 10 feet above the ground and 4 feet horizontally from a post or tree.
- Carry out all trash. If you can pack it in, you can pack it out.
- Hold a valid Wyoming state fishing permit if you're fishing the waters of Grand Teton.

In Grand Teton, you must not:
- Feed, touch, tease, frighten, or intentionally disturb wildlife.
- Take pets into the backcountry.
- Make campsite "improvements" such as fire rings, rock walls, log benches, drainage, trenches, etc.
- Possess or operate a motorized vehicle, bicycle, wheeled vehicle, or cart in any undeveloped area or on any backcountry trail.

- Dispose of human waste within 200 feet of any water source or campsite or within sight of a trail.
- Possess, destroy, injure, deface, remove, dig, or disturb from its natural state any plant, rock, animal, mineral, cultural, or archeological resource.
- Use or possess weapons, traps, or nets.
- Cut switchbacks.
- Wash dishes or bathe in park streams or lakes.

FINDING MAPS

In addition to the USGS quads for each hike (specific maps are listed with each trip), there are two excellent map sources for Grand Teton National Park. A local company, Earthwalk Press, owned by a couple (a ranger-naturalist team) who have worked for the park for many years, produces a wonderful map, Hiking Map and Guide: Grand Teton National Park. Trails Illustrated also publishes an excellent map for the park. Both maps are available at the Moose Visitor Center or local sporting goods stores. In advance of your trip, you can order both maps from the Grand Teton Natural History Association (with the profit going to benefit the park) through their Web site: www.grand tetonpark.org.

You can also contact the association as follows:

Grand Teton Natural History Association
P.O. Box 170
Moose, WY 83012
Phone: (307) 739–3606
e-mail: info@grandtetonpark.org

The NPS hands out a free map when you enter the park. Take this along as a reference, too. It is not detailed enough to satisfy your needs, but it often has the most current information concerning trail reroutings, closures or regulations.

FOR MORE INFORMATION

For a great summary of basic facts on visiting Grand Teton, call the main park number (see below) and ask for a copy of *Teewinot,* a free newspaper published by the Grand Teton Natural History Association. You can also get a copy at the entrance station when you enter the park. The paper contains a list of commercial services available in and near the park, updates on park road construction, lists of ranger-led activities, events, and guided tours, campgrounds, medical and emergency services and facilities, area museums, special exhibits, and lots more useful information. *Teewinot* will answer most of your questions about services in the park. Because of budget cuts, the NPS is sometimes unable to keep up with all visitor inquiries, so please be patient when trying to get your questions answered. There are many books and other publications on Grand

Teton that provide a wealth of excellent information, and there are often better ways to get information than calling the NPS directly. Many of these publications are available at park visitor centers.

Contact Grand Teton National Park by mail, phone, or Internet:

National Park Service, Park Headquarters, P.O. Drawer 170, Moose, WY 83012-0170; (307) 739–3600; www.grand.teton.national-park.com/.

For information on lodging within the park, contact the Grand Teton Lodge Company:

Grand Teton Lodge Company, P.O. Box 250, Moran, WY 83013; (307) 543–2881; www.gtlc.com.

A moose visits our camp at Phelps Lake on the Grand Teton loop.

23

The Teton Crest

General description: A multiday adventure starting from 10,450 feet elevation

Special attractions: The best trip on trails through the high country of Grand Teton National Park, featuring truly spectacular scenery

Type of trip: A long shuttle

Total distance: 35.4 miles

Difficulty: Difficult

Traffic: Moderate

Maps: Earthwalk Press Grand Teton map; NPS handout map; Teton Village, Rendezvous Peak, Mt. Bannon, Grand Teton, Granite Basin, Mt. Moran, and Jenny Lake USGS quads

Starting point: Top of Aerial Tramway at Teton Village

Finding the trailhead: Take the Aerial Tramway behind the main ski lodge in Teton Village to the top of Rendezvous Mountain to start this hike. Teton Village is 12.5 miles northwest of Jackson. From Jackson, take Wyoming Highway 22 west of Jackson for 6 miles to the Moose-Wilson Road junction, just before entering the small town of Wilson. Turn right (north) here, and go 6.5 miles, and turn left (west) into Teton Village.

Leave a vehicle at the Leigh Lake Trailhead at the String Lake Picnic Area. To find this trailhead take U.S. 89 north of Jackson for 11.5 miles and turn left (west) at the Moose junction. Drive past the visitor center and through the entrance station (1 mile after turning off the highway). Follow this paved park road for another 9.7 miles from the entrance station to the Jenny Lake turnoff. Turn left (west) here and drive 0.6 mile (follow the signs and take two right turns) to the String Lake Trailhead and the 0.3 mile farther to the String Lake Picnic Area. The Leigh Lake Trailhead is in the northwest corner of the picnic area. If you're coming from the north, drive 9.9 miles from the Jackson Lake junction and turn right (west) at the Jenny Lake turnoff. There are toilet facilities in the picnic area at the Leigh Lake Trailhead.

Parking and trailhead facilities: Parking in the main ski lodge parking lot; restaurants, shopping, and rest rooms in the Teton Village Lodge.

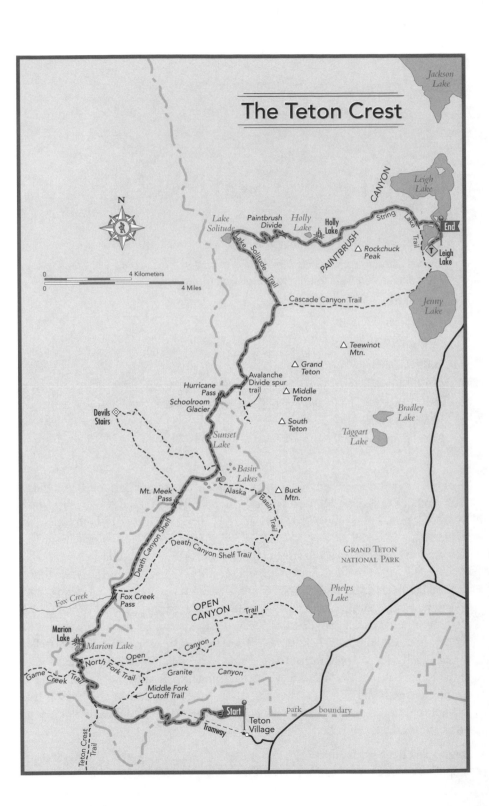

The Teton Crest

Jackson Lake

Leigh Lake

CANYON

Lake Solitude *Paintbrush Divide* *Holly Lake* **Holly Lake** String Lake Trail **End**

N

PAINTBRUSH △ Rockchuck Peak **Leigh Lake**

Lake Solitude Trail

Cascade Canyon Trail *Jenny Lake*

0   4 Kilometers
0   4 Miles

△ Teewinot Mtn.

△ Grand Teton

Avalanche Divide spur trail

Hurricane Pass △ Middle Teton

Schoolroom Glacier *Bradley Lake*

Devils Stairs ◇ *Sunset Lake* △ South Teton *Taggart Lake*

Basin Lakes

Mt. Meek Pass Alaska Basin △ Buck Mtn.

Basin Trail

Death Canyon Shelf

Death Canyon Shelf Trail **GRAND TETON NATIONAL PARK**

Fox Creek *Phelps Lake*

Fox Creek Pass **OPEN CANYON** Trail

Marion Lake

Marion Lake Open Canyon

North Fork Trail Granite Canyon

Game Creek Trail

Middle Fork Cutoff Trail **Start**

Tramway Teton Village park   boundary

Teton Crest Trail

0.4 m.	Junction with tram service road and park boundary; turn right
3.9	Junction with Middle Fork Cutoff Trail; turn left
4.4	Junction with Teton Crest Trail; turn right
5.4	Junction with Game Creek Trail; turn right
6.0	Junction with North Fork Trail; turn left
6.6	Marion Lake
7.0	Park boundary
8.8	Junction with trail down Fox Creek; turn right
8.9	Fox Creek Pass and junction with Death Canyon Shelf Trail; turn left
12.4.	Mount Meek Pass and park boundary
12.6	Junction with trail to Devils Stairs; turn right
14.4	Basin Lakes
14.6	Junction with trail to Buck Mountain Pass; turn left
15.4	Junction with second trail to Buck Mountain Pass; turn left
15.7	Sunset Lake
17.4	Schoolroom Glacier and Hurricane Pass
19.0	Junction with trail to Avalanche Divide; turn left
22.5	Junction with Cascade Canyon Trail; turn left
25.2	Lake Solitude
27.6	Paintbrush Divide
28.9	Junction with spur trail to Holly Lake; turn left
29.2	Holly Lake
29.7	Return to main trail in Paintbrush Canyon; turn left
33.9	Junction with String Lake Trail; turn left
34.6	Junction with Leigh Lake Trail; turn right
35.4	Leigh Lake Trailhead and String Lake Picnic Area

Recommended itinerary:

First night:	Marion Lake
Second night:	Death Canyon Shelf
Third night:	South Fork Cascade Canyon
Fourth night:	North Fork Cascade Canyon
Fifth night:	Holly Lake

The hike: It really doesn't get any better than this. The Teton Crest and the Grand Teton Loop represent the two truly classic backpacking trips in Grand Teton National Park. This trip is longer but easier since it has the incredible luxury of starting at 10,450 feet and ending at 6,875 feet, a net loss of 3,575. That's not to say, however, that there is not any hill climbing. Quite to the contrary, you get to sweat your way up three big hills, including the two most famous in the park—Hurricane Pass and Paintbrush Divide. And, of course, you go by the three most famous high country lakes—Marion Lake, Lake Solitude, and Holly Lake. And lastly, you get the best mountain scenery possible, including several miles in the shadow of the Grand Teton.

What more could you want? Well, you want good weather, a week off, and the advanced physical conditioning necessary to enjoy it all.

There aren't many hikes that start out downhill, but if you take the aerial tramway from Teton Village, this can be one of them. As you stand at the main ski lodge in Teton Village, you have a tough choice. You can carry your backpack stuffed with six days of food and gas up 4,100 feet over 6.6 miles of constantly switchbacking service road or you can ride up the tram in ten minutes without breaking a sweat. Think about it!

Obviously, most people choose the tram, which leaves every fifteen minutes from 9:00 A.M. to 7:30 P.M. There is a small fee.

Be sure to keep your map out. This route has an unusually high number of junctions, and it would be possible to get on the wrong trail without carefully following the map.

From the tram hike down a steep ridgeline to the junction with the tram service road and the park boundary. Take this first leg of your trip slowly so you can soak in the incredible view of the Teton Range to the north, including Grand Teton peeping over the skyline (you'll be on the other side of it three days later).

At the park boundary turn right and take one big switchback down the steep slope of Rendezvous Mountain into a bowl. You can see the trail heading up on the other side of the bowl. After the descent through some talus and subalpine vegetation, you move into spruce forest interspersed with large meadows. You hike through this type of terrain until Marion Lake where you climb up to the alpine country along the Teton Crest Trail. In August and September this route can be dry, as several intermittent streams dry up, so carry plenty of water. Horses are not allowed on the first 3.9 miles of this trail.

When you get to the next junction, take a left (northeast) and then turn right (north) at the next two junctions to Moose Creek Pass and Game Creek, until you drop down into the North Fork of Granite Creek below Marion Lake, where you hit another junction. Turn left (north) and tackle a short but steep climb up to the lake.

Marion Lake is a little jewel tucked in the shadow of mighty Housetop Mountain and surrounded by wildflower-carpeted meadows. Even if you aren't camping here, plan on spending some serious time at the lake. It's too nice to view quickly and then abandon, so this makes a good spot for the first night out.

After you stay at Marion Lake, you face a 0.4-mile hill up to the park boundary and an unnamed divide on the flanks of Housetop Mountain. From here over to Fox Creek Pass is mostly level, alpine hiking with great views all around, especially aptly named Spearhead Mountain off to your right (east).

Just before reaching Fox Creek Pass, there is a slightly confusing junction (no sign when we were there) with a trail heading off to the left (west) down Fox Creek into the Jedediah Smith Wilderness. Turn right (north) here, and just over a small hill you'll see Fox Creek Pass and the park boundary. At the pass you can go right down Death Canyon or left (south) and continue along the Teton Crest Trail on Death Canyon Shelf.

Day hikers on the first leg of the Teton Crest.

The next 11 miles—from Marion Lake to Fox Creek Pass, along Death Canyon Shelf, over Mount Meek Divide, through Alaska Basin, and up to Hurricane Pass—are the absolute essence of the Teton Range, the choicest of the choice for mountain scenery. Even though I have been backpacking for more than thirty years, this was a truly memorable stretch of trail, and I'm sure it will be for you, too.

Death Canyon Shelf is a flat bench on the east flanks of a series of awesome peaks—Fossil Mountain, Bannon Peak, Mount Jedediah Smith and Mount Meek. To the east you can look down Death Canyon all the way to Jackson Hole looming in the distance. The shelf is a great choice for the second night out. It's exposed to weather, so be prepared. Also, water can be hard to find late in the season.

From Mount Meek Divide, you drop down into gorgeous Alaska Basin. Several small lakes dot the basin—and there is a labyrinth of trails. All are distinct and well signed, however, so you should not have a problem finding your way past Basin Lakes and Sunset Lake and up to Hurricane Pass. There was a hurricane wind when we were there, and I suspect this is a common occurrence.

From the pass you can see it all, including the Grand Teton (and Middle and South Teton), Mount Moran to the north, and right below you, Schoolroom Glacier. Unless the weather prohibits a long stay (as it did when we were there) spend some quality time on Hurricane Pass identifying all the peaks.

The trip from Marion Lake to Hurricane Pass might have been the best ever, but the section between the pass and Holly Lake rivals it for scenic beauty. The trail down Hurricane Pass is steep right at top, but soon becomes a nicely switchbacked trail. If you

Hurricane Pass.

have some extra time, set up camp near the top of the South Fork Camping Zone and take a side trip up toward the Avalanche Divide for a close-up view of the three tetons.

After a night along the South Fork of Cascade Creek, drop down to the junction with the main trail up Cascade Canyon. You could bail out at this point and go down to the Jenny Lake west shore boat dock, but if you do, you miss Lake Solitude and the Paintbrush Divide, so go left (northwest) at this junction.

The trail up the North Fork of Cascade Creek is forested at first, but soon breaks out into subalpine meadows and a virtual kaleidoscope of wildflowers. It's 2.7 miles to Lake Solitude, but you probably want to set up your fourth camp somewhere near the top of the North Fork Camping Zone. Then, it will only be a short walk up to Lake Solitude after camp has been set up. Lake Solitude is remote, but sometimes not as quiet as it used to be. It's now a popular destination, so during the day, expect to see other hikers in the area.

After the fourth night below Lake Solitude, psyche yourself up for the biggest hill of the trip, the 2.4 miles up to 10,700-foot Paintbrush Divide. The trail is in great shape, and when you stop to rest, you have some great scenery to enjoy—Lake Solitude and Mica Lake below and Grand Teton off to the southeast.

The Paintbrush Divide is not quite as awesome as Hurricane Pass, but it's a very close second. After soaking up the scenery for a while, start down the divide into Paintbrush Canyon on one big switchback through a talus slope and, even in September, over some snowbanks clinging to this north-facing slope. In fact, in many years it's dangerous until August to try this slope without an ice axe. Before you leave on this trip, be sure to quiz a ranger on the snow conditions on the Paintbrush Divide. If an ice axe is recommended, be sure you know how to use it for self-rescue if you fall. If this is beyond your capabilities, delay this trip until snow conditions improve.

If you're going the entire five-night trip, plan on Holly Lake for your last night in paradise. The junction is only 1.3 miles from the divide, but it's another 0.3 mile uphill to the lake and about that far over to the campsites on the east end of the cirque containing Holly Lake.

After your stay at Holly Lake, take the rest of the cutoff trail left (east) from the lake and rejoin the main trail down Paintbrush Canyon 0.4 mile from the lake. From here, you gradually drop out of the high country into the mature forest of the low country.

When you get to the junction with the String Lake Trail, go left (east) and hike a mere 0.7 mile to the bridge over the short stream between String Lake and Leigh Lake and to the junction with the Leigh Lake Trail just on the other side of the bridge. From here turn right (south) and hike a super-flat 0.8 mile along String Lake back to the Leigh Lake Trailhead and String Lake Picnic Area parking lot, where you are likely to feel somewhat remorseful for realizing this is the end of a truly remarkable backpacking trip.

Options: This hike can be taken in reverse, but you face more climbing because you won't start at the top of Rendezvous Mountain. You can bail out and make the trip shorter by coming down Death Canyon or Cascade Canyon.

Side trips: If you have the time and energy, try the side trips up to the Static Peak Divide and the Avalanche Divide.

Camping: For the first night out, you have four choices. Marion Lake has three heavily used campsites with a good water source, nice views (although you can only see the lake

Hikers coming down the Paintbrush Divide into Lake Solitude.

Holly Lake with Leigh and Jackson Lakes in the distance.

from the first campsite and then just barely) and two raised tent pads each. This lake may be the best choice for the first night out because it's nicely located at 6.6 miles from the aerial tram. Although they would not be as convenient, the Middle Fork or Upper Granite Canyon Camping Zones are also possibilities. Upper Granite has nicer campsites along the stream with good water sources. The Middle Fork campsites generally offer better views, but water can be scarce in many areas, especially in late August and September when intermittent streams dry up. Marion Lake has designated campsites, but the two camping zones allow you to find your own campsite. For the fourth choice you can hike past Marion Lake and camp outside the park.

For the second night you probably want to strive for the Death Canyon Shelf, an open camping zone with no designated campsites. Water is scarce on the south part of the shelf, but adequately abundant from the midpoint on. The scenery from camp will be the best possible. There's enough room to find privacy, and rest assured that the air conditioning will be on.

If you're trying to cover this route with four nights out, hike past the shelf and camp anywhere in Alaska Basin. This is outside the park, so NPS regulations don't apply. However, be sure to walk softly and set up a zero-impact camp in this fragile highland.

For the next night out, you can go for either the South Fork or North Fork camping zones. Both areas have indicated sites, but you can camp anywhere in these zones. The indicated sites are nicely set up, however, so I can't imagine wanting to find something new. All of these campsites (and there are plenty), are five- or four-star. The main issue is how far you want to go that day. You won't be disappointed with the campsite. The camping in the North Fork is probably even nicer than in the South Fork because most sites come with a stunning view of Grand Teton.

Holly Lake has three designated campsites. These campsites are about a quarter mile from the lake at the end of a trail that crosses the outlet on rocks and goes up on a slope above the lake. Campsite No. 3 is the most private, but surprisingly, the campsites do not have a good view right from camp. Water is fairly accessible from all three sites, which have two tent pads each and share a bear box.

The lower Paintbrush Canyon camping zone has nine indicated campsites strategically located on high points above the trail. Most of them are private (about 100 yards from the trail) but have only one tent pad (the NPS plans to add more later). Some of them have a fairly long hike to water. Most of the campsites are five-star with a good view.

You can also camp in the Upper Paintbrush Camping Zone along the main trail below Holly Lake. This zone requires a different permit than camping at Holly Lake even though they are not far apart.

Fishing: No real fishing opportunities on this route.

Snow banks linger until early August in Alaska Basin.

24

The Grand Teton Loop

General description: A classic circuit around the high peaks of the Teton Range

Special attractions: A rare opportunity to experience both the austere high country and the gentle low country of Grand Teton National Park on the same trip

Type of trip: Loop

Total distance: 32.6 miles

Difficulty: Difficult

Traffic: Moderate to heavy

Maps: Earthwalk Press Grand Teton map; NPS handout map; and Jenny Lake, Mt. Moran, Granite Basin, Mt. Bannon, Grand Teton, and Moose USGS quads

Starting point: Jenny Lake west shore boat dock

Finding the trailhead: Take U.S. 89 north of Jackson for 11.5 miles and turn left (west) at the Moose junction. Drive past the visitor center and through the entrance station (1 mile after turning off the highway). Follow this paved park road for another 6.8 miles from the entrance station to the South Jenny Lake turnoff. Turn left (west) here and drive less than a half mile to the South Jenny Lake boat dock and visitor center. If you're coming from the north, drive 12.8 miles from the Jackson Lake junction and turn right (west) at the South Jenny Lake turnoff. From the South Jenny boat dock, take the short boat ride across the lake to the west shore boat dock. The boat leaves every fifteen to twenty minutes; there is a small fee. If you have two vehicles, you can leave one of them at the Lupine Meadows Trailhead (about a mile walk to the south). The turnoff to Lupine Meadows is about a quarter mile south of the South Jenny turnoff on the main park road.

Parking and trailhead facilities: The South Jenny Lake area has a general store, visitor center, boat dock, toilet facilities—and usually plenty of room to park. This is a heavily used area, and the boat ride across the lake is very popular, so in midday during the summer, the parking lot can be full. There are no facilities at the west shore boat dock. Lupine Meadows Trailhead also has toilet facilities and plenty of room to park, but can also fill up by midday.

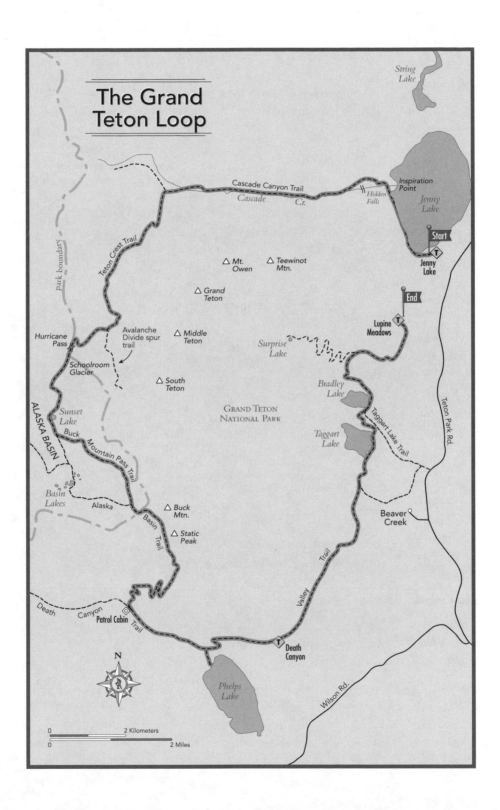

The Grand
Teton Loop

String
Lake

Cascade Canyon Trail

Cascade   Cr.

Hidden
Falls

Inspiration
Point

Jenny
Lake

Teton Crest Trail

△ Mt.
    Owen

△ Teewinot
    Mtn.

Start

T

Jenny
Lake

△ Grand
    Teton

End

Lupine
Meadows

T

Park boundary

Hurricane
Pass

Avalanche
Divide spur
trail

△ Middle
    Teton

Surprise
Lake

Schoolroom
Glacier

△ South
    Teton

Bradley
Lake

Taggart Lake Trail

ALASKA BASIN

Sunset
Lake

Buck

Taggart
Lake

GRAND TETON
NATIONAL PARK

Mountain Pass Trail

Basin
Lakes

Alaska

△ Buck
    Mtn.

Beaver
Creek

Basin Trail

△ Static
    Peak

Teton Park Rd.

Death   Canyon   Trail

Patrol Cabin

Valley   Trail

T Death
   Canyon

N

Phelps
Lake

Wilson Rd.

0   2 Kilometers

0   2 Miles

0.2 m.	Junction with Jenny Lake Trail; go straight
0.5	Hidden Falls and junction with spur trail to Hidden Falls overlook
0.9	Inspiration Point
1.6	Horse bypass trail
4.9	Junction with South and North Fork Cascade Canyon Trails; turn left
8.4	Junction with spur trail to Avalanche Divide; turn right
10.0	Schoolroom Glacier, Hurricane Pass, and park boundary
11.7	Sunset Lake
12.0	Junction with Buck Mountain Trail; turn left
14.1	Junction with Alaska Basin Trail; turn left
14.7	Buck Mountain Pass and park boundary
15.9	Static Peak Divide
19.9	Patrol cabin and Death Canyon Trail; turn left
22.4	Junction with trail to Phelps Lake; turn right
22.8	Phelps Lake
23.2	Junction with Valley Trail; turn right
23.9	Phelps Lake Overlook
24.7	Junction with trail to Death Canyon Trailhead; turn left
27.6	Junction with Beaver Creek Trail; turn left
28.4	Taggart Lake
28.5	Junction with Taggart Lake Trail; turn left
29.5	Bradley Lake
29.6	Junction with Taggart Lake Trail; turn left
30.9	Junction with Surprise Lake Trail; turn right
32.6	Lupine Meadows Trailhead

Recommended itinerary:

First night: Lower section of South Fork Cascade Canyon
Second night: Basin Lakes area in Alaska Basin
Third night: Phelps Lake

The hike: This hike, along with the Teton Crest, offers up the real stuff. It's difficult to really capture the true essence of the Teton Range in a day hike, but with a night or two in the shadows of the high peaks, it creeps into your insides and takes root.

You need at least four days to hike the entire loop and have the time for relaxing and for side trips. Even four days makes this a tough trip. Because of the position of the camping zones, you are looking at 10-plus-mile days on the last two days. There is no camping zone between Alaska Basin and Phelps Lake (11 miles) or between Phelps Lake and the trailhead (10 miles). This hike description outlines a four-day trip, but check the options section below for ways to shorten or lengthen the trip.

The trip starts with a pleasant boat ride across Jenny Lake. You can clearly see the beginning of your route, the mouth of Cascade Canyon, during the fifteen-minute ride.

The mouth of Cascade Canyon around Hidden Falls is perhaps the most heavily used spot in Grand Teton National Park. Thousands of park visitors take the scenic boat ride across Jenny Lake, mill around the falls and Inspiration Point awhile, and then return. The area shows the wear and tear of this heavy use. But there's a reason for the traffic. The falls are spectacular, and you can get really inspired from Inspiration Point.

Most visitors to Hidden Falls do not take the scenic hike up Cascade Canyon, so once you've gone past Inspiration Point, the traffic thins out dramatically.

The hike up the canyon climbs seriously for about the first mile and then goes into a gradual, almost unnoticeable ascent along the, of course, cascading stream. However, Cascade Creek also pauses in some smooth-water sections to give a quiet contrast to the steep canyon walls on each side. Mount Owen and Teewinot Peak dominate the southern horizon. The steep canyon gives you one outstanding view after another all the way to the junction where the trail splits into the South Fork up to Hurricane Pass and the North Fork to Lake Solitude and the Paintbrush Divide.

Go left (southwest) here. The grade becomes slightly more precipitous as you head toward Hurricane Pass. Look for a campsite in the early part of the camping zone, which starts shortly after the junction.

Cascade Canyon from the east shore of Jenny Lake.

Starting up Hurricane Pass.

The next morning, start early enough to have time for a side trip up to the Avalanche Divide. When you get to the junction with the Avalanche Divide, hang your packs and take two or three hours enjoying a truly fantastic view of the Grand Teton, Middle Teton, and South Teton, the best view of all three I found anywhere in the park. The trail to the divide is steep (Category 2 hill) and gets a little hard to follow near the divide, but the incredible vistas make the pain and exhaustion go away.

Once back at the junction, start the Category 2 climb up to Hurricane Pass—a gap in the Wall, a steep cliff along the park boundary. It's a respectable but not brutal climb to the pass. The trail is in great shape and nicely switchbacked. It may give you some comfort to know that this route would be more difficult in reverse with the over 10 miles of steep upgrade in Death Canyon and up to the Static Peak Divide.

On top, true to its namesake, Hurricane Pass may get a bit breezy (equal to about a category three hurricane when I was there), but hang onto something long enough to get a memorable view of everything. In addition to the incredible mountain scenery, you can see Schoolroom Glacier right below the pass.

From the pass, it's a short walk on the ridge before dropping down into Alaska Basin. You could call this the "no wimp zone." Anything up here is hardy—the alpine sunflowers, the little willows that might be a hundred years old, the overstuffed marmots running around—and even the mighty backpackers who make it to Alaska Basin.

Once over the ridge and into the basin, you get a sweeping view of the entire basin and Battleship Mountain to the west. The trail goes along the west shore of Sunset Lake and shortly thereafter meets the first of many junctions. To stay on this route, go left (east), but you may want to go over to the Basin Lakes area for your second night out. In this case, go right (south) and then left (east) at the junction just before the lakes. Both routes take you to Buck Mountain Pass and are about the same length, but the Basin Lakes route involves a slightly tougher climb—still a gentle Category 4 hill, though.

When you get to Buck Mountain Pass, you may have the impression that it's all downhill from here. That would be true if you were on Hurricane Pass going the other way, but not so this direction. You still have a mild upgrade ahead of you to get to the Static Peak Divide, the third pass on this route.

The trip up to the Static Peak Divide and the divide itself can get your adrenaline flowing. For a short stretch you hike on a trail gouged out of a steep cliff, so be careful. If you have young children with you, this would be a good place to keep them close to you. Static Peak Divide is quite austere and ruggedly spectacular, but don't get caught in a lightning storm.

From the divide it's a nice high-country hike for about a mile, and then you drop into the forested south slope of Death Canyon. From here the trail switchbacks endlessly down to the floor of Death Canyon, the junction with the Death Canyon Trail, and a patrol cabin (not on map). Walking down this hill will make you happy with your decision not to do this trip in reverse because it would be a real calf-stretching, Category 1 climb to get up to the Static Creek Divide from Death Canyon.

When you reach the Death Canyon Trail, go left (east) and continue your downhill hike on a much more gradual grade on a fairly rocky trail down Death Canyon. You can see Phelps Lake ahead, which will probably be your next campsite. If so, go right

Happy hikers on Hurricane Pass, with Grand Teton and Middle Teton in the background.

Watch your step on the way to Static Peak Divide.

(east) at the junction above the lake. Later, as you approach the shore of the lake, watch for a spur trail to the left (north) going around to the campsites on the north shore of the lake.

After your stay at Phelps Lake, retrace your steps back up to the Valley Trail above the lake and take a right (north) and hike along the base of the Teton Range for about 10 miles to the trailhead. This last day is quite the contrast to the first three days of the hike spent in the high country. Here, you go through mature forest with a few aspen groves and meadows. Watch for moose, black bears, and other wildlife, especially around Phelps Lake, where we also saw a rare rubber boa on the trail.

There is an unexpectedly steep but short hill coming out of Phelps Lake, but this is somewhat indicative of the rest of this last day. When you hike back up from your campsite at Phelps Lake, you'll be back on the Valley Trail. Turn right (north).

The Valley Trail isn't one of the high-country adventures that most people visualize when they think of Grand Teton National Park. Instead, this is a walk in the woods similar to what you would find in many western mountain ranges. The entire Valley Trail goes through a forest mixed with lodgepole, Englemann spruce, Douglas-fir, and aspen.

The Valley Trail passes three low-elevation lakes—Phelps, Taggart, and Bradley— and also five spur trails back to trailheads along the eastern slope of the Teton Range, so you can cut your hike short and bail out at several points along the way. The Grand Teton Loop, however, follows the Valley Trail all the way to Lupine Trailhead.

As you go from Phelps Lake to Taggart Lake to Bradley Lake to the Lupine Meadows Trailhead, you climb a ridge (actually moraines) between each point—nothing very steep, but constantly up and down.

About 2 miles after Phelps Lake, you go left (north) at the junction with the trail to the Death Canyon Trailhead. Also take left turns at Beaver Creek, Taggart Lake, and Bradley Lake trail junctions. Glaciers created these three lakes by flowing out of the canyons, melting and leaving a moraine to form a natural dam. The view from Taggart Lake with Grand Teton as a backdrop is a great candidate for a postcard.

After Bradley Lake, you reach the junction with the trail to Garnet Canyon and Surprise and Amphitheater Lakes. Go right (north) here, and hike the last 1.7 miles to the Lupine Meadows Trailhead. If you didn't leave a vehicle here, elect the person with the most remaining energy to drop his or her pack and walk about a mile over to the South Jenny Lake area where you left your vehicle to take the boat ride four days earlier.

Options: I have never hiked up from Death Canyon to the Static Peak Divide, but while hiking down it, I was left with the impression that I didn't want to do this trip in reverse.

You have the option of shortening your trip by leaving vehicles at the Death Canyon or Taggart Lake Trailheads.

You could lengthen you trip by one day by spending a night on the Death Canyon Shelf. If this interests you, keep going south from Basin Lakes until you find one of many five-star campsites on the shelf. Then, the next morning, go back to Alaska Basin and on to Buck Mountain Pass and the rest of the trip.

If the Phelps Lake campsites are taken, you can camp in the Death Canyon Camping Zone above the patrol cabin at the junction of the Static Peak Trail. This adds 2 to 3 miles to the trip. It also leaves a very long last day if you go all the way to Lupine Meadows, but you can spend a night at the Bradley Lake campsite reserved just for hikers doing this loop.

It's difficult to get the spacing correct on the last section of this trip, and it's easy to end up with more miles in one day than you really want. One alternative is to hang packs somewhere near the Death Canyon Trailhead and walk the rest of the trip with a daypack. If you do this, be sure to hang your packs out of reach of bears. Then, after reaching the Lupine Meadows Trailhead, drive back to the Death Canyon Trailhead for your over-night packs.

Side trips: If you get an early start and don't mind some extra climbing on your first day, hang your packs at the junction of the North Fork and South Fork trails (4.9 miles from the boat dock) and day hike up to Lake Solitude (5.2 miles round trip). The very ambitious can climb another 2.4 miles up the Paintbrush Divide (adding another 4.8 miles). The scenery is worth the trip, especially the constant view of Grand Teton coming down from Lake Solitude.

You'll really miss something if you don't do the side trip up to the Avalanche Divide, but it's a difficult climb to get there, leaving it for the fit and energetic only. If you have extra time after setting up camp in Alaska Basin, there are several short trails for interesting side trips. In addition, the basin is open, subalpine country, which makes off-trail hiking easy.

Camping: The South Fork Camping Zone has at least fifteen campsites that are indicated but you can camp anywhere, all the way up to a great site at the junction with the Avalanche Divide Trail. Most indicated campsites are four- or five-star with nice views and privacy and good access to water, but a few are very exposed, so shy away from these sites if the weather looks ominous. Keep in mind that you aren't required to camp at the indicated sites. To keep the distance fairly equitable each day of your trip, camp in the lower part of this camping zone.

Alaska Basin is outside of the park in the Jedediah Smith Wilderness, so you can set up a zero-impact camp anywhere in the basin. If you camp at Sunset Lake, don't camp on the shoreline. There are several great campsites safely away from the beautiful but fragile alpine lake.

Phelps Lake has three five-star designated campsites. As you approach the lake, watch for a junction with a trail going to the left (north) to the campsites. All of them are on the north shore of the lake with a terrific view of the lake, fire pits, room for two tents, and a shared bear box. The campsites are out of sight of the main trail, but the campsites are fairly close to each other so please talk softly to respect the privacy of others.

Fishing: Like most trips in Grand Teton, this route is not made for the angler. Except for a few trout (brook, lake, and cutthroat) in Phelps Lake, there are no meaningful fishing opportunities.

25

Moose Basin Divide

General description: A long backpacking trip into the most remote section of Grand Teton National Park

Special attractions: A little-used section of Grand Teton National Park, featuring a more gentle terrain than the high peaks in the southern sections of the park.

Type of trip: A "lollipop" loop

Total distance: 41.2 miles

Difficulty: Difficult

Traffic: Very light

Maps: Earthwalk Press Grand Teton map; NPS handout map; and Coltec Bay, Ranger Peak, Grassy Lake Reservoir, and Huckleberry Mountain USGS quads

Starting point: Glade Creek Trailhead

Finding the trailhead: Drive 4.4 miles west of Flagg Ranch on Grassy Lake Road (also know as Ashton–Flagg Ranch Road) and park at the trailhead on the left (south) side of the road.

Parking and trailhead facilities: Small lot at the trailhead; pit toilet.

Recommended itinerary: This route is nicely suited for a five-day trip.

First night:	Lower Moose Creek before entering Webb Canyon
Second night:	Moose Basin
Third night:	About halfway down Owl Creek
Fourth night:	Jackson Lake shoreline north of patrol cabin or lower Berry Creek

The hike: Most people don't think about this section of Grand Teton National Park, so you can plan on having Glade Creek and most of the north trails to yourself. This hike actually starts outside of the park on the John D. Rockefeller Jr. Memorial Parkway, but the area is just as undeveloped as the park itself—in fact, more wild than many parts of the park. The trailhead sign says that it's 3.5 miles to the park boundary, but this is probably exaggerated by a half mile or more.

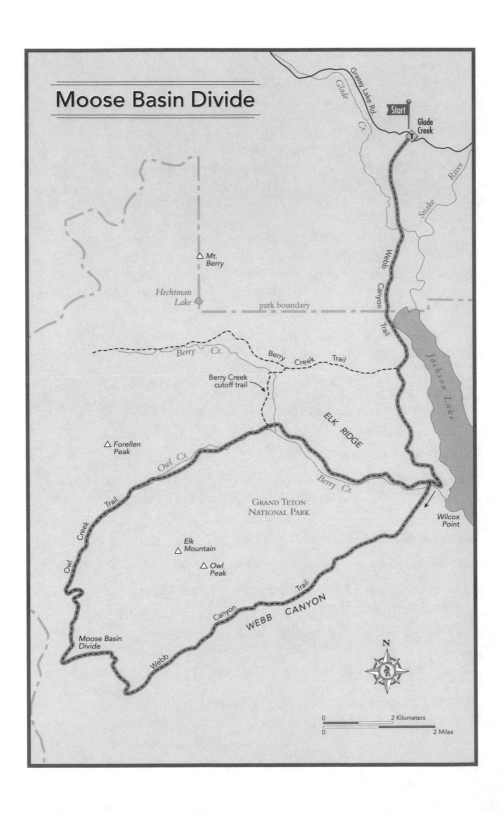

Moose Basin Divide

Grassy Lake Rd

Glade Cr.

Start

Glade
Creek

Snake River

Webb Canyon Trail

Mt. Berry

Hechtman Lake

park boundary

Jackson Lake

Berry   Cr.

Berry   Creek   Trail

Berry Creek
cutoff trail

ELK RIDGE

Forellen
Peak

Owl Cr.

Berry Cr.

GRAND TETON
NATIONAL PARK

Owl Creek Trail

Wilcox
Point

Elk
Mountain

Owl
Peak

Owl

Canyon

Trail

WEBB CANYON

Moose Basin
Divide

Webb

N

0   2 Kilometers
0   2 Miles

1.5 m.	Cross the Glade Creek footbridge
2.0	Break out into a big meadow
3.5	Park boundary
4.9	Berry Creek Trail; turn left
8.0	Jackson Lake, patrol cabin, and junction with Owl Creek Trail; turn right
8.1	Junction with Webb Canyon Trail; turn left and ford creek
9.1	Webb Canyon
19.1	Moose Basin Divide and Owl Creek Trail
29.1	Berry Creek cutoff trail; turn right
33.1	Junction with Webb Canyon Trail; turn left
33.2	Jackson Lake and patrol cabin
36.3	Berry Creek Trail; turn right
37.7	Park boundary
41.2	Glade Creek Trailhead

The trail starts out through a mature lodgepole forest. You cross Glade Creek on a footbridge at about the 1.5-mile mark. Shortly thereafter, you drop down a fairly steep hill to a vast meadow. To the left, you can see the Snake River flowing into Jackson Lake and a huge freshwater marsh, the second largest freshwater marsh found in the park. (The other is just south and west of Jackson Lake Lodge.) You can also see Jackson Lake off to the south, and you also may see some moose, swans, and other wildlife, especially in the early morning or near sunset. Even the mighty grizzly bear frequently roams through this rich habitat.

But be forewarned. There is one wildlife species you will see and not enjoy. This is the only section of trail in the park where I had to stop and get out the mosquito repellent and netting.

At the junction with the Berry Creek Trail, go left (south) and continue to hike through a mature forest interspersed with huge meadows. The trail is in great shape all the way to the patrol cabin, and you get some nice views of Jackson Lake over the last mile or so before the cabin. It seems like a short 8 miles from the Glade Creek trailhead to the patrol cabin.

At the junction in front of the patrol cabin, go right (west) and hike another 0.1 mile to the junction with the loop trail over Moose Basin Divide. If you're following the clockwise route outlined here, go left (south), and ford Berry Creek. Sorry, no footbridge, which means getting your feet wet just before setting up camp.

After Berry Creek, the trail goes through an open bench and then over into Moose Creek. This vicinity is a good choice for the first night out.

Moose Creek.

About a mile up the trail, you enter Webb Canyon, a steep and narrow section of the Moose Creek drainage, and stay there for several miles. The trail stays close to the stream most of the way, and Moose Creek is mighty impressive as it crescendos out of the high country. It's a constant cascade through the steep canyon. The scenery almost makes you forget the big hill you're climbing.

After about 6 or 7 miles of canyon hiking, you break out into gorgeous subalpine country in Moose Basin. You can camp anywhere in the basin, and it will be a memorable night in paradise. When we were there, it was a monstrous "moose-less" meadow, but in most cases, you should be able to see moose, elk, and other large wildlife in this rich high country—including the grizzly, so be alert.

From the basin, it's 2 to 3 miles to the divide. In the last 2 miles, the trail becomes a series of cairns in spots, and it's a wildflower carpet all the way. Actually, this last pull to the divide rates as a Category 1 hill, but it doesn't feel that bad once you get to Moose Basin. Instead, it seems like much of the serious climbing is behind you back in Webb Canyon. The map shows a patrol cabin, which is indeed there but difficult to find.

Save some water for lunch at the top. Late in the season, water is scarce for a mile or so on each side of the divide.

After a good rest on the 9,700-foot divide, drop sharply down toward upper Owl Creek and onto a bench covered with whitebark pine, a favorite food of Old Griz. Be especially alert late in the year when the bears are up here fattening up on whitebark pine nuts for their winter sleep.

Owl Creek is the mirror image of Moose Creek. Instead of steeply climbing through a canyon and then mellowing out for a gentle push to the top, Owl Creek drops sharply at top and then goes into a gentle open valley. Owl Creek is a gigantic meadow with lots of great campsites and probably more moose than Moose Creek and more berries than Berry Creek. You have two stream crossings (one on Owl Creek and one on Berry Creek)—again, sorry, no footbridges.

When you reach the junction with the cutoff trail to Berry Creek, go right (east) and ford Berry Creek before it merges with Owl Creek. From this point, Berry Creek goes into a narrow canyon, and the trail climbs way above it and stays there for 4 miles until it drops down to the junction with the Webb Canyon Trail.

From here, retrace your steps back to the Glade Creek Trailhead.

Options: You can cut 16 miles off your trip by getting a boat ride or taking a canoe across Jackson Lake from Leeks Marina to Wilcox Point. Be sure to go early in the morning and in good weather. You do not want to get caught in a storm on Jackson Lake. You can also take the loop in reverse, but I believe the hill is more precipitous on the Owl Creek side, and it's 14 miles uphill instead of 11 from the Moose Creek side.

You can also go back via the Berry Creek Cutoff Trail instead of taking the last 4 miles down Berry Creek to the patrol cabin. This only adds about a mile to your trip, but it does mean a big climb to get over a ridge.

Side trips: There are several appealing off-trail side trips in the alpine country on both sides of Moose Basin Divide. If you want to stay another day or two, you can take the Berry Creek Cutoff Trail over to Berry Creek, set up a base camp, and spend a day hiking up to Jackass Pass and back. Instead of coming directly back, you can hike around Survey Peak via the Teton Crest Trail and the Survey Peak Trail. Do this loop clockwise to avoid the very steep climb on the Survey Peak Trail. This side trip adds about 16 miles

The view from Moose Basin Divide.

Owl Creek is lined by large, lush meadows most of the way.

to your overall distance, but it's a terrific day hike and it allows you to spend two nights in the open beauty of Berry Creek.

Camping: This is an open camping area, so you can set up a zero-impact camp anywhere along this route, before or after entering the park, but you need a permit after crossing the park boundary. It won't be difficult to find scenic campsites, especially in Owl Creek and in upper Moose Creek. You can find a good camp in the low country around the patrol cabin or by going up the Webb Canyon trail less than a mile. However, campsites in Webb Canyon itself are marginal. When you break out of the canyon, sites are plentiful and very scenic. Likewise, when you drop down into Owl Creek, it's easy to find a five-star campsite, but camping locations are scarce in the section between the Berry Creek Cutoff Trail and the patrol cabin.

Fishing: No fishing along this route.

WIND RIVER RANGE

The incredible Wind River Range runs 110 miles from Togwotee Pass to South Pass in western Wyoming, south of Grand Teton National Park. The Wind River Range offers a lifetime of backpacking vacations. It contains dozens of peaks over 12,000 feet, including many over 13,000 feet as well as Wyoming's highest point, Gannett Peak, 13,804 feet. The Continental Divide follows the crest of the Wind River Range, and the Forest Service is currently constructing new sections of the trail due for completion in 2004. Most of the 100-mile-plus CD trail will follow existing trails.

Of its 2.4 million acres, 901,649 acres of the range are protected in four wilderness areas: Bridger (428,168 acres), administered by the Bridger-Teton National Forest; Popo Agie (101,991 acres) and Fitzpatrick (191,103 acres), administered by the Shoshone National Forest; and the Wind River Roadless Area (180,387 acres), administered by the Wind River Indian Reservation.

Water from more than 2,000 lakes and countless tarns feeds three major river systems (the Yellowstone, Snake, and Colorado Rivers) and provides some of the best high-mountain fishing in the country. Climbers also adore the range and its endless precipitous challenges.

Although the Wind River Range is very popular, in most cases it doesn't seem crowded. That's because there is so much country to explore, on trail or off-trail, that you can almost always find a campsite of your own. There are exceptions such as Lonesome Lake, Titcomb Basin, and Big Sandy Lake, but once out of these high-use areas, you will feel the spirit of the wilderness.

Although backpackers far outnumber parties using livestock, expect to see a few horses and llamas. Backpackers who like to take their dogs, which are prohibited in nearby Grand Teton and Yellowstone National Parks, also tend to flock to the Wind Rivers, so don't be surprised by a barking dog at night.

Like any hiking area, the Wind Rivers feature good day hikes, but more than most areas, this wilderness is suited for long backpacking trips. This isn't really an area for beginners or small children. The long routes and high-elevation hiking are more suited to experienced backpackers, especially those with a passion for either fishing or climbing.

Unlike many areas, the Wind River Range's land managers don't give much attention to accurate signs, which tends to promote this area's wild character. Most signs do not have mileage on them, and those that do are usually overestimated. This should help teach us that the exact mileage really isn't important to our wilderness experience, and not knowing it might actually enhance that experience, sort of like leaving your watch in the car at the trailhead.

After your long, exhilarating hike in the Wind Rivers, you'll probably need to replenish your protein and fat supply, so stop at the Sugar Shack drive-in in Pinedale for a Grizzly Adams, a real mountain man of a burger, that puts to shame the Grizzly burgers of Roscoe and Ennis, Montana.

The Wind River Range is known for its large, deep lakes, such as Graves Lake.

GETTING TO THE WIND RIVER RANGE

The two routes in this book are best accessed from Pinedale, 76 miles south of Jackson or 99 miles north of Rock Springs, Wyoming. Jackson is the closest airport, but you can also fly to Idaho Falls or Salt Lake City.

BACKCOUNTRY REGULATIONS

To preserve the high wilderness character of the Wind Rivers, the Forest Service has established a few key regulations.

Camping and campfires are not allowed within 200 feet of lakes or trails, or within 100 feet of any stream. Campfires are discouraged but allowed, but below timberline only, which is usually about 10,400 feet in the Wind Rivers. Use only dead and downed wood—and don't ravage the fragile *krummholz* for firewood. Group size is limited to fifteen people, and any organized group (church groups, commercial tours, and so on) must have a special permit.

Be sure to check the information board at each trailhead for current changes in regulations. For example, special regulations are frequently imposed in dry years to help prevent forest fires.

FINDING MAPS

Earthwalk Press publishes a terrific set of two topo maps for the Wind River Ranges by splitting the mountains into the Northern Wind River Range and Southern Wind River Range. These maps are, by far, the best choice. In fact, they are so good, that I really didn't use my USGS quads when I hiked these routes. You can pick up these maps at local sport stores or order them directly from the Grand Teton Natural History Association at the following address.

Grand Teton National History Association
Box 170
Moose, WY 83012
Phone: (307) 739–3606
e-mail: info@grandtetonpark.org

FOR MORE INFORMATION

Like the Lee Metcalf and Absaroka-Beartooth Wildernesses, management of the Wind Rivers Range is complicated. The Bridger–Teton National Forest administers sections west of the crest of the range with the Shoshone National Forest and the Wind River Indian Reservation managing the eastern sections. For the two routes in this book, you can get information from the following addresses:

Bridger–Teton National Forest, Pinedale Ranger District, 29 East Fremont Lake Road, P.O. Box 220, Pinedale, WY 82941; (307) 367–4326.

Shoshone National Forest, Washakie Ranger District, 600 North Highway 287, Lander, WY 82520; (307) 332–5460.

26

Sky Pilot

General description: A spectacular loop through the northern heart of the Wind River Range

Special attractions: Sky Pilot Peak and the precipitous peaks of the west rim of the Titcomb Basin as well as numerous sparkling mountain lakes

Type of trip: Loop

Total distance: 37 miles

Difficulty: Moderate with the exception of one strenuous climb up to Glimpse Lake on the first day

Traffic: Moderate on most of the trip, but heavy on the last leg from Little Senaca Lake to the trailhead

Maps: The Earthwalk Press Northern Wind River Range map and Fremont Lake North, Bridger Lakes, Squaretop Mountain, and Gannett Peak USGS quads

Starting point: Elkhart Park Trailhead

Finding the trailhead: From the south edge of Pinedale, Wyoming (76 miles south of Jackson or 99 miles north of Rock Springs on U.S. Highway 191), turn north onto a paved road signed for Half Moon and Fremont Lakes. From here, it's 14.5 miles of pavement ending at the trailhead. Because of the easy access, Elkhart Park is the most popular trailhead for the Wind River Range. Two trails leave Elkhart Park Trailhead. You want the Pine Creek Canyon Trail on the far end of the trailhead, not the Pole Creek Trail.

Parking and trailhead facilities: Pit toilet, small campground, picnic area, drinking water, and two large parking lots, which are usually nearly full. There are also several undeveloped camping areas on the way to the trailhead.

Recommended itinerary: This route is suited for four nights out, but with the addition of rest days for day hiking, this trip can easily be stretched to six or seven days.

First night:	Glimpse Lake or Prospector Lake
Second night:	Borum Lake or Summit Lake
Third night:	Elbow Lake or Upper Jean Lake
Fourth night:	Lost Lake, Little Senaca Lake, or Hobbs Lake

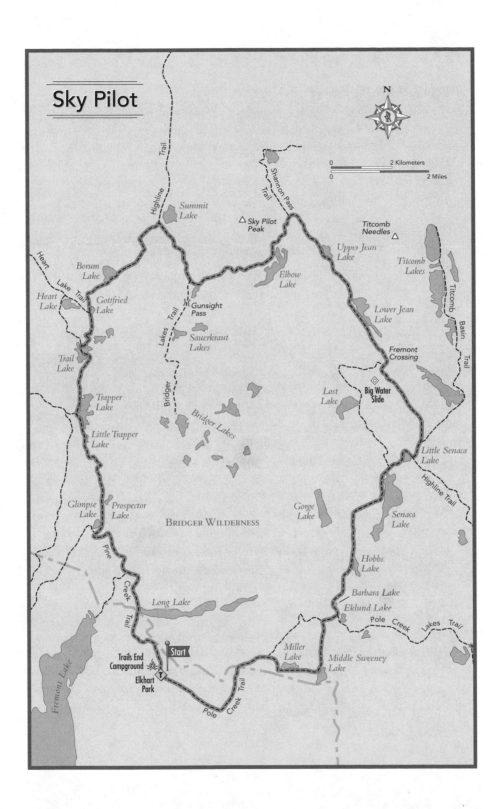

Sky Pilot

N

0   2 Kilometers
0   2 Miles

Highline Trail

Shannon Pass Trail

Summit Lake

△ Sky Pilot Peak

Titcomb Needles △

Upper Jean Lake

Titcomb Lakes

Heart

Borum Lake

Elbow Lake

Lake Trail

Heart Lake

Gottfried Lake

Gunsight Pass

Lower Jean Lake

Titcomb Basin Trail

Lakes Trail

Sauerkraut Lakes

Fremont Crossing

Trail Lake

Bridger

Lost Lake

Big Water Slide

Trapper Lake

Bridger Lakes

Little Trapper Lake

Little Senaca Lake

Highline Trail

Glimpse Lake

Prospector Lake

BRIDGER WILDERNESS

Gorge Lake

Senaca Lake

Pine

Hobbs Lake

Creek

Barbara Lake

Long Lake

Trail

Eklund Lake

Pole Creek Lakes Trail

Start

Fremont Lake

Miller Lake

Middle Sweeney Lake

Trails End Campground

Elkhart Park

T

Pole Creek Trail

2.1 m.	Long Lake
3.2	Junction with trail to Fremont Lake; turn right
3.4	Bridge over Pine Creek.
6.0	Glimpse Lake and junction with Glimpse Lake Trail; turn right
6.8	Prospector Lake
9.2	Little Trapper Lake
9.7	Trapper Lake and junction with Trapper Creek Trail; turn right
11.2	Trail Lake and junction with Heart Lake Trail; turn right
12.2	Gottfried Lake and second junction with Heart Lake Trail; turn right
13.3	Borum Lake
15.0	Summit Lake and junction with Highline Trail; turn right
17.0	Gunsight Pass and junction with Bridger Lakes Trail; turn left
19.5	Elbow Lake
20.5	Junction with Shannon Pass Trail; turn right
21.5	Upper Jean Lake
22.5	Lower Jean Lake
24.0	Junction with trail to Big Water Slide and Lost Lake; turn left
24.1	Fremont Crossing and bridge over Fremont Creek
26.0	Junction with Titcomb Basin Trail; turn right
26.5	Little Senaca Lake and junction with Highline Trail; turn right
27.3	Junction with trail to Lost Lake; turn left
27.5	Senaca Lake
30.0	Hobbs Lake
31.0	Barbara Lake
31.3	Eklund Lake and junction with trail to Pole Creek Lakes; turn right
31.8	Junction with trail to Sweeney Lakes; turn left
33.5	Junction with trail to Miller Lake; turn right
34.1	Junction with Pole Creek Trail; turn left
37.0	Elkhart Park Trailhead

The hike: This route makes a nice loop through the heart of the northern Wind River Range from the ultrapopular Elkhart Park Trailhead. Most hikers prefer the out-and-back option and set up a base camp in the Titcomb Basin, which is, along with Cirque of the Towers, among the most heavily visited spots in the entire mountain range. This loop option avoids the crowded Titcomb Basin and Island Lake. Regrettably, the only way to get a loop route from Elkhart Park is to drop down to Long Lake and Pine Creek and climb back up a Category 1 hill.

Long Lake.

From the trailhead you drop sharply to Long Lake, a definitely long expanse of water. Even though beautiful Long Lake is only 2 miles from a major trailhead, it gets moderate use. Most hikers head for Island Lake on a flat trail instead of braving the big hill either direction out of Long Lake.

After Long Lake you go over a small knoll and turn right (north) at the junction with the trail going to Fremont Lake. After crossing the bridge over Pine Creek, you instantly start the Category 1 climb up to Glimpse Lake, ascending about 1,800 feet in 2.5 miles. There is no nice way to describe this hill. It's extremely steep, ugly, hot, and shadeless, and it's on a lousy trail. If you wonder why you aren't seeing any horse apples on the trail, that's because this section is so steep it isn't recommended for livestock. The only good thing I can say about this section of trail is that it doesn't stretch out the agony with miles of nearly level switchbacks. Take it slow and steady and keep in mind that the rest of the route is quite easy.

When you finally conquer the climb, after a long break, of course, it's an easy walk to your first campsite, either at Glimpse Lake or if you aren't too weary, Prospector Lake or even Little Trapper Lake. If you go to Prospector Lake, you have a small, 200-foot hump to get over. This becomes the norm on this route—a small hill between each of the series of lakes you pass by.

Most of the route to Trapper Lake goes through forest mixed with frequent lush meadows. The trail junction at Trapper Lake can be confusing, so heads up to make sure

Crossing Pine Creek.

you don't get on the Corner Trail. In addition, you'll find frequent, well-defined social trails throughout this section, especially around Summit Lake and Shannon Pass; keep the map out and make sure you're still on the official trail.

At Trail Lake you can go around Heart Lake on an official trail or around Neil Lake to the foot of Gottfried Lake on a social trail—or you can hang your pack at Trail Lake or Gottfried Lake and do a day hike around the lake-filled basin. If you decide to camp at Borum Lake, you might want to save time for an off-trail day hike over to Cutthroat Lakes or No Name Lakes. You'll find lots of campsites all along the way to Borum Lake where you finally break above timberline and head for Summit Lake, a popular base camp in the shadow of mighty Mount Oeneis.

Here you cross Pine Creek again, just after it comes out of its source, Summit Lake. Gunsight Pass is a minor bump on the road, hardly a noticeable rise, but the hill just before Elbow Lake will get you sweating again. If you have extra time, consider a side trip down to beautiful Sauerkraut Lakes.

The scenery has been excellent all the way, of course, but now it gets exceptional after Elbow Lake. Perhaps the highlight is the prominent Sky Pilot Peak to the north, dominating the northern horizon for a long section of trail. After you turn right (south) at the Shannon Pass trail junction and gradually climb to an 11,000-foot divide between the Elbow Lake and Jean Lakes Basin, the incredible Titcomb Needles, including the Great Needle, dictate the eastern horizon along with Brimstone Mountain and Shroud Peak. This is probably the most scenic section of the heavily hiked Highline Trail.

After Lower Jean Lake you reach Fremont Crossing, which is a huge bridge (with steel beams no less) over Fremont Creek. Without the bridge this could be a difficult ford. From the bridge take a short side trip over to see the Big Water Slide, an unusual waterfall where Fremont Creek "slides" over a smooth granite wall long ago polished by passing glaciers. If you don't mind a taking a social trail, you can take an alternative route via Lost Lake and down to the Pole Creek Trail. This trail is rougher than the official trail, but about the same distance.

After an enjoyable side trip to the Big Water Slide (a great lunch spot, incidentally), you can enjoy a pleasant walk down to Little Senaca Lake, taking a right (west) turn at the junction with the Titcomb Basin Trail and another right (west) at the lake as you leave the Highline Trail and move to the Pole Creek Trail.

At this point in the trip, expect to see a steady stream of hikers going in and out of the Titcomb Basin, a rage among climbers and backpackers alike because of the string of incredible 13,000-foot peaks rising above the basin along the Continental Divide to the west and the Titcomb Needles jutting up on the east side of the basin.

From here you start gradually dipping down toward timberline again as you hike along the west shore of mighty Senaca Lake, which looks big and deep enough to have its own monster. At Hobbs Lake, next along the trail, you're solidly below timberline. Watch for moose. At Hobbs we were fortunate enough to sit under a gnarly old white-bark pine and watch a moose and two calves swim across the lake, one of those wilderness moments you always remember.

After Hobbs Lake you walk through similar environs past Barbara Lake (with a super-scenic overlook where you can look back and see Arrowhead, Sky Pilot, Jackson,

Big Water Slide.

Camping at Hobbs Lake.

Titcomb Needles, and many other peaks you have passed earlier in the trip) and Eklund Lake (not visible from the trail), taking rights (west) at junctions to Pole Creek Lakes and Miller Lake, unless you decide on a slightly longer alternative route via Sweeney Lakes and Miller Lake.

The last leg is a nice 3-mile walk on a well-traveled trail through a lodgepole pine forest sprinkled with meadows just right for those last glimpses back into the mountain wonderland you just left.

Options: This route might serve as a contrast in philosophies. I prefer to plan my hardest days as early as possible in the trip and easy days late in the trip. This route has only one big climb, the monster hill up from Pine Creek to Glimpse Lake, and I suggest getting it behind you on the first day out. However, if you have the opposite philosophy, you can do this trip in reverse and save the big climb for the last day, crawling into the trailhead after climbing up from Long Lake.

This loop can be expanded in at least three ways—skipping Borum Lake and taking the loop trail around Cutthroat and No Name Lakes before getting back on the route at Summit Lake; taking the Lost Lake alternative route; or checking out Sweeney Lakes and Miller Lake on the last day when headed back to the trailhead.

Side trips: The possibilities are almost countless. If you have an extra day from your second night out, you can take the loop around Dean Lake, Cutthroat Lakes, and No Name Lakes. Shorter possibilities are Corner Lake, Heart Lake, Neil Lake, and Sauerkraut Lakes. Another long side trip is Bridger Lakes, but this would be a tough day and probably only possible if you camped around Pass Lake or Sauerkraut Lakes.

Two more ideal side trips are a trip up to Shannon Pass combined with a strenuous but not technically difficult walk up Stroud Peak and a daylong trip past Island Lake and into the Titcomb Basin.

Add these possibilities to dozens of peaks begging to be bagged, and you could spend two weeks on this route.

Camping: You can camp anywhere along the route, but be sure to set up a zero-impact camp and follow the special regulation for the area—camp 200 feet from lakes and trails and 100 feet from streams. Avoid campfires—firewood is sparse and scenic.

Fishing: Most lakes along this route are loaded with trout, so an angler can have a field day with little chance of disappointment.

27

Lizard Head

General description: A long circuit through the southern Wind River Range

Special attractions: Lizard Head Peak, two trips over the Continental Divide, and many other high alpine views, spectacular mountain lakes, and endless climbing opportunities

Type of trip: Loop

Total distance: 42.5 miles

Difficulty: Difficult

Traffic: Heavy around Big Sandy Lake, Jackass Pass, and Lonesome Lake; moderate on the rest of the trip

Maps: The Earthwalk Press Southern Wind River Range map and Mount Bonneville, Lizard Head Peak, Dickinson Park, Big Sandy Opening, and Temple Peak USGS quads

Starting point: Big Sandy Trailhead

Finding the trailhead: From Pinedale (drive 76 miles south of Jackson or 99 miles north of Rock Springs on U.S. Highway 191), drive south for 11.5 miles on U.S. 191 and turn left (east) onto Wyoming Highway 353. After 18 miles the pavement ends, and the highway becomes a seemingly endless gravel road, continuing on for another 26.5 miles to the trailhead, passing by several well-signed junctions. Stay on the main road in any unmarked junction. The road ends at the trailhead. You can reach the trailhead in any vehicle. It takes about two hours to get from Pinedale to the trailhead, the most remote trailhead for the Wind River Range.

Parking and trailhead facilities: Pit toilet, campground, picnic area, and large parking lot for forty to fifty vehicles, often close to full. In addition to the small vehicle campground at the trailhead, there are several undeveloped camping areas on the way to the trailhead.

Recommended itinerary: For ambitious hikers this trip is nicely suited for four nights out. For the slightly less ambitious, five nights is more realistic. In either case consider adding one or two days by staying in campsites two nights and taking day hikes on the rest days.

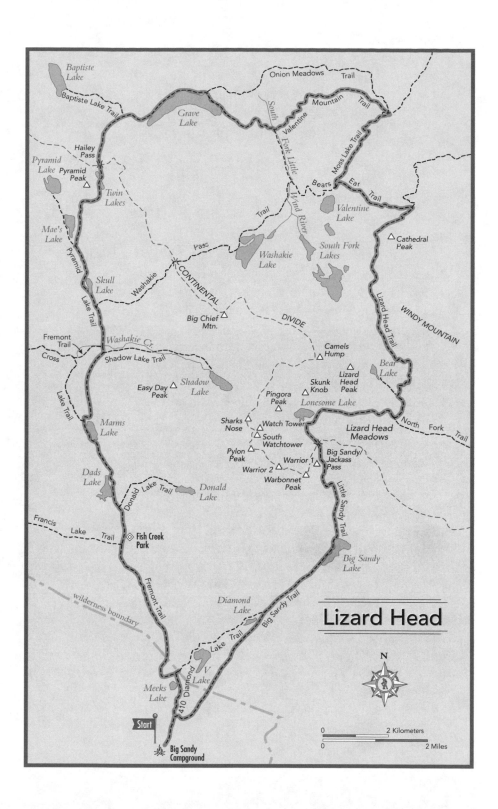

Baptiste Lake

Baptiste Lake Trail

Grave Lake

Onion Meadows Trail

South Fork Little

Valentine Mountain Trail

Moss Lake Trail

Hailey Pass

Pyramid Lake

Pyramid Peak

Twin Lakes

Bears Ear Trail

Valentine Lake

Mae's Lake

Trail

Wind River

South Fork Lakes

Cathedral Peak

Skull Lake

Pass

Washakie

CONTINENTAL

Washakie Lake

Lake Trail

DIVIDE

Lizard Head Trail

WINDY MOUNTAIN

Big Chief Mtn.

Fremont Trail

Washakie Cr.

Cross

Shadow Lake Trail

Camels Hump

Bear Lake

Easy Day Peak

Shadow Lake

Skunk Knob

Lizard Head Peak

Lake Trail

Sharks Nose

Pingora Peak

Lonesome Lake

Marms Lake

Watch Tower

South Watchtower

Lizard Head Meadows

North Fork Trail

Dads Lake

Pylon Peak

Warrior 2

Warrior 1

Big Sandy Jackass Pass

Donald Lake Trail

Donald Lake

Warbonnet Peak

Francis

Lake Trail

◇ Fish Creek Park

Little Sandy Trail

Big Sandy Lake

wilderness boundary

Fremont Trail

Diamond Lake

Big Sandy Trail

Lake Trail

410 Diamond

V Lake

Meeks Lake

🚩 Start

🔥 Big Sandy Campground

Lizard Head

N

0   2 Kilometers
0   2 Miles

0.5 m.	Junction with Meeks Lake Trail 410; turn right
1.2	Bridger Wilderness Boundary
3.5	Junction with Diamond Lake Trail; turn right
5.0	Foot of Big Sandy Lake
5.5	Upper end of Big Sandy Lake and junction with Little Sandy Trail; turn left
8.0	Jackass Pass/Big Sandy Pass
9.0	Lonesome Lake
10.5	Lizard Head Meadows
11.0	Junction with Lizard Head and Bears Ear trails; turn left
12.5	Junction with social trail to Bear Lakes; turn right
17.5	Junction with Bears Ear Trail; turn left
20.0	Junction with Moss Lake Trail; turn left
21.0	Valentine Lake
23.0	Little Wind River, junction with Washaskie Trail; turn right
24.0	Junction with Valentine Mountain Trail; turn left
25.5	Foot of Grave Lake
25.7	Junction with Onion Meadows Trail; turn left
27.0	Junction with Baptiste Lake Trail; turn left
29.0	Hailey Pass
29.2	Twin Lakes
31.5	Mae's Lake
31.7	Junction with Pyramid Lake Trail; turn left
32.5	Skull Lake
33.0	Junction with Washakie Pass Trail; turn right
33.8	Washakie Creek, junction with Fremont Trail; turn left
34.0	Junction with Shadow Lake Trail; turn right
35.2	Marms Lake, junction with Cross Lake Trail; turn left
36.5	Dads Lake
37.0	Junction with Donald Lake Trail; turn right
37.7	Mirror Lake
38.0	Fish Creek Park, first junction with Francis Lake Trail; turn left
38.5	Second junction with Francis Lake Trail; turn left
41.0	Meeks Lake, junction with Diamond Lake Trail; turn left
41.5	Junction with V Lake Trail; turn right
42.0	Junction with Big Sandy Trail; turn right
42.5	Big Sandy Trailhead

Four nights:

First night:	Big Sandy Lake
Second night:	Bear Lakes
Third night:	Little Wind River or Grave Lake
Fourth night:	Skull Lake

Five nights:

First night:	Big Sandy Lake
Second night:	Lizard Head Meadows
Third night:	Valentine Lake or Little Wind River
Fourth night:	Mae's Lake or Pyramid Lake
Fifth night:	Dads Lake or Donald Lake

The hike: This route takes you through the prime scenery of the southern Wind River Range. However, the trip may be frustrating because even though you hike through so much superb scenery, you have to let many special places pass by unseen because there aren't enough hours in the day (or energy in the body) for all the desired side trips. It would take ten days to cover everything you would like to see on this route.

The route involves three big ascents, so it isn't for the faint-hearted. It can, however, be hiked in reasonably short segments to make it less strenuous.

Probably the most important factor in this trip is the weather. If it's clear and sunny, backpacking doesn't get much better than this. If you get caught in socked-in, low-hanging clouds and rain, it can be a veerrrry loonnng trip, and you would miss most of the incredible vistas. So check the weather forecast before you head for the southern Wind River Range.

The first leg of the trip to Big Sandy Lake is a heavily used trail following Big Sandy Creek. You get some great views of Schlestler Peak as a backdrop over meadows along the slow-moving stream. The trail to Big Sandy Lake is a hardly noticeable upgrade. At the lake itself, Haystack, Dogtooth, and Big Sandy Mountains join Schlestler to provide a stunning landscape.

Because of the long drive to the trailhead, most hikers don't hit the trail until midday, which makes Big Sandy Lake a logical first campsite. Unfortunately, everybody has this plan, so expect lots of company, including dogs barking at every pine squirrel that comes by. Other hikers use Big Sandy as a base camp to visit Cirque of the Towers, Black Joe Lake, and other nearby destinations. Fortunately, the lake has lots of good campsites. You can avoid the congestion of Big Sandy Lake by camping at Black Joe or Clear Lake, but this adds a few miles to your trip and you might find almost as many people at these spots.

The high use at Big Sandy Lake has attracted black bears, and some campers have, regrettably, allowed the bears to get food and garbage. So, while camped here, use the bear-resistant food storage containers at the lower and upper ends of the lake or carefully hang food and garbage well out of reach of bears.

From the upper end of Big Sandy Lake, you immediately start climbing toward Jackass Pass (also called Big Sandy Pass). Jackass Pass is about 1,100 feet above Big Sandy Lake, but it turns out to be about 1,600 feet of climbing to get there because you go up, then

Plan on a fairly rough hike up Jackass Pass.

down, to North Lake, then up, then down, to Arrowhead Lake, then up, finally, to the pass. Overall, it's a tough Category 1 climb involving rock hopping and scrambling. Take it slow and enjoy the incredible scenery. In addition, this stretch of trail, the roughest on the entire route, goes through a field of huge boulders, making it impassable for livestock. Watch for cairns to show the way in a few places, and just before the pass, look for an unofficial junction with good social trails heading to the left to Arrowhead Lake and straight to Hidden Lake. You want the right-hand trail climbing up another quarter-mile to the pass.

When you get to 10,800-foot Jackass Pass, the scenic wonder known as the Cirque of the Towers spreads out before you—mountain scenery at its finest, no doubt. It's hard to find an adequate adjective for this scene, but cathedralistic might be close. You could spend an hour just trying to identify all the peaks. Not only are they great peaks but they have great names like Warbonnet, Watchtower, Warrior, Big Chief, Wolfs Head, Skunk Knob, and Sharks Nose.

But don't plan on having it to yourself. On most sunny days you can expect to see several other hiking parties enjoying the same vista. On the pass you cross over the Continental Divide and move from the Bridger Wilderness to the Popo Agie Wilderness.

Besides being a scenic wonderland, the Cirque of the Towers is the Mecca for climbers, perhaps the most popular backcountry climbing destination in the Northern Rockies. Because of extremely heavy use, the FS has prohibited camping within a quarter mile of Lonesome Lake nestled in the bottom of the cirque—perhaps the most poorly named lake in the range because it's hardly lonesome. The lake is about a mile below the pass on a steep, rutted trail.

After skirting (and braiding) along the south shore of Not-so-Lonesome Lake, the trail turns east after crossing at the outlet of the lake, the beginning of the North Popo Agie River. In early season you have to wade this stream, but in August, you can usually cross on rocks without getting your feet wet. From here you drop slowly down toward Lizard Head Meadows, about a mile downstream on an excellent trail.

Walking from Big Sandy Lake to Lizard Head Meadows is like traveling through one postcard and into the next. Take your time and relish every moment.

From Lizard Head Meadows take a left (north) turn up toward Bear Lakes. Just before the lakes, the trail forks with a good social trail going to the lower lake. Take this if you plan to camp there or enjoy it as a short side trip, but your main route is the right-hand fork toward the flanks of Windy Mountain and Cathedral Peak, a stretch of trail I unofficially call the Lizard Head plateau. From the meadows to the highest point on the plateau, you climb about 1,800 feet, with most of the climbing coming in the first 2.5 miles, another Category 1 climb.

Both Lizard Head Meadows and Bear Lakes have excellent campsites. From the meadows on you have a better sense of being in the wilderness because the human population decreases dramatically.

When you clear the timberline around Bear Lakes, you have no questions on how this route received its name. To the west rises the colossal Lizard Head Peak. From the plateau, it doesn't take much imagination to visualize a giant lizard watching you. It sort of seems like you are being allowed to pass through the Great Lizard's domain, as long as you're careful not to break any of its rules. You also get a last incredible view of Cirque

Cirque of the Towers.

Lizard Head Meadows.

of the Towers to the west and an unusual rock glacier to the south between Mitchell and Dogtooth Mountains.

The trail across the plateau is better than you might expect, rocky in a few places with a string of cairns in a few others, but in general it's in great shape and easy to follow. It is, however, impassable for horses. If you have time for side trips, you can bag Cathedral or Windy Mountains. Watch for bighorn sheep, commonly seen in this alpine area.

Roll out early and start hiking as early as possible on the day you plan to hike over the plateau. You definitely don't want to be caught up here in a late afternoon thunderstorm.

After you reach the Bears Ear Trail and turn left (west), you drop sharply into Valentine Lake. After the lake, the trail continues to drop all the way down to the Little Wind River, a handsome stream through a flat-bottomed, open valley. It's smaller than many mountain creeks, but big enough to force you to get your feet wet for the first time on this trip. From the valley you can look back and see Lizard Head Peak and plateau. You turn right (north) at the junction just after fording the stream.

After turning left (west) at the junction with the Valentine Mountain Trail, you climb over a small 250-foot hump to the foot of Grave Lake, where you'll find an impressive footbridge over the outlet stream. Grave Lake has an abundance of five-star campsites and is a favorite destination for both backpackers and stock parties.

Toward the end of the mile-long lake, the trail climbs steeply away from the lakeshore up to the base of Pilot Knob to get above a field of truck-sized boulders. Shortly after leaving the lake, turn left (west) at the junction with the trail from Baptiste Lake and then cross Baptiste Creek. Rest and filter water here to psyche yourself up for the assault of Hailey Pass.

This pass is impassable by horses and close to impassable by backpackers. It's a short, Category H climb up the last half mile. As you approach it and look ahead to the pass, it can be daunting. From Baptiste Creek to the base of the pass is a gradual grade and pleasant stroll amidst magnificent scenery, but then, the trail goes straight up on a series of zigzags too small to be called switchbacks. The trail doesn't prolong the pain. Instead, it gets you to the 11,200-foot pass as fast as possible. You won't need to stretch out your calf muscles after climbing Hailey Pass.

Like the hike up the Lizard Head plateau, start as early as possible to avoid being on Hailey Pass in a hailstorm. At the pass, you cross the Continental Divide again and go back into the Bridger Wilderness.

Twin Lakes is essentially on the pass, and the trail drops down about 200 feet and goes between the lakes. This is a rough section of trail with a few serious scrambles, so be careful. After the second lake the trail gets better and drops quickly to Mae's Lake and the junction with the trail to Pyramid Lake. Both lakes lie in the shadow of well-named Pyramid Peak.

From Mae's Lake to Skull Lake to Marms Lake to Dads Lake and onto Fish Creek Park, you pass through open, dry mountain terrain, gorgeous in a more gentle way than the austerity of the Cirque of the Towers and Lizard Head on the east side of the divide. The lakes along this section of trail are similar, shallow, and scenic. The trail is in great shape, but can get dusty in August.

After Fish Creek Park and Divide Lake, the trail drops into lower, forested elevation and stays there, past Meeks Lake, and back to the Big Sandy Trailhead. At Meeks Lake you can also go right and reach the trailhead, but stock parties more commonly use this route.

When we hiked this route in August 2001, a forest fire was burning on both sides of Fish Creek Park, so you might see signs of it. The FS sometimes allows wilderness fires, such as this one, to burn naturally because fire is a key element of the nature of wilderness.

Options: You can do this trip in reverse with about the same level of difficulty. Hailey Pass would be easier from the west, but you would face a steep climb above Valentine Lake, just as steep as climbing up from Lizard Head Meadows. Jackass Pass is difficult from both sides.

If you have extra time on the first day on the way to Big Sandy Lake, you can extend your trip by about 2 miles by taking the route by V Lake and Diamond Lake.

Also, you can cut this route short by turning left (south) at Little Wind River and going over Washakie Pass instead of Hailey Pass. This cuts about 8 miles off your trip. If you take this option, you can do the shortened route with three nights out.

When you come off of the Lizard Head on the Bears Ear Trail, you can take a right (north) at the Moss Lake Trail and go to Dutch Oven and Moss Lake and around Valentine Mountain before heading down to the Little Wind River. This would add about 7 miles, including a serious climb up to Dutch Oven Lake and more elevation gain to reach Moss Lake. Basically, this option would add a day to your trip.

Side trips: This route offers a huge number of possibilities for side trips, but you may have to base camp along the way, spending an extra night at a campsite to have the time to see

Heading up Hailey Pass.

the sights. From Big Sandy Lake you can easily hike to Black Joe, Clear, and Deep Lakes. From Lizard Head Meadows you can check out Papoose Lake and Bear Lakes before heading up to the plateau. If you want an easy climb, try Windy Mountain or Cathedral Peak on the way over the plateau or Easy Day Peak from Marms Lake. If you want a hard climb, well, you can have an endless summer in the Cirque of the Towers.

Another great side trip would be from a base camp in the Little Wind River. Take a day to explore Loch Leven, Washakie, and South Fork Lakes. You could also visit Dutch Oven and Moss Lakes from the same base camp, but this would take another day.

If you aren't camping at Pyramid Lake, you can see it with a short side trip. On the way to the trailhead, you can check out Donald, Francis, or Divide Lakes.

And these are only a few of the possibilities for great side trips.

Camping: There are no designated campsites, so camp almost anywhere, but be sure to set up a zero-impact camp to avoid signs of overuse in this fragile area. Don't forget that backcountry regulations prevent camping within a quarter mile of Lonesome Lake and within 200 feet of any lake or trail or 100 feet from any stream.

Fishing: The fishing opportunities along this high-elevation route are not as productive as in northern reaches of the range and in lower elevation lakes and streams in the southern sections. However, you can find big trout in Graves Lake and in the South Fork and Washakie Lakes and small fish (cutthroats and brookies) in all the lakes on the west side of the divide, as well as some of the streams, especially Little Wind River and Graves Creek. This is, however, not the ideal trip for the fanatic angler.

THE WILDERNESS CHALLENGE

Many hikers, I suspect, view the "wilderness challenge" as the adventure of braving wild country with only what they can carry on their backs. They briefly flee the comfortable life to risk survival along some austere divide, and then return home the victor.

We've almost come to consider it our right to have the opportunity to visit places on earth that have been affected primarily by the forces of nature, where the imprint of man's hand is substantially unnoticeable.

Yes, we can "challenge" the wilderness. We can climb the highest peak, float the wildest river, seek out the most hidden of the mountain's secrets. In the northern Rockies, we can even challenge the mighty grizzly bear, the wilderness king, and temporarily become the most feared creature on the mountain.

This challenge lures us to the blank spots on the map. It seems ingrained in our birthright and most likely will for generations to come.

But today's hikers face an even more fierce, more difficult, more time-consuming, and more frustrating challenge. Now we must rise to the challenge of saving the last wilderness.

Never has the oft-quoted adage of Will Rogers—"They ain't makin' any more of it"—been so relevant. Another famous thinker, Aldo Leopold, also emphasized the point by writing, "Wilderness is a resource that can shrink, but not grow." How true. But the amount of wilderness must grow to help dilute the rapidly increasing number of hikers.

I suppose the day will come when most wilderness areas have restrictions on the number of human visitors. However, increasing the size of the wilderness resource would certainly make this day a more distant probability.

It's also true that the label "wilderness," when officially designated by Congress, can attract hikers, leading to more crowded conditions. However, limitations on recreational use are undoubtedly preferable to the alternative—gradual destruction.

Knowing this, it hurts to hear politicians talk of "balance" as they prepare to give their support to the destruction of another roadless area. In the lower forty-eight states, the ratio is now 99 percent nonwilderness to 1 percent wilderness, as legally defined by the Wilderness Act of 1964. If every remaining acre of roadless country south of Canada became part of the Wilderness Preservation System (created by the Wilderness Act of 1964), we still wouldn't come close to balance. The pitiful 1 percent might, at best, climb to 3 percent.

Yet in almost every speech by wilderness opponents or politicians trying to please everybody, we hear cries for balance. "I'm in favor of wilderness," they predictably say, "but not in this area. We need balance; we can't have all wilderness." This means, of course, that we need to reduce that paltry 3 percent to make room for more roads.

I wonder how many of these podium-thumpers really understand the existing inequity. Herein lies our challenge—to make Americans understand the wisdom of wilderness, to keep the bulldozer out of the last remnants of wild country, to preserve a few more examples of what America used to be like.

This challenge can't be taken lightly. Compared to winning congressional protection for a threatened roadless area, climbing the highest peak or surviving the elements is remarkably easy. In a time when economics dictates most decision-making, pleas to designate wilderness aren't always eagerly received. But wilderness can be an economic bonanza to a community.

Claims that wilderness destroys the local economy illustrate only one of the many myths plaguing wilderness preservation efforts. Other myths include:

- Only the rich, elite, young, and strong use wilderness.
- Domestic livestock grazing isn't possible or practical in wilderness.
- Wilderness locks out sportsmen and other recreationists.
- Wilderness is bad for wildlife.
- Wilderness isn't multiple-use.
- Wilderness locks up vital minerals.
- We have too much wilderness already.

These are all myths, and quite the opposite is true in each case. So if you're confronted with these false statements, get the facts and set the record straight. Don't let an opportunity pass without providing a reply. There's too much at stake. The integrity of the last American wilderness is on the line. And even more important, the decisions on what to do with the remaining roadless areas will be made in the next few years.

The conservation groups listed at the end of this book have the facts to support pro-wilderness claims and dispel myths. Making the decision-makers listen to these facts is your challenge. In America one person can make a big difference.

I dislike projecting wilderness as a giant battleground. But in reality that's a fair description. The battle over wilderness has been and will be as bitterly fought as any domestic political issue.

Hikers and other people who use and adore wilderness must be the soldiers in this war. Otherwise, the day when the last roadless area is protected as wilderness will soon dawn.

APPENDIX

CONSERVATION ORGANIZATIONS

Montana Wilderness Association
P.O. Box 635
Helena, MT 59624
(406) 443–7350
www.wildmontana.org

The Wilderness Society
1615 M Street, NW
Washington, DC 20036
(800) THE–WILD
www.wilderness.org

National Parks and Conservation Association
1300 19th Street NW, Suite 200
Washington, DC 20036
(800) NAT–PARK
www.npca.org

Alliance of the Wild Rockies
P.O. Box 8731
Missoula, MT 59807
(406) 721–5420
www.wildrockiesalliance.org

THE BACKPACKER'S CHECKLIST

As every well-prepared backpacker knows, without a complete checklist it's remarkably easy to forget an essential item. It's always good sense to take a final look at a checklist before loading the pack into your vehicle. The following list may be "over-complete" because it includes items backpackers may not really need, but just in case you're one of the people who likes to take an optional item, this checklist will serve as a handy reminder.

Equipment: Equipment does not have to be new or fancy (or expensive), but make sure you test everything before you leave home.

❑ Tent with waterproof fly
❑ Sleeping bag (Good to 20° F or warmer) and stuff sack
❑ Sleeping pad

- ☐ Full-size backpack
- ☐ Day pack
- ☐ Water bottle
- ☐ Water filter
- ☐ Water purification tablets
- ☐ Compass
- ☐ Maps
- ☐ Toilet trowel
- ☐ Toilet paper
- ☐ Sun screen and lip lotion
- ☐ Insect repellent
- ☐ Headlamp or flashlight and extra batteries and bulb
- ☐ Multitool pocketknife
- ☐ Sunglasses
- ☐ Cooking pots and pot holder
- ☐ Cup, bowl, and eating utensils
- ☐ Lightweight backpacking stove, adequate fuel, and funnel
- ☐ Matches in waterproof container
- ☐ Trash compactor bags
- ☐ Zip-locked bags
- ☐ Nylon cord (50 ft.)
- ☐ Small towel
- ☐ Notebook and pencil
- ☐ Personal toilet kit
- ☐ First-aid kit
- ☐ Survival kit
- ☐ ID, credit card, and cash
- ☐ Car keys

First-Aid kit: For more information on wilderness first-aid kits, see *Wilderness First Aid* by Gilbert Preston, M.D.

- ☐ Ace bandage
- ☐ Adhesive bandages (Band-Aids®)
- ☐ Adhesive tape
- ☐ Antibiotic ointment packets or small tube of Neosporin®
- ☐ Triangular bandage

- [ ] 4 x 4 inch gauze pads (four)
- [ ] Gauze rollers
- [ ] Medications (laxative, antidiarrhea, allergy, aspirin or Ibuprofen®)
- [ ] Nonadhesive bandage for burns
- [ ] Nylon bag
- [ ] Rubber/vinyl gloves
- [ ] Safety pins
- [ ] Scissors
- [ ] Tweezers or forceps
- [ ] Wound closure strips
- [ ] Moleskin® or Molefoam®
- [ ] Personal medicine as required (for example, allergy pills)
- [ ] Snake-bite kit if in snake country

Survival kit: Always bring a survival kit with these items.

- [ ] Candle
- [ ] Cigarette lighters (2, in waterproof wrapper)
- [ ] Compass with signal mirror
- [ ] Emergency fire starter in film case
- [ ] Emergency food bars (2)
- [ ] Iodine water purification tablets
- [ ] Matches (with strike strip in waterproof container)
- [ ] Plastic whistle
- [ ] Space blanket
- [ ] Pocket knife or multipurpose tool

Clothing: Strive for natural fibers such as cotton and wool, and "earth tones" instead of bright colors. Dig around in the closet for something "dull." Your wilderness partners will appreciate it. Try out the clothing before leaving home to make sure everything fits loosely with no chafing. In particular, make sure your boots are broken in, lest they break you on the first day of the hike.

- [ ] Windproof wilderness coat
- [ ] Quality raingear
- [ ] Sturdy hiking boots
- [ ] Socks (two or three pairs)
- [ ] Lightweight, loose-fitting hiking shorts
- [ ] Lightweight, loose-fitting long pants

- [ ] Long-sleeve shirt
- [ ] Short-sleeve shirt
- [ ] Large-brimmed hat or cap
- [ ] Warm hat (e.g., stocking cap)
- [ ] Mittens or gloves
- [ ] Long underwear
- [ ] Sweater and/or insulated vest
- [ ] Extra underwear
- [ ] Sandals or lightweight shoes for wearing in camp and fording streams

Food: Backpackers commonly burden themselves with too much food. Plan meals carefully, bringing just enough food plus some emergency rations. Freeze-dried foods are the lightest and safest in bear country, but they are expensive and not really necessary. Don't forget hot and cold drinks. Bring high-energy snacks for lunching during the day.

Optional Equipment: Most backpackers take additional equipment even though they might not really need it, such as:

- [ ] Binoculars
- [ ] Camera and extra film
- [ ] Extra ditty bags or stuff sacks
- [ ] Paper towels
- [ ] Fishing equipment
- [ ] Climbing equipment
- [ ] Extra water bottle
- [ ] Padded chair
- [ ] Extra shirts
- [ ] Bandana
- [ ] Trekking poles
- [ ] Books

FOR MORE INFORMATION ON NATIONAL PARKS AND FORESTS

You can obtain online information on backpacking in national parks, including regulations and safety advice on the National Park Service Web site. Take the following steps:

1. Go to www.nps.gov.
2. Click on "Visit Your Parks."
3. Select desired park.
4. Click on "Activities."

5. Click on "Backpacking."

You can also contact the national parks directly:

Glacier National Park
West Glacier, MT 59936
(406) 888–7800, fax: (406) 888–7808
E-mail: glac_park_info@nps.gov

Yellowstone National Park
P.O. Box 168
Yellowstone National Park, WY 82190-0168
(307) 344–7381, fax: (307) 344–2005
E-mail: yell_visitor_services@nps.gov

Grand Teton National Park
P.O. Drawer 170
Moose, WY 83012-0170
(307) 739–3300, fax: (307) 739–3438
E-mail: grte_info@nps.gov

For online information on the national forests (albeit less detailed than information available online for national parks), follow these steps:

1. Go to www.fs.fed.us.
2. Click on "National Forest Web Sites."
3. Click on "National Forest by Name."
4. Select desired forest.

Or contact individual national forests at the following addresses:

Bridger-Teton National Forest
340 N. Cache
P.O. Box 1888
Jackson, WY 83001
(307) 739–5500, fax: (307) 739–5503

Bridger-Teton National Forest
Pinedale Ranger District
P.O. Box 220
Pinedale, WY 82941
(307) 367–4326, fax: (307) 739–5750

Shoshone National Forest
Washakie Ranger District
600 North Highway 287
Lander, WY 82520
(307) 332–5460

Beaverhead-Deerlodge National Forest
420 Barrett Street
Dillion, MT 59725-3572
(405) 683–3900, fax: (406) 683–3855

Beaverhead-Deerlodge National Forest
Madison Ranger District
5 Forest Service Road
Ennis, MT 59729
(406) 682–4253

Custer National Forest
1310 Main Street
P.O. Box 50760
Billings, MT 59105
(406) 657–6200, fax: (406) 657–6222

Custer National Forest
Beartooth Ranger District
HC 49, Box 3420
Highway 212 S of Red Lodge
Red Lodge, MT 59068
(406) 446–2103, fax: (406) 446–3918

Flathead National Forest
1835 Third Avenue E
Kalispell, MT 59901
(406) 758–5200

Flathead National Forest
Swan Lake Ranger District
200 Ranger District Road
Bigfork, MT 59911
(406) 837–7500

Gallatin National Forest
10 East Babcock Avenue
P.O. Box 130
Bozeman, MT 59771
(406) 587–6702, fax: (406) 587–6758

Gallatin National Forest
Big Timber Ranger District
Highway 10 East
P.O. Box 1130
Big Timber, MT 59011
(406) 932–5155, fax: (406) 932–5777

Gallatin National Forest
Gardiner Ranger District
Highway 89
P.O. Box 5
Gardiner, MT 59030
(406) 848–7375, fax: (406) 848–7485

Lewis and Clark National Forest
1101 15th Street N
P.O. Box 869
Great Falls, MT 59403
(406) 791–7700, fax: (406) 761–1972

Lewis and Clark National Forest
Rocky Mountain Ranger District
1102 Main Street NW
P.O. Box 340
Choteau, MT 59422
(406) 466–5341, fax: (406) 466–2237

LIVING LIFE ONE MILE AT A TIME

Bill Schneider has spent more than thirty years hiking trails all across America, primarily in the northern Rockies.

During college in the mid-1960s, he worked on a trail crew in Glacier National Park. He then spent the 1970s launching and publishing the *Montana Outdoors* magazine for the Montana Department of Fish, Wildlife & Parks and covering as many miles of trails as possible on weekends and holidays.

In 1979 Bill and his partner, Mike Sample, created Falcon Publishing Company and released two guidebooks that first year. Bill wrote one of them, *Hiking Montana*, which is still popular. Since then, he has written seventeen more books and many magazine articles on wildlife, outdoor recreation, and environmental issues. Along the way, on a part-time basis over a span of twelve years, Bill has taught classes on bicycling, backpacking, no-trace camping, and hiking in bear country for the Yellowstone Institute, a nonprofit educational organization in Yellowstone National Park.

Under Bill's direction, Falcon Publishing (now part of The Globe Pequot Press), became the leading national publisher of recreational guidebooks with more than 700 titles in print, including the popular FalconGuide® series. Bill now works as a publishing consultant and freelance writer based in Helena, Montana.

Another day at the office—the author studying the map on Electric Pass.

WHAT'S SO SPECIAL ABOUT UNSPOILED, NATURAL PLACES?

Beauty   Solitude   Wildness   Freedom   Quiet   Adventure
Serenity   Inspiration   Wonder   Excitement
Relaxation   Challenge

There's a lot to love about our treasured public lands, and the reasons are different for each of us. Whatever your reasons are, the national **Leave No Trace** education program will help you discover special outdoor places, enjoy them, and preserve them—today and for those who follow. By practicing and passing along these simple principles, you can help protect the special places you love from being loved to death.

THE PRINCIPLES OF **LEAVE NO TRACE**

- Plan ahead and prepare
- Travel and camp on durable surfaces
- Dispose of waste properly
- Leave what you find
- Minimize campfire impacts
- Respect wildlife
- Be considerate of other visitors

Leave No Trace is a national nonprofit organization dedicated to teaching responsible outdoor recreation skills and ethics to everyone who enjoys spending time outdoors.

To learn more or to become a member, please visit us at www.LNT.org or call (800) 332–4100.

Leave No Trace, P.O. Box 997, Boulder, CO 80306